Accounting, Finance, and Taxation in the Gulf Countries

Accounting, Finance, and Taxation in the Gulf Countries

Wagdy M. Abdallah

palgrave
macmillan

ACCOUNTING, FINANCE, AND TAXATION IN THE GULF COUNTRIES

First published in 2008 by
PALGRAVE MACMILLAN®
in the US—a division of St. Martin's Press LLC,
175 Fifth Avenue, New York, NY 10010.

Where this book is distributed in the UK, Europe and the rest of the world, this is by Palgrave Macmillan, a division of Macmillan Publishers Limited, registered in England, company number 785998, of Houndmills, Basingstoke, Hampshire RG21 6XS.

Palgrave Macmillan is the global academic imprint of the above companies and has companies and representatives throughout the world.

ISBN-13: 978–1–4039–7798–4
ISBN-10: 1–4039–7798–4

Library of Congress Cataloging-in-Publication Data

Accounting, finance, and taxation in the Gulf countries / edited by Wagdy M. Abdallah.
p. cm.
Includes index.
ISBN 1–4039–7798–4
1. Accounting—Persian Gulf Region. 2. Finance—Persian Gulf Region. 3. Taxation—Persian Gulf Region. I. Abdallah, Wagdy M. (Wagdy Moustafa)

HF5616.P35A33 2008
658.15′9909536—dc22 2008002504

A catalogue record of the book is available from the British Library.

Design by Newgen Imaging Systems (P) Ltd., Chennai, India.

First edition: September 2008

10 9 8 7 6 5 4 3 2 1

Printed in the United States of America.

To my wife for her love, support, and understanding, and to the memory and souls of my parents

Contents

List of Tables and Figures

Tables

Figures

Contributors

Wagdy M. Abdallah is a certified management accountant and a professor of Accounting at the Stillman School of Business-Seton Hall University, New Jersey, USA, where his teaching expertise spans several areas including managerial, cost, and international accounting including accounting and tax in the Middle East countries. He specializes in international accounting and gives seminars on various aspects of doing business in the Middle East, including the Gulf countries. Among his specialties are international transfer-pricing guidelines and practices, American joint ventures in the Asian and Middle East countries, and managing multinationals in the Middle East. He has presented his scholarly work at many national and international academic conferences. He has authored several books on transfer pricing and the Middle East. He was selected by the U.S. Fulbright Foreign Scholarship Board for a Fulbright award in 2005. He obtained his Ph.D. degree (majoring in accounting) from the University of North Texas, United States, in 1982.

Thoraya Al-Hajj has an MBA degree from the University of Sharjah, the United Arab Emirates, and is currently the financial manager at the Sharjah Women's Club.

Sabri Al-Segini is an assistant professor of Accounting at the University of Sharjah, United Arab Emirates, and teaches Financial Reporting, Advanced Accounting, Accounting Information Systems, and Managerial and Cost Accounting. He started teaching Oil and Gas Accounting in 2005. He has published many articles and is the coauthor of three textbooks (in Arabic). His research focuses on corporate governance and financial reporting. He received his Ph.D. degree from the University of Warwick, England.

Mohamed E. Ibrahim obtained his Ph.D. degree (majoring in Accounting) from the University of North Texas, United States, in 1985. He gained his academic and administrative experience through his association with Concordia University (Montreal, Canada) and University of Sharjah (UAE). He served as head of the department of Accounting at both institutions for about nine years and as dean of the College of Business at the University of Sharjah. Now, he is the vice president for Academic Affairs at the University of Jazeera in Dubai, UAE. He also served as an academic at the University of Manitoba (Canada) and the Hong Kong Polytechnic University.

Professor Ibrahim's main lines of research include performance evaluation, heuristics in professional judgment, and the role of information in professional decision making. His research output has appeared in several national and international journals. In addition, he has written and coauthored four books in the areas of financial and management accounting. He is currently affiliated to the University of Jazeera.

Athar Murtuza is a South-Asian by birth and a U.S. citizen since 1973. He obtained his Ph.D. in literature and went on to get an MBA and was certified as a Certified Management Accountant (CMA). As an associate professor of accounting at Seton Hall University, he teaches Cost and Managerial Accounting courses and has interests in effective communication of accounting information as well as in promoting accounting literacy as a requirement of effective citizenship in a civil society. His research interest includes accounting ethics, interdisciplinary perception of accounting, and the regulation of commerce and the pursuit of wealth in the Islamic world from the seventh- to seventeenth century. He is currently working on a monograph about functions performed by Muhtasib in the Islamic world from the seventh- to the seventeenth century.

Sivakumar Velayutham is an associate professor in accounting at the University of Sharjah. He has previously published in the *British Accounting Review*; *Critical Perspectives on Accounting*; *Advances in International Accounting*; *International Journal of Accounting*; and *Accounting Historians' Journal*.

1

Introduction

Wagdy M. Abdallah

When multinational companies are looking ahead for a new country in the Middle East or the Gulf area to invest in is not an easy task. However, one key factor in making a decision is the map of the country. If you want to know how important the country you want to invest in is, just take a look at the country's map from economic, cultural, and political perspectives. Here is Kuwait, here is Saudi Arabia, and here is the United Arab Emirates. If you stand in one of the Gulf countries, you are at the heart of World oil reserves, history, and a unique tradition of culture. The Gulf countries, with some 65 percent of the world's known oil reserves, have occupied a position of primary strategic importance for multinational companies since the Second World War.

Unlike other areas in the world, the Gulf region has been suffering with major conflicts and problems that go beyond disagreements over territory or fears concerning a rival's geopolitical and economic strategies. Making long-term peace agreements or settlements with Israel may look like the mission impossible because it requires not only carefully drawn compromises backed by international powers, but also fundamental changes in the attitudes of people toward each enemies. Whether the Gulf region will have a more stable and peaceful political and economic environment in the twenty-first century is definitely uncertain.

In the past two decades, several significant political and economic events have changed the political and economic conditions of the Gulf countries. These environmental factors made the history of the Gulf countries a unique one. Every political and/or economic event swings every one of the Gulf countries as a roller coaster. The 1979 revolution in Iran, the 1980–88 Iran-Iraq war, the 1990 Iraqi Invasion of Kuwait, the Gulf War in 1991, invasion of Iraq by the U.S. military forces in 2003, the surge of the death of Iraqi civilians and U.S. troops in Iraq, the significant increase in crude oil prices over $100 a barrel in the year of 2008, the Israeli invasion of Lebanon in 2006, and the execution of the former president of Iraq on December 30, 2006, all shaped the Gulf countries and the relationship with American and European businesses in a different way than before.

There are eight Gulf countries; they are Bahrain, Kuwait, Iraq, Iran, Oman, Qatar, Saudi Arabia, and United Arab Emirates. However, this book covers six out of eight Gulf countries; these are the Arab Gulf countries. However, Iraq and Iran are excluded from this book for the following reasons: (1) the six countries covered have many things in common that are not present in either Iraq or Iran, such as the political and economic stability; (2) the available information about Iraq and Iran is not sufficient and is contradictory, which makes it hard to form an objective opinion and may prevent this book from achieving its ultimate goals; (3) Iran is not an Arabic country and the spoken language, Persian, is different from that spoken in the other seven Arab Gulf countries; and (4) with the tensions between the United States and Iran, at the present time, it is not an easy task for American scholars to formulate an objective opinion about the economic or political conditions in Iran without visiting the country. The difficulties Americans face in getting a visa to visit Iran makes things more complicated. In the pages that follow, the term Gulf countries refers to the Arab Gulf countries.

The Gulf region is an economically diverse region that includes countries with a common heritage, at various stages of economic development, and with a very distinct endowment of natural resources. Despite undertaking economic reforms in many Gulf countries, and having considerable success in avoiding crises and achieving macroeconomic stability, the region's economic performance in the past 30 years has been below its potential (Abed and Davoodi 2003). Historically, dependence on oil revenues and a legacy of central planning in the Gulf countries have played major roles in shaping the region's development strategies. The six oil-rich countries of the Gulf Cooperation Council (GCC) have the highest per capita GDP in the region (ibid.).

As global business and economic expansion continue, Gulf countries witness a gradual move from state-owned and family-owned enterprises to international joint venture participation and ownership; from small business firms to large-scale multinational manufacturing companies from all over the world, with more competitive global markets; from short-term financing requirements to long-term credits and capital investments. Combining all these changes with the continuing need for efficient utilization of scarce resources (both oil and non-oil), there is an urgent need for a more relevant, timely, comprehensive, and sophisticated management accounting system associated with transparent financial reporting systems for both MNCs and local partners.

This book looks at the accounting and auditing systems and practices and their cultural, legal, and economic environment in Gulf countries. Understanding the accounting implications of environmental factors requires the coverage of (1) the economic, political, educational, and legal issues of the Gulf countries; (2) the Islamic culture and its impact on management and accounting of national companies and MNCs operating in the Gulf region; (3) international accounting financial reporting standards promulgated by the International Accounting Standard Board and its relevance to the Gulf countries; (4) the practice of corporate governance and the key drivers for the changes in corporate governance; (5) tax rules and regulations of the six Arab Gulf countries to look at regional opportunities for cost saving and tax-liability minimization; and (6) the stock markets and the forces contributing to its development and its efficiency.

The aforementioned topics are of interest for readers for the following four different reasons: (1) they represent great varieties in accounting systems and practices, (2) they have the best investment opportunities in the world, (3) they are representative countries from the Arab Gulf countries with different economic, political, cultural (including religion), and other important environmental factors, and (4) American readers most often associate with the Gulf countries; therefore, they are important to the executive officers of American and non-American MNCs and the U.S. foreign policy.

Multinational Companies in the Gulf Region

To help American and other foreign MNCs plan, manage, finance, control, and account for their Gulf countries' business activities in the most effective and efficient ways, it was essential to identify representative countries from the Gulf region with different economic, political, cultural, and other important environmental factors. This book concentrates on the countries American readers most often associate with the Gulf region, those that are important to the executive officers of American MNCs and U.S. foreign trade policy. Moreover, this book uses the term "Gulf countries" to refer to the Persian Gulf Arab countries, the countries in the southern shores of the Persian Gulf, excluding Iran and Iraq. The main reason for exclusion of both Iran and Iraq in this book is the nonavailability of sufficient data for research to be conducted in the case of Iran, and the high degree of political risk and instability of the economic conditions in Iraq.

For MNCs, the Gulf region has a significant level of global trade as represented by the existence of over 1,000 different MNCs of different nationalities investing approximately over $30 billion in the region. There are more than one hundred million people living in the area in more than 10 countries. For managers of these MNCs, Middle East region's major international advantages include the presence of major oil and natural gas reserves, major international airports, ports along the gulf, high personal income per capita in some countries, highly skilled educated labor force at very low costs, and a growing tax-free zone to be used as an industrial base (Kavoossi 1995: 5). The Middle East countries have long been interconnected to the rest of the world through international trade and several economic agreements.

The six chosen Gulf countries, Bahrain, Kuwait, Oman, Qatar, Saudi Arabia, and the United Arab Emirates (UAE), are unquestionably dissimilar in many respects, including levels of development, workings of the market, integration with the world economy, accounting and financial reporting standards and practices, the level of the efficiency of their stock markets, and systems of governance and legitimization. However, they all have had to confront the difficult choices involved in readjusting an economy that showed signs of serious deterioration and stagnation. Understanding the economic, legal, financial, and political history of the Gulf region is so important for accountants, corporate executive officers, and local managers.

As they enter a Gulf country, managers of MNCs have to cope with cultural practices, local competitive conditions, different laws, and different business conditions, different accounting standards and practices. To meet all these challenges, American MNCs found that joining up with companies or governments familiar with local practices and culture was the only way to be successful in doing business in Middle East countries.

In the Gulf region, every country runs joint ventures for the purpose of expanding economic and technical cooperation with other countries, absorbing foreign capital, introducing advanced technology and equipment and advanced managerial experience, and recruiting qualified trained personnel so as to speed up its modernization programs. Most of the countries have designed laws, regulations, and practices to attract foreign investments to participate in the development of the local economy, especially in those areas that need the use of their advanced technology, through the transfer of technology.

In some Gulf countries, joint ventures with local partners are allowed without restrictions on minimum or maximum percentage of ownership for local or foreign partners, such as in the UAE in the free-zone areas. However, in other countries, such as Kuwait and Saudi Arabia, a foreign company is not allowed to do business, not even a branch of the foreign company, without associating itself with a local partner or a local agent.

Despite the uncertainty factor associated with foreign investments and the hostile international business climate in the Gulf countries, interest in joint ventures has never been keener. Moreover, for more than three decades, many changes have taken place in Europe, Eastern Europe, Russia, and the United States of America, the most important one being the rapid internationalization of its medium- and large-sized businesses. U.S. manufacturers, for instance, can no longer rely exclusively on the domestic market to sell their products. While maintaining dependence on their domestic resources, these companies can systematically seek out joint ventures in other countries for expansion and larger international market share.

The Gulf Countries and the Business Environment

For corporate executive officers (CEOs) of MNCs operating or planning to start business activities in the Gulf countries, potential investors for the Gulf countries, American citizens who are willing to work or are thinking of working in the Gulf region, and for global businesses, understanding the business environment and people of the Gulf countries is a must to grasp some of the economic, cultural, legal, and political factors of the area. These environmental factors, especially economic and cultural ones, have significant impact on MNCs and on every global businessman, indirectly through their effect, and on the perception and behavior of outside participants. They also affect them directly through their effects on the behavior of internal participants as they manage, operate, and control their business operations in the Gulf countries including accounting, auditing, taxation, finance, and management control systems.

Economic, Political, and Social Factors

Every single day you hear, in the American or European media, about what they call a terror attack somewhere in one of the countries of the Middle East or the Gulf region. It may be in Iraq, Pakistan, Afghanistan, or Saudi Arabia. Then, an important question comes to mind: Why do MNCs invest in the Gulf or Middle East countries even though these countries are associated with a high degree of political and economic risks?

Despite all the talk of terror attacks and a hostile business climate, interest in doing business in the Gulf countries has never been keener as in the present time for many reasons. These reasons include (1) improving their competitive position, (2) exploring new markets, (3) maximizing profits, (4) meeting tariffs and quota restrictions of the Gulf countries, (5) securing otherwise unobtainable raw materials, such as crude oil, for the needs of their home countries, (6) exploring the scarce economic resources in the Gulf countries, (7) choosing countries with low income taxes (or tax heaven countries) on foreign investments, and (8) manufacturing their products in the least cost producing countries, such as the UAE or Saudi Arabia, and selling the products in the best-selling markets, such as Europe (Abdallah 2001).

The Gulf region is so important for the United States, the United Kingdom, Japan, China, and many other industrial countries because the Gulf countries are an important source of petroleum for the rest of the world. Over the past few decades, this region has been the site of several wars, an Islamic revolution in Iran, and political and economic developments that have affected every country in Asia, Europe, the United States, and several other countries of the world, but contrary to popular belief, the relative importance of the Gulf region as a source of oil supply is set to expand, not decline.

According to the Energy Information Administration of the United States, Persian Gulf countries currently produce over 23 million barrels per day of total oil liquids and it is expected to increase its market share over the next 2 decades. In 2006, the Persian Gulf countries had estimated net oil exports of 18.2 million bbl/d of oil. Saudi Arabia exported the most oil among all Persian Gulf countries in 2006, with an estimated 8.7 million bbl/d. Also, Iran had an estimated net export of about 2.5 million bbl/d, followed by the UAE (2.5 million bbl/d), Kuwait (2.2 million bbl/d), Iraq (1.4 million bbl/d), Qatar (1.0 million bbl/d), and Bahrain (0.02 million bbl/d). According to the Energy Information Administration's journal *International Energy Outlook 2007*, Persian Gulf oil production is expected to moderately grow and reach 26 million bbl/d by 2015, approximately 30 million bbl/d by 2020, and over 38 million bbl/d by 2030, compared to over 23 million bbl/d in 2006. This would increase the share of Persian Gulf oil production to 33 percent of the world total by 2030, up from 28 percent in 2006 (EIA 2007).

If we take a look at the history of the Gulf countries over the past two decades, all of us would agree that it as a unique one. These countries have experienced events that have swung them from one end to the other like a roller coaster. However, unlike the roller coaster that moves in every direction, the events in the Gulf countries have unfurled toward pulling these countries down rather than in propelling them in the upward direction. The diversity of the Gulf region has always made it a difficult region for biased American and European scholars to define politically and to treat objectively It is a region in which the political has dominated the economic and where the interests of the state have often eclipsed those of society. It is a region in which states and governments are preoccupied with war and peace, with survival, with basic democratic currents, and with constant challenges to their power and authority. In an environment such as this, accounting, taxation, and finance issues have often been relegated to the bottom of their lists of priorities.

In the Gulf countries, as oil-rich countries, the oil sectors are quite large in relation to their non-oil sectors. In all of these countries, the oil sectors being nationalized, their foreign exchange revenues accrue to the respective governments and are used to support imports of technology to sustain industrial or service activities and the gathering of foreign assets. However, the ability of the Gulf countries to use oil revenues for domestic development depends on their ability to translate these resources into useful imported goods (Campell 2005).

One of the most important things for the Gulf countries to do in a competitive global business environment is to integrate their economic and financial activities. In 1981, the six Arab Gulf states of Bahrain, Kuwait, Oman, Qatar, Saudi Arabia, and the UAE formally ratified the charter of the organization named Co-operation Council for the Arab States in the Arabian Gulf (GCC). The fundamental common factors of the GCC countries are the Arabic language, Islam, similarity in societal and social structures, and shared cultural backgrounds. Another common factor among the Gulf countries, which give them a considerable advantage over the European Economic Union, is that they share almost the same level of economic development (GCC.org).

The objectives of the GCC include (1) formulating similar regulations in various economic and financial fields; (2) fostering scientific and technical progress in industry, mining, agriculture, water and animal resources; (3) establishing scientific research centers; (4) setting up joint ventures among Gulf countries; (5) encouraging cooperation of the private sector; (6) strengthening ties between their peoples; and (7) establishing a common currency by 2010 (IMF 2002). The GCC sets among its policy goals that of establishing a common market by 2007 and a monetary unit by 2010. However, before introducing the single currency in the Gulf countries, the following two issues should be achieved: maintaining a strong fiscal position and adopting a common code of fiscal conduct consisting of fiscal convergence criteria, a common accounting framework for public accounting, and adequate budgetary procedures (IMF 2003).

The foregoing trends suggest that financial and management accounting techniques and methods should be more responsive to changes in the economic conditions in the Gulf countries. They should be ready to meet the major trends and changes that are expected to prevail in the twenty-first century in the Gulf countries. In the developed countries, the accounting techniques are more likely responsive to economic and social changes and will continue to be adaptable and dynamic. However, in the Gulf countries, the accounting techniques are not responsive to the economic changes in the local environment (Farag 1991).

From the perspective of Gulf countries, the domestic policy reforms should be redesigned to promote and support the demand for more accounting, tax, and finance information to help managers to make relevant decisions related to the Gulf countries' environment, and to put more emphasis on shaping the accounting profession to be relevant and more flexible in order to report and disclose the necessary transparent financial and economic information to help both MNCs and host countries in meeting the significant economic challenges in the twenty-first century.

The Islamic Business Ethics and Its Impact on Accounting and Finance

Besides understanding the economic environmental factors, religion plays an important role in determining the local culture in the Gulf countries, and other Muslim countries, and can have a significant effect on business practices including accounting practices, auditing practices, tax rules, and financial institutions. Under Islam, for example, the Qur'an provides guidance with respect to issues such as charging interest on loans (a usury or money on money), making charitable contributions, bankruptcy, written contracts, business transactions, business planning, family affairs, marriage, and documentation. In some Islamic countries, banks operate under the Shari'ah, the Islamic law of human conduct derived from the Qur'an. Because traditional accounting rules do not cover many of the transactions carried out by Islamic financial institutions, the Accounting and Auditing Organization for Islamic Financial Institutions, a standard-setting body based in Bahrain, has been active in developing and promoting Islamic accounting standards to be used in financial institutions (Doupnik and Perara 2007).

The most important question for MNCs is how to make their joint ventures or wholly owned subsidiaries in the Gulf countries not only more profitable but also more successful in both the short- and long run? To be successful, you have to have useful knowledge about how the Gulf region's customers think, behave, make decisions, and above all about their unique culture or social life. This unique culture is not just a part of their lives; it is their way of life. It has a significant effect on their daily decisions, such as working, thinking, planning, managing, financing, investing, among many others. This unique culture is not only for individuals but also for businessmen, business entities, and the government.

The unique culture of the Gulf countries may include religious mores, behavior, attitudes toward growth and stability, and others. Some of these variables might have significant impact on MNCs operating in different Gulf countries and each may affect upon the nature and degree of success of accounting and management control systems of MNCs needed in each Gulf country. The feelings and attitudes of people in a country are reflected in the regulations and rules that the country has established with respect to MNC's activities. Several empirical studies have proved that cultural variables have more a significant impact on MNCs' financial performance operating overseas than economic environmental variables (Abdallah 2001).

Therefore, it is so important for MNCs, which are planning or are already investing in the Gulf countries and/or in any other Muslim country around the world, to understand this unique culture and adjust their business planning, marketing, managing, and financing strategies to fit into the unique environment accordingly. This unique culture is called "Islam." In trying to explore how the unique culture, or Islam, affects MNCs in managing, financing, and accounting their overseas activities, a brief look at the religion of Islam and how it affects different kinds of businesses operating, especially financial institutions, in the Gulf countries is presented in chapter 3. Also, the effect of religion on accounting and finance systems and practices is discussed. Due to the fact that almost 1.5 billion (including 27.4 million in the Gulf countries, 133.1 million in China, 133.3 million in India, 196.3 million in Indonesia, and 9.9 million in the United States) people follow Islam in the world today (CIA 2006), it may also be important to stress on the global aspects of Islam.

While the accounting literature is still in a developmental stage with respect to the culture, many accounting scholars have addressed the issue of the influence of culture on the development of accounting systems and practices. The earliest one included a list of environmental variables and explained the differences in accounting practices (Mueller 1968; American Accounting Association 1977). Radebaugh (1975) extended the approach and made a comprehensive framework in an attempt to incorporate the Farmer and Richman model of business environment into a preliminary accounting model.

However, the impact of culture upon accounting has yet to be established. Most of the research endeavors in this area (Hofstede 1980; Gray 1988; Perera 1989; Nobes and Parker 2006; Violet 1983; Belkaoui and Picur 1991;

Fechner and Kilgore 1994; Doupnik and Salter 1995; Doupnik and Perara 2007) have been the acknowledgment of the significance of environmental factors and, in particular, cultural factors in shaping a nation's accounting systems and practices. Violet (1983) argued that accounting is determined by culture and Hofstede (1987) emphasized that the lack of consensus in accounting practices between countries is because their purpose is not technical but rather cultural. Therefore, there is a general agreement that the culture of a country influences the choice of accounting systems and practices.

Most of the prior research efforts have claimed that local accounting systems are determined by environmental factors. Gray (1988) made a significant attempt to develop a model by identifying the mechanism by which societal-level values are related to the accounting subculture that directly influences accounting practices. Doupnik and Perara (2007) emphasized that the religion plays an important role in determining the local culture in a country and can have a significant effect on business and accounting practices. Gray used Hofstede's culture-based societal value dimensions as the basis for his analysis. He also identified four value dimensions of the accounting subculture, which are also related to the following societal values: professionalism, uniformity, conservatism, and secrecy. Furthermore, he classified accounting systems on the basis of each of the four values. Perera (1989) stressed the relationship between cultural values and the accounting subculture. They proposed a number of hypotheses, as did Gray, of the relationship between cultural values and accounting values.

A preliminary empirical test of the general model was made by Doupnik and Salter (1995). They examined the relationship between countries' accounting systems and practices, and they made a preliminary empirical test of the general model by examining the relationship between countries' accounting practices and a set of environmental factors and cultural dimensions hypothesized as relevant elements of the model. The results of their research lend support to the general model and provide insight into the importance of various factors in explaining existing diversity in accounting practices.

It had been emphasized by many management scholars that religion is the most distinctive factor and the mainspring of culture. Educational systems, political organization, and social relations such as the role of women are all significantly affected by the religion of the society in which we live in. Moreover, religion in many countries has a significant impact at the practical level and also on the ethics of the business firm (Gomez-Mejia and Palich 1997).

The foregoing trends suggest that understanding the meaning of the word "Islam" has become an important issue to clarify any misunderstanding or confusion and to avoid any barriers toward conducting business in the Gulf countries. The word "Islam" means a submission to the will of the All-Mighty God, or the surrender of the believer to One God, or submission of one's heart and actions to One and only One God. The Muslim is thus one who gives himself/herself entirely to God and exclusively to One God. This is the basic idea of the religion started in 609 by the Prophet Muhammad (peace be upon him). Muslims believe that Judaism and Christianity prepared the way for Islam and that Muhammad revealed the final true religion, and no one can be a Muslim without believing in Moses and Jesus as great prophets of God.

Islam is not just one component of its believers' lives, a set of beliefs remembered on special occasions. Rather, for the devout, it is a way of life. Its tenets and rules permeate almost everything, often including politics and government. Islam is an ancient religion with profound historical and theological ties to Judaism and Christianity. All three religions worship the same God, acknowledge large parts of the same Bible and revere Adam, Noah, Abraham, and Moses. And, as do Christians, Muslims regard Jesus as the messiah (Ruff 1998).

In fact, Islam teaches that it represents the modern mainstream of a primordial, monotheistic religion that began with the earliest humans. Over millennia, the religion took form with the early Jewish prophets, was modified significantly by Jesus, and was finally shaped by Muhammad, the final prophet who died in 632 (Ruff 1998). There is much truth in the assertion that "Islam is an egalitarian religion." If we compare both the principles and practice of Islam at the time of its advent with these societies that surrounded it, the Islamic religion did really bring a message of equality. Not only did Islam not endorse such systems of social and tribal discrimination, it explicitly rejected them (Lewis 1995).

A common mistake is to look upon the religion of Islam as a separate entity, in the way that other monotheistic religions do. Islam is both the state and the society, and its followers embrace it completely and wholly as a way of life. It is based on the fact that God has created all of us, the humans, to worship him, and He has created everything, such as food, life, health, work, children, and money for us, and it is not fair to be so busy with what has been created for us and in the process forget the creator.

Religious, moral, and law values may not have direct impact on economic theories, as a branch of pure social science, but they have affect the behavior, policies, and principles that make up the real-world economics including the economic systems. Consequently, religious values affect the consumer behavior, his/her utility, preferences, and allocation of resources. It also has effect upon the producers' behavior, choices, pricing decisions for both internal transfers and final products. It also impacts upon the role of the country in designing its economic policies, especially if it is a Muslim country, on the basis of Islamic regulations. In conclusion, religion may have significant impact upon the designing of economic policies and systems. It is obvious, from the above analysis, that Islam is "a religion and state" and a belief with rules (El-Mahjoob 1986).

Understanding the implications of Islam on accounting, tax, and finance is the issue that all MNCs operating in the Gulf countries should consider while setting up or conducting their businesses. It is true that the Islamic culture is completely different from the prevailing Western perspective, which is based on individualism and material gains. Now, it is important to recognize the relationship between accounting and Islam. It may affect managing, controlling, accounting for, and social responsibility of foreign subsidiaries or joint ventures in the Gulf countries. There are several issues that might show the impact of Islam on international business, for both accounting and management, in the Gulf countries and other Islamic countries as well. These issues include (1) working hours, (2) interest and Islamic banking, (3) relationship between debtor and creditor, (4) business contributions or monetary donations, (5) taxation, (6) bankruptcy, (7) business ethics, and (8) equality.

In the last 25 years, Islamic banking has emerged as a major form of banking and the Gulf countries represent the center of Islamic banking. The strong appeal of Islamic banking and financial service industry can be seen by the interest being shown in it by the leading Western banks such as Citibank, Chase, and HSBC Bank. Since 9/11 a large amount of Arab money is leaving the United States and finding home elsewhere and this is no doubt a major reason for the growth in the Islamic financial services being made available. Another important event is the establishment of the Dow Jones Islamic Fund on June 30, 2000 in response to the needs of Muslim investors, who not only want to have a financially rewarding investment, but a Shari'ah-compatible one as well. The Fund invests in foreign securities that involve risks relating to adverse political, social, and economic developments abroad, as well as currency risks and differences in accounting methods. Chapter 3 provides an update on Islamic banking and financial services.

Success in achieving the highest profits and creating the best-motivated work team in the Gulf countries, as in many aspects of international business, depends on how MNCs accommodate the Islamic concepts in their strategic management decisions. By looking at the situation from a businessman's viewpoint, Gulf countries' subsidiary- or joint-venture managers can turn the business around to their company's best advantage and get the needed production results in the most efficient way at the lowest cost with the lowest restrictions.

For MNCs to know how to manage their business successfully and how their accounting systems and practices would work in the Gulf countries, it is essential for them to understand the culture of the Gulf countries and how it affects the business practices there and accounting systems as well. Obviously, any effort to examine and analyze the Gulf countries' cultural influence on accounting should identify (1) a set of specific cultural factors that are likely to be directly associated with accounting systems and practices; tax rules and regulations; and stock markets of the Gulf countries, and (2) the manner by which the association between cultural factors and accounting systems and practices, in the Gulf countries, occurs (Perera 1989).

Financial Reporting and Auditing

In an attempt to attract higher levels of foreign investment, Gulf countries should be responding with several tools; these include the following: (1) increasing the flow of economic information to investors, (2) broadening the use of international accounting standards, and (3) improving the efficiency of their capital markets. Due to the fact that the quality of financial disclosure influences the quality of decisions made by the investors and creditors, it is essential for foreign investors and creditors to understand the accounting systems and practices of Gulf countries. For them the following aspects should be looked into:

(1) Compare the financial reports of MNCs operating in the Gulf countries,
(2) Analyze the differences in financial reporting systems and auditing standards and practices of Gulf countries,
(3) Know the effect of accounting differences on asset valuation and income determination of local or joint ventures operating in Gulf countries,
(4) Decide where to invest at a high rate of return and a low rate of political risk, and
(5) Look for the possibility of designing the appropriate harmonized financial reporting systems and practices of the Gulf countries.

In a world of growing global relationships of a political, social, and economic nature it has become essential to recognize the importance of international accounting. The issue of using common accounting standards in the global market has come under attack. What magnifies the issue is the question of the extent to which a firm's securities can be issued and traded in a foreign country while adhering only to the home country's accounting standards. A global environmental and cultural framework was proposed by Gray (1989) as a basis for identifying international forces for change and their impact on accounting systems and practices at the national level.

Gulf countries, which maintain their own local GAAP, may claim that their local GAAP is "based on" or "similar to" or "nearly identical to" International Financial Reporting Standards (IFRSs). In some cases the changes in wording seem minor, and in other cases the wording is quite different. Sometimes, in a country such as the Saudi Arabia, the regional GAAP, such as the Gulf Cooperation Council Accounting and Auditing Organization (GCCAAO), is written in Arabic language, not in English, and the English translation are not be official Often, not all IASs/IFRSs have been adopted locally. Frequently, there is a time lag in adopting the IFRSs as the local GAAP (IASB 2007).

Most Gulf countries still regulate the accounting and auditing profession through the codes of commercial law. Therefore, the main concern of Gulf countries is how to record (not recognize) economic transactions, keep source documents, prepare financial statements, and perform the auditing function by a registered accountant (Al-Qahtani 2005). Recently, the GCC countries have adopted the IASs, but there are some differences in their accounting standards/systems (Hussain et al. 2002).

Although there is a growing cooperation among the Gulf countries in many aspects, the area of accounting appears to be neglected. Hence, there should be harmonization or at least elimination of the major differences of accounting standards and practices in GCC countries. Thus, this book presents an in-depth analysis of the similarities and differences in accounting standards and practices in the six Gulf countries as compared with both International Accounting Standards (IASs) promulgated by the International Accounting Standards Board (IASB); the Local Accounting Standards (LAS) as developed in each Gulf country, and the regional accounting standards as developed by the GCCAAO.

In Bahrain, the Commercial Company Law of 2001 requires all business entities' accounting books, records, and financial reports to be in full compliance with IASs issued by the IASB (Ernst & Young 2003). Law No. 26 of 1996 was issued in accordance with the GCC regulations for practicing accounting. Law No. 26 is similar to other GCC states' laws in all material aspects. It also requires that auditors should comply with International Auditing Standards issued by the IFAC. In 1983, the Ministry of Trade and Agricultural encouraged leading national and international accounting firms to join a committee charged with the responsibility of setting uniform accounting standards. The committee recommended the adoption of all IASs with the exception of Standard No. 15, "Information reflecting the effects of changing prices" (Al-Qahtani 2005).

In Kuwait, the accounting profession developed tangibly in the early 1950s. Driven by need, the Kuwait government passed legislation that required public firms to report audited financial statements. The stock market crash of 1982 had a lot to do with a lack of accounting, accountability, and professionally credible auditing. The Kuwaiti Association of Accountants and Auditors is the only local professional body of accounting. Law No. 5 of 1981, in setting legal rules governing the auditing profession, requires that registered auditors should be persons of Kuwaiti nationality. In Kuwait, three rules of IASs have had a significant impact on accounting and financial reporting; these are (1) IAS No. 24, "Related Party Transactions," which affected the reporting of related party transactions and the quantification of such transactions; (2) IAS No. 27, "Consolidated Financial Statements and Accounting for Investments in Subsidiaries," which was introduced for the first time in Kuwait to the large family trading groups; and (3) IAS No. 30, "Disclosures in Financial Statements of Banks and Similar Financial Institutions," which improved significantly the disclosures of Kuwaiti banks' financial statements.

In Oman, the Law 53 of 1996 requires business enterprises to follow IASs. Otherwise principles and practices of accounting are not codified. Joint stock companies must prepare audited financial statements within three months after the end of the year and provide their shareholders with audited balance sheet and profit-and-loss statements. Companies listed on the Muscat Securities Market are required to publish unaudited financial information on a quarterly basis and should comply with certain disclosure standards. The Omani Law regulates the accountancy and auditing profession. By June 2001, it was mandatory for accounting and auditing firms doing business in Oman to have at least one Omani partner with a minimum participation of 35 percent (Ernst & Young 2003).

In Qatar, since the middle of the 1990s, the Ministry of Media and Information has started the privatization program and the creation of the national stock market. The authorities are further debating the possibility of establishing a national association of accountants with the responsibility of issuing accounting standards (Al-Khatar and Naser 2003). There is a gap between the degree of economic development and the development of the accounting and auditing systems and practices in Qatar. The main problem that faces Qatar is the lack of specific accounting standards that govern the activities of companies. Until now Qatar neither developed its own standards nor adopted the IASs. However, most large companies operating in Qatar are using the IASs promulgated by the IASB (ibid.)

In Saudi Arabia, the accounting profession is controlled by the Ministry of Commerce (MOC). The Saudi accounting profession was given a formal standing by a Royal Decree in August 1974. The decree was titled Nezam Al Muhasibean, which translates as "Rules and Regulation for Public Accountants." This was followed by the formation of The High Commission of Public Accountants composed of representatives from the Ministry of Commerce, General Public Accounting Office, representatives from the academia and the accountant profession.

In the UAE, the federal law requires that all banks and financial institutions prepare their financial statements according to the IASs. The Federal law No. 22 of 1995 organizes the auditing profession. Article 6 states that auditors, as in other GCC countries, are not allowed to be employees in other organizations. However, in the UAE, academics are exempt from this requirement (Al-Qahtani 2005). The central bank has made it mandatory for all commercial banks in the UAE to prepare their accounts in accordance with IASs from 1999 onward (Hussain et al. 2002).

With respect to auditing in the Gulf countries, the necessary institutions and their infrastructures are required for a truly functional profession ; however, they are still in the early developmental stage in some countries and do not exist at all in some others. In some countries, such as Saudi Arabia, a national profession body has been established to set accounting and auditing standards and monitor practices. In some others, such as the UAE and Sultanate of Oman, such national bodies do not exist. That is to say, the auditing profession is still a young one and it will be sometime before it occupies a professional status similar to the one in Western societies.

However, the actual practices and services of the auditing profession in the Gulf countries are not that different from the practices known in Western societies in terms of service types, scope, and the qualifications of the individuals involved in performing such services. However, there is one unique culture-based characteristic of actual auditing practices in the Gulf countries that is less known in the Western society—the auditing services related to Islamic banking. The Kingdom of Bahrain is the leading champion in this area where a set of auditing standards have been developed and practiced.

Accounting Profession and Accounting Education

In the last 15 years the GCC economies have experienced high growth rates as well as high population growth, which have contributed to a huge demand for accounting professionals. Much of the demand has mainly been met by a growing expatriate workforce.

In the past five years, the higher education sector has gone through a major change, mainly in the form of the opening up of many private universities. Whilst the opportunities for higher education in accounting has grown exponentially, the approach to accounting education has not changed much. The focus of accounting education has continued to be the mastery of knowledge rather than the mastery of skills. It is argued that the weak state of the accounting profession could be a reason for this as well as little connection between the practice environment and the academic programs, which are based on the traditional American accounting curriculum.

It is pointed out that a major reason for the weak and poorly developed accounting profession in GCC countries is the government control over registration of accountants and auditors and the non-requirement of membership of the local body provides little incentive for accountants to be members of the local professional body. The small size of the professional bodies and hence their limited financial resources does not allow them to carry out the normal activities of a professional body such as improving accounting education, funding research and knowledge development, developing and enforcing work standards and ethical standards, and quality control.

Corporate Governance and Financial Transparency

In recent years, several events came to light around major business failures such as Enron Corporation, Dynergy, Tyco, Rite Aide, and Worldcom; most of the multinational companies, including the ones operating in the developing countries, especially in the Gulf region, have recently been forced to ensure that the goals of the management of the corporation are in line with the goals of the other major stakeholders through efficient corporate governance systems. In general, corporate governance systems vary all over the world; therefore, it is almost impossible to find one corporate governance system that fits all countries (Cruz 2006). For example, if the UAE or Kuwait adopts the American model, how will this affect the financial and nonfinancial performance of owned companies of Saudi, Qatar, or Bahrain? And what is the best practice of corporate governance systems that would better align the interests of the board of directors and management with the interest of long-term stockholders in the Gulf countries?

For global business community, corporate governance is essential for companies in developed as well as developing countries. A sound and high-quality corporate governance system is expected to improve access to capital, attract premium valuations, offer financing on better terms, and definitely improve financial and nonfinancial performance of the company. Moreover, it may result in better leadership, oversight and strategic direction, efficient information flows and work processes, and better compliance, accountability, and less conflict, all of which lead to better decision making and affect the long-term prosperity of companies.

Investors, in the Gulf countries, are concerned about corporate governance, as well-governed companies tend to outperform their competitors, safeguard and provide for higher returns on investment, protect shareholder rights, and provide assurance that the management acts in the best interest of the company and all shareholders. On the other hand, governments of Gulf countries should care about corporate governance, as it develops the local capital markets, reduces vulnerability to financial crises, and improves a country's ability to organize, properly allocate, and monitor investments, all of which foster long-run economic growth. Therefore, it is necessary for every corporation in the Gulf region to ensure that they have and maintain a sound and high-quality corporate governance system in order to move forward.

Tax Rules and Regulations

Tax rules and regulations of the Gulf countries are not coded to the same extent as those in industrialized countries such the United States and the United Kingdom. In general, the political regimes of the Gulf countries are well aware that taxation without representation can lead to such politically unstable conditions. For this very reason, "no representation without taxation" is the collective choice in these countries (Gordon 1999). Regional trends in establishing taxation policies, governments have to balance between the need for non-oil revenues and the encouragement of new foreign investment. Several Gulf countries have recently reformed their tax systems and the common theme is a reduction in the maximum corporate tax rate to levels common in industrial countries. However, Saudi Arabia reduced the maximum corporate tax rate from 47 to 20 percent.

In the developed countries, the ability to successfully impose and collect taxes includes a great deal of institutional sophistication. However, most Gulf countries lack this sophistication and strenuously avoid using direct taxation as a means of revenue. Efficient institutions offer states great deals of credibility, and Arabs throughout the region remain suspicious about their governments' abilities to effectively run the affairs of the country (ibid.).

It often comes as a surprise to foreign businessmen that not only are corporate taxes imposed on business profits in some Gulf countries, but also the rates are sometimes very high compared with Western countries. Generally speaking, the six Gulf countries impose no personal income tax until this time. However, in Kuwait, there is a proposal to impose tax on personal income at rates between 5 and 30 percent, but the proposal has not yet been approved as of today.

With respect to customs duties in the Gulf countries, in January 2003 the GCC Summit approved the application of a unified customs tariff of 5 percent on goods imported to GCC countries. All six Gulf countries presently charge customs duties at a single rate of 5 percent as part of an overall plan for greater GCC economic integration, with the exception of the UAE that uses a 4 percent rate on customs duties. In theory, the Customs Union means the members have adopted unified customs laws and procedures, single point-of-entry with internally free movement of goods, and treatment of goods as national origin within the GCC. The GCC has set 2010 as the target date for adoption of a single currency, with 2005 as a deadline for agreement on convergence criteria.

With respect to allowing operating losses to be carried forward or backward, none of the six Gulf countries discussed here allow losses to be carried backward; however, there are varying periods for which losses can be carried forward. In Kuwait and Saudi Arabia, operating losses are allowed to be carried forward for unlimited period of time. In Oman and Qatar, operating losses can be carried forward for five and three years, respectively. However, in Bahrain and the UAE, these losses are not allowed to be either carried forward or backward.

Most countries offer tax incentives that can be of significant benefit to MNCs investing in the Gulf countries. The main incentive is the tax holiday. Tax holidays, combined with other incentives, such as subsidized loans to finance local expenditure, customs duty exemptions, and a lack of exchange controls in most countries, help to make the Gulf region an attractive place to invest, despite the high tax rates that are still imposed in certain countries (Bartlett 1997).

This book discusses the rates of corporate income tax, personal income tax, customs duties, tax holidays, withholding taxes, and other information about the six Gulf countries. In chapter 9, tax rules and tax regulations of every Gulf country is discussed including taxable income, corporate tax rates, personal income tax, customs duties, capital gains, transfer pricing, dividends, interests, royalties, tax incentives, and tax holidays.

Stock Markets and Financial Institutions

The first official Stock Exchange in a Gulf country was established in Kuwait in 1977. The establishment of the stock exchange followed a long period (since the 1950s) of domestic equity trading (Al-Rimawi 2001). The establishment of the official stock exchange was motivated by spiraling levels of speculation in the stocks of local companies ending with the first market collapse in early 1977 when share values dropped by nearly 20 percent (Al-Yahya 1993). Al-Rimawi (2001) attributes the lack of official interest in regulating the domestic Kuwaiti securities market to Kuwait's official active interest in investing substantial funds abroad. In December 1977 the government opened and regulated an official stock exchange and intervened to maintain share prices (Seznec 1987).

In Saudi Arabia, the Stock Market was formed in 1985 although informal trading has been in existence since the 1950s. The formation of the Saudi Arabian Stock Market was followed by the Muscat Securities Market in Oman in 1988 and the Bahrain Stock Market in 1989. Qatar and the UAE, however, did not establish their official stock markets until 1997 and 2000, respectively. In Saudi Arabia and Bahrain the respective monetary agencies (Saudi Arabian Monetary Authority [SAMA] and Bahrain Monetary Agency [BMA]) were charged with the day-to-day regulation of the Market. In Oman, the Muscat Securities Market (MSM) was set up as an independent self-regulating organization.

The first GCC country to issue a formal securities law and establish an independent securities regulator was Oman in 1998. Royal Decree 80/98 dated November 9, 1998, provided for the establishment of two separate entities: a regulator, to be named the Capital Market Authority (CMA), which will be a governmental authority responsible for organizing and overseeing the issue and trading of securities in the Sultanate; and an exchange, to be named the Muscat Securities Market (MSM) where all listed securities shall be traded. The exchange shall also be a governmental entity, financially and administratively independent from the authority but subject to its supervision. The Board of Directors of the Capital Market Authority is chaired by the minister of commerce and industry.

The UAE Federal Number 4 of 2000 established the Emirates Securities and Commodities Authority (ESCA) in February 2000. The UAE is probably one of few countries to establish an independent securities regulator prior to formation of stock exchanges. This could probably be attributed to the UAE being made up of seven semiautonomous emirates (states). The desire by both Abu Dhabi and Dubai to have independent stock exchanges probably contributed to a feeling in the federal government that an independent securities regulator would contribute to the development of a more organized securities market in the UAE without resulting in undue competition between the two stock exchanges. Following the establishment of the ESCA in February 2000 the Dubai Financial Market commenced operation in March 2000 and Abu Dhabi Securities Market was established in November 2000.

The Saudi Arabian government followed Oman and the UAE in establishing an independent regulator—the Saudi Arabian Securities and Exchange Commission (SASEC)—by passing the Capital Markets Law in June 2003. The Commission is to be governed by five commissioners, who will be appointed by the Royal Decree. The commissioners were only appointed in April 2004 and the SASEC is to be chaired by deputy chairman of the Saudi Arabian Monetary Authority.

In February 2004, the Capital Market Supervision Directorate of the Bahrain Monetary Agency (renamed the Central Bank of Bahrain) issued a Consultation Paper on Securities and Exchange Regulation and it is expected to be adopted soon. The consultation paper provides for a comprehensive securities regulation although it does not envision the establishment of an independent regulator. The Bahrain Monetary Agency is to continue regulation of the securities market. The youngest securities regulator in the GCC is the Qatar Financial Markets Authority (QFMA) created in 2005 through Law No. 33 of year 2005. It is to operate as an independent regulatory authority managing the regulatory regime of financial markets in Qatar. The securities market in Kuwait is regulated by the Kuwait Stock Exchange Committee, which is chaired by the minister of commerce and industry, and includes representatives from the Ministry of Finance and the Central Bank. The Committee issues orders relating to share dealings, work of jobbers, and related areas.

An Overview of the Book

This book covers five main themes. In Part I, the issue of environmental factors affecting investment and management of national and multinational (MNCs) in the Gulf countries is covered in chapters 2 and 3. Part II focuses on the following four issues: (1) accounting systems, standards, and practices of Gulf countries, (2) international financial reporting standards and its relevance to the Gulf countries, (3) auditing standards and practices of the Gulf countries, and (4) the accounting profession and accounting education in the Gulf countries. All four issues are discussed in chapters 4 through 7. In Part III, the following three major issues are stressed: (1) corporate governance, (2) tax rules and regulations of the Gulf countries, and (3) stock markets of the Gulf countries. These topics are analyzed in chapters 8 through 10. Finally, in Part IV, the summary and conclusions including the future outlook of global business trends and its impact on accounting, taxation, and auditing developments in the Gulf countries are explored in chapter 11.

In Part I, a general overview of the history of the Gulf countries, the characteristics or environmental factors of the Gulf countries, and the Islamic culture and its impact on management and accounting of companies doing business in the Gulf countries are introduced. In chapter 2, I examine the main characteristics or environmental features of the Gulf countries. The impact of environmental factors on accounting including economic, political, and social aspects are discussed briefly. In chapter 3, the focus is on the Islamic business ethics and its impact on accounting, tax, and finance of national and multinational companies in the Gulf countries.

In Part II, I focus on accounting and auditing standards and practices of the Gulf countries. Chapter 4 is a discussion of the accounting systems, standards, and practices of the Gulf countries. The accounting differences and similarities between Accounting Standards of the Gulf countries and International Accounting Standards are included. In chapter 5, the history and the developments of auditing standards and practices of the Gulf countries are presented. In chapter 6, I discuss the harmonization of accounting standards and the use of the International Financial Reporting Standards issued by the International Accounting Standards Board and supported and recognized by both the International Organization of Securities Commissions, Financial Accounting Standards Board, and International Federation of Accountants. In chapter 7, the developments and the contributions of accounting education and the accounting profession to the economic development of the Gulf countries' economies are evaluated.

In Part III, I focus on corporate governance, tax regulations, and the stock markets. In chapter 8, I examine the most important corporate governance issues and financial reporting transparency of the companies in the developing countries, with special attention to Gulf countries. In chapter 9, I examine and discuss the tax rules and regulations of the Gulf countries in general and emphasize the essential need for successful and effective tax planning for MNCs. In chapter 10, new insights into the development of securities regulation and an evaluation of the securities regulation in the Gulf countries and the performance of their stock markets are provided.

Part IV includes the future outlook of global business trends in the Gulf countries and its impact on the application and use of accounting and auditing standards. In chapter 11, I explore the future of global business environment in the Gulf countries in the twenty-first century, emphasizing on the effect of culture on the development of accounting systems.

References

Abdallah, Wagdy M. 2001. *Managing Multinationals in the Middle East: Accounting and Tax Issues.* Westport, CT: Quorum books.

Abed, George T. and Hamid R. Davoodi. 2003. "Challenges of Growth and Globalization in the Middle East and North Africa." International Monetary Fund.

Al-Khatar, Khalid and Kamal Naser. 2003. "User's Perceptions of Corporate Social Responsibility and Accountability: Evidence from an Emerging Economy." *Managerial Auditing Journal* 18 (6/7): 538–549.

Al-Qahtani, Abdulla K. 2005. "The Development of Accounting Regulation in the GCC." *Managerial Auditing Journal* 20 (3): 217–226.

Al-Rimawi, L.M. 2001. "Jordanian, Kuwaiti and Omani Securities Regulation: Can They Be the Subject Matter of a Viable Comparative Study with EU Securities Regulation?" *Journal of Financial Regulation and Compliance* 9 (3): 253–273.

Al-Yahya, M. 1993. *Kuwait: Fall and Rebirth.* London: Kegan Paul.

American Accounting Association. 1977. Report of the 1975–76 Committee on International Accounting Operations and Education. *Accounting Review* (Supplement): 65–132.

Bartlett, Sam. 1997. "Middle East Low Tax Myth Dispelled." *International Tax Review* (March) 8 (6): 19–22 (London: Euromoney Institutional Investor).

Belkaoui, Ahmed Riahi and Ronald D. Picur. 1991. "Cultural Determinism and the Perception of Accounting Concepts." *The International Journal of Accounting* 26: 118–130.

Campbell, Dennis. 2005. "Introduction." In Christian Campbell, ed., *Legal Aspects of Doing Business in the Middle East.* United Kingdom: Yorkhil Law Publishing.

Central Intelligence Agency (CIA). 2006. "World's Facts Book," http://www.odci.gov/cia/publications/factbook.

Cruz, Elfren S. 2006. "Framework." *Business World*, Manila, July 8, 1.

Doupnik, Timothy S. and Stephen B. Salter. 1995. "External Environment, Culture, and Accounting Practice: A Preliminary Test of a General Model of International Accounting Development." *The International Journal of Accounting* 30: 189–207.

El-Mahjoob, Rafaat. 1986. *Islamic Economic Studies.* Cairo, Egypt: The Institute of Islamic Studies. In Arabic.

Energy Information Administration (EIA). 2007. "Persian Gulf Region-Oil," http://www.eia.doe.gov/emeu/cabs/Persian_Gulf/Oil.html-June 2007.

Ernst & Young. 2003. "Doing Business in Bahrain." *Ernst and Young Global*, New York. www.ey.com.

Farag, Shawki M. 1991. "Accounting in the 1990s: An International Perspective." *The International Journal of Accounting* 26: 243–251.

Fechner, Harry H.E. and Alan Kilgore. 1994. "The Influence of Cultural Factors on Accounting Practice." *The International Journal of Accounting* 29: 265–277.

Financial Accounting Standards Board. *Financial Reporting for Segments of a Business Enterprise*. Statement of Financial Accounting Standards No. 14. Stamford, CT: FASB.

Gomez-Mejia, Luis R. and Leslie E. Palich. 1997. "Cultural Diversity and the Performance of Multinational Firms." *Journal of International Business Studies* (2nd Quarter): 309–335.

Gordon, Michael. 1999. "No Representation without Taxation." *Middle East*, London, March 1999, 19–20.

Gray, S.J. 1988. "Towards a Theory of Cultural Influence on the Development of Accounting Systems Internationally." *ABACUS* 24 (1): 1–15.

Gulf Cooperation Council. 2007, http://www.gcc-sg.org.

Hofstede, G. 1980. *Culture Consequences*. Beverly Hills, CA: Sage Publication.

———. 1987. *Accounting and Culture*. Barry E, ed. Cushing: American Accounting Association.

Hussain, Mostaque, Mazhar M. Islam, A. Gunasekaran, and Kooros Maskooki. 2002. "Accounting Standards and Practices of Financial Institutions in GCC Countries." *Managerial Auditing Journal* 17 (7): 350–368.

International Accounting Standards Board (IASB). 2007. http://www.iasc.org. August 14.

International Monetary Fund (IMF). 2002. "The Gulf Countries Council." http://www.IMF.org/external/np/sec/decdo/gcc.htm. August 26.

International Monetary Fund. 2003. "GCC Countries: From Oil Dependence to Diversification." By Ugo Fasano and Zubair Iqbal.

Kavoossi, M. 1995. "Improving International Competitiveness in the Gulf Region: An Assessment." *International Journal of Commerce and Management* 5 (3): 5–16.

Lewis, Bernard. 1995. *The Middle East: A Brief History of the Last 2,000 years*. New York: Scribner.

Mueller, G.G. 1968. "Accounting Principles Generally Accepted in the United States versus Those Generally Accepted Elsewhere." *International Journal of Accounting Education and Research* 3 (2) (Spring): 91–103.

Nobes, Christopher and Robert Parker. 2006. "Comparative International Accounting," 9th edition; Prentice Hall/Financial Times—Pearson Educational Limited; England: London.

Perera, M.H.B. 1989. "Toward a Framework to Analyze the Impact of Culture on Accounting." *International Journal of Accounting* 24: 42–56.

Radebaugh, L.H. 1975. "Environmental Factors Influencing the Development of Accounting Objectives Standards and Practices in Peru." *International Journal of Accounting Education and Research* 11 (1) (Fall): 39–56.

Ruff, Carolyn. 1998. "Islam Is a Way of Life." Staten Island, NY: Staten Island Advance, August 1, B1-B2.

Seznec, J. (1987). *The Financial Markets of the Arabian Gulf*. London: Croom Helm.

Violet, W.J. 1983. "The Development of International Accounting Standards: An Anthropological Perspectives." *International Journal of Accounting Education and Research* 18 (2) (Spring): 1–12.

Part I

Environmental Factors Affecting Investment and Management of National and Multinational Companies in the Gulf Countries

2

The Economic and Political Factors and Their Impact on Accounting and Management in the Gulf Countries

Wagdy M. Abdallah

The purpose of this chapter is to understand and discuss the economic and political factors and their impact on accounting systems and management practices in the Gulf countries. Prior research has indicated that there are difficulties in harmonizing international accounting and auditing standards of the Gulf countries because of the significant impact of economic, religious, and political factors on the internationalization of accounting and auditing standards. Moreover, as international comparisons of accounting practices have revealed differences, research has identified that those environmental factors have a considerable effect on a country's accounting and auditing system and practices.

Given the conflicting social, political, and economic factors, American and foreign investors in the Gulf area are not immune to turbulence in global financial markets. This, in turn, exerts impact on how multinational companies do business in the Gulf countries in the twenty-first century. This chapter investigates and analyzes the impact of economic and political factors on business, accounting, and auditing systems and practices of the Gulf countries and suggest relevant, appropriate accounting systems and practices to fit the Gulf countries' environment. The first section presents the main characters of the Gulf countries with a historical and general background of the economic and political issues affecting multinational companies in managing and accounting their Gulf activities. Second, the objectives, process, and actions of Gulf Cooperation Council (GCC) of the Gulf countries are discussed. Third, the impact, key factors for success, responses, and challenges facing MNCs are analyzed. Fourth, the efficiency and the key factors of financial stock markets of the Gulf countries and their effect on financial reporting and accounting standards and practices are examined. The last section of the chapter presents the effect of environmental variables on accounting in the Gulf countries.

Historical and General Background

The Persian Gulf, also known as the Arabian Gulf, is a 600-mile-long body of water which separates Iran from the Arabian Peninsula, and one of the most important strategic waterways in the world due to its strategic importance in world oil transportation. The Persian Gulf States, also called the Gulf States (which may cause a confusion with the Gulf States of the United States, which are those areas along the Gulf of Mexico), are the countries in Southwest Asia or the Middle East that border the Persian Gulf. These countries are Bahrain, Iran, Iraq, Kuwait, Oman, Qatar, Saudi Arabia, and the United Arab Emirates (UAE).

Due to the fact that the Gulf countries have been a major source of oil for the major industrialized countries including the United States, the Gulf region has become a theater of several wars, invasion, and political instability. It has been reported that the Persian Gulf oil production is expected to be increased by 20 percent in 2010 and 61 percent in 2020 from the production in 2000 (Energy Information Administration 2004).

The Gulf countries' diversity of mixing up the politics with economic issues and the intensive number of family-owned business have made the financial reporting and disclosure issues the less important items on of the countries' priorities. For the corporate executive officers (CEOs) of MNCs to make their business in the Gulf countries favorable investment and economic opportunities, they should understand the cultural environmental conditions and make their management control system a flexible one to be appropriate for the environment of the Gulf countries.

For accountants, it is the environment in which the accounting systems, practices, and the profession have been developed and grown; therefore, the environmental variables are the basis for the accounting and auditing standards and practices in the Gulf countries. To corporate executive officers and managers of MNCs, keeping pace with the most recent economic, financial, cultural, and political developments is so important for the success of their Gulf region's operations, business, competition, and investments.

Over the past three decades, the Gulf countries have witnessed an extraordinary economic and social transformation (IMF 2003a). Low inflation rates, an average of 4 percent overall real economic growth a year during the past three decades, with the constant increase of the non-oil economic activities are reflecting the efforts of the GCC countries for economic diversification (ibid.). Moreover, the completion of major infrastructural projects has reduced the role of government spending in the growth of non-oil sectors. However, the national labor force of the Gulf countries has been increased as a result of the high growth in population and the rising participation of women in the labor force (ibid.).

Unlike other areas, the Gulf region has been suffering with major conflicts that resemble a mission impossible. Conflicts between Arabs and Israelis, Iranians and Iraqis, Sunni and Shai'a Muslims, Iraqis' civil war coupled with the occupation of Iraq by the United States and allied troops, and other problems go beyond disagreements over territory or fears concerning a rival's geopolitical, political, and economic strategies. Whether the twenty-first century will produce a more stable and peaceful political, financial, and economic condition in the Gulf region depends on the intentions, efforts, and actions of both the international community and all the countries directly involved.

The six Gulf countries share many economic characteristics. Oil production contributes almost one-third to total GDP and three-fourths to annual government revenues and exports (IMF 2003a). The GCC countries have significant revenues from oil and gas and have considerably small local populations, which resulted in higher per capita incomes than those of their neighboring Arab countries. Oil wealth has helped some of the Gulf countries to accumulate significant financial resources that are significant in formulating their foreign policies. The region still maintains its importance in the production process despite the discovery of new alternative sources of energy, such as solar and nuclear energy. As can be seen from table 2.1, the six Gulf countries, excluding Iran, account for almost 46 percent of the total world oil reserves and 25 percent of crude oil exports (Saudi Arabia is the largest world oil exporter), possess at least 20.5 percent of the proven global natural gas reserves (Anonymous 2005a).

From the 1960s to the 1980s, the Gulf countries enjoyed rising prosperity. They were ahead of all other developing regions except East Asia in per capital income growth. By the second half of the 1980s the growth had collapsed. In the GCC countries, per capita incomes declined. Oil export countries, such as Saudi Arabia and Kuwait, which used to generate unlimited wealth during the early 1970s, suddenly were forced to make cuts in budgets, governmental services, and aid sent to poor Arab countries. In the 1990s, most Gulf countries consumed their own resources toward

Table 2.1 Gulf countries and the U.S. reserves by country as of January 1, 2006 (billions barrels)

Country	*Oil Reserves*	*Percentage*
Saudi Arabia	264.3	20.5
Iraq	115.0	8.9
Kuwait	101.5	7.9
UAE	97.8	7.6
United States	21.4	1.7
Qatar	15.2	1.2
Rest of the world	677.3	52.4
World total	1,292.5	100.0
Gulf countries' total	593.8	45.9

Source: Anonymous (2005a).

war efforts and advanced weapons. Other economic problems included massive foreign debt, scarcity of water resources, and a population boom in several poor countries (Diller and Moore 1994).

In 1995, several important factors adversely affected the availability of energy supplies from the Gulf region. Consequently, the competition among neighboring countries over anticipated energy resources had heightened tensions in this volatile region. Likewise, the growing concentration of world oil production among Gulf countries, who are also members of the Organization of Petroleum Exporting Countries (OPEC), increases the political dimension that could affect world oil supplies. Ongoing rifts between OPEC members over oil production quotas, market share, and pricing strategies will further erode prospects for greater unity among the membership. A weakened and debt-ridden OPEC could threaten the stability of the region's oil-based economies and negatively impact the world's oil-consuming countries. Balancing supply with demand will be a central issue if Gulf producers are to avoid instability in their respective economies (EIA 2007).

Contrary to popular belief, the consumption of world oil is set to rise over the next two decades and the United States will import more, not less, oil from the Gulf countries. Oil will remain the world's primary source of energy fuel for the anticipated future. Reinforced by projections for increased demand from industrialized countries as well as emerging third-world nations, the importance of oil and its availability will be a principal concern for global economies well into the next century (Air Force 2002). Emerging as a significant trend in the world oil market is the growing centralization of world oil production in the Arabian Gulf. The area's share of the world supply is projected to increase from one-fourth today to about one-third within the next 10 years. Adding significance to the level of Arabian Gulf oil production is the expected decline in oil production elsewhere. With fewer alternatives to Arabian Gulf oil reserves, production, and exports, supply disruptions within the region would cause great challenges (ibid.).

It is estimated that 12 percent of the oil used by the United States comes from the Gulf region. However, the key allies of the United States now depend more than ever on the Arabian Gulf oil. Oil from the Gulf fills over one-quarter of Western Europe's needs, and more than two-thirds of that of Japan. With 66 percent of the world's known oil reserves in its territory, the region will be the key oil-producing area in the foreseeable future. As global economies become increasingly dependent on Gulf oil, any threat to the free-market access to the region is a threat to global security. Strategic points such as the Strait of Hormuz, the Bab el Mandeb, and the Suez Canal remain vulnerable to disruption, and Iraqi or Iranian aggression against these waterways could disrupt not only a large portion of world oil supply, but also more than 15 percent of all world commerce that is routed through these strategic waterways (ibid.).

For multinational companies, it is also important to understand the common characteristics that the Gulf countries share. These include (1) a free enterprise economic system; (2) the Arabic language; (3) the cultural and social tradition, with a significant impact of the Islamic religion; and (4) similar political and legal systems—religion has a significant effect on the Gulf countries' legal system. All the aforementioned factors are very important for both multinational companies and accountants, because the greater the similarities among the countries the better the chance to establish a harmonized accounting system in the region (AlHashim 1985).

However, there are risks in generalizing the economic growth performance of the Gulf region as a whole because each of the six economies has had its own experience, which in some ways remains unique. There are obvious differences between countries that introduced reforms, and hence grew at higher rates, and those that were slower and less aggressive in pursuing reforms and thereby fell behind. Nevertheless, the economic structures and institutions of the Gulf countries do tend to exhibit common features and, given the need for a policy focus on the challenges and opportunities that face the region, there is a strong case for treating the region as a unit of analysis.

Many important international forces have made significant changes in the global market, especially the Gulf region, including international economic/political interdependence, foreign direct investment and multinational corporate strategy, new technology, international financial markets, the growth of business services, and the activities of international regulatory organizations. Economic groupings, such as the World Trade Organization (WTO), European Union (EU), and the Gulf Cooperation Council (GCC) discussed later, have been a major influence in promoting economic integration through the free movement of invested capital, goods, technology, services, and people between countries.

International organizations, such as the United Nations (UN), are also involved in the development of global business. The United Nations is responsible for the emergence of organizations such as the World Bank Group, the International Monetary Fund (IMF), the UN Conference on Trade and Development, the Conference on the Law of Sea, the General Agreement on Tariffs and Trade (GATT), and the Economic and Social Council (ECOSOC). ECOSOC includes a Commission on Transnational Corporations (UNCTC) designed to promote an effective international framework for the operations of MNCs and to monitor the nature and effects of their activities. The UNCTC is involved, among other activities, in initiatives to develop international standards of accounting and reporting.

The Organization for Economic Co-operation and Development (OECD), unlike the United Nations, is focused on the development of the industrialized developed countries of the world. The main objective of the OECD is to foster international economic and social development and to this end a Code of Conduct, including information disclosure guidelines, has been issued relating to the operations of MNCs to encourage them to develop positive relationships with host countries and their governments.

One of the most important aspects that has emerged with the overwhelming movement toward a global economy is that a society's economic well-being and survival depends on its international competitiveness. In their bid to become more competitive, Gulf countries have found that their choices are increasingly limited by the dynamism of not only their industrialized and developed counterparts, but also by the more successful newly industrializing neighbor, such as Israel. Another factor in favor of greater competitiveness is the increasingly free trade oriented international trade regime institutionalized through the GATT and other agreements.

In a global business environment, international accounting has been recognized as a vital key for both investors and creditors. For issuing and trading securities of a MNC, there is no substitute for using well-recognized and accepted international accounting standards by the international financial community (Gray 1989).

The Gulf Cooperation Council

On May 25, 1981, the six Arab states of Bahrain, Kuwait, Oman, Qatar, Saudi Arabia, and the UAE formally ratified the charter of the organization named Co-operation Council for the Arab States in the Arabian Gulf. This has become more popularly known as the Gulf Cooperation Council or GCC. Iran is deliberately excluded, and up to 2003 Iraq acted as a security barrier for the Gulf Arab states against Iran. In 2006, Yemen did make negotiations for GCC membership, and will more likely join the Council by 2016 (Wikipedia 2007).

The fundamental common factors of the GCC countries are the Arabic language, Islam, similarity of societies and social structures, and shared cultural backgrounds. Another common factor among the Gulf countries, which gives them considerable advantage over the European Economic Union, is that they share almost the same level of economic development.

The GCC stated seven objectives, mentioned in chapter 1, combined with two interesting policy goals that are to establish a common market by 2007 and a common monetary unit by 2010; however, at the time of writing this book (2008), neither the first one is achieved nor any preparation for the second has started. While these objectives are ambitious, the economic conditions of the Gulf countries for achieving these are favorable, given a market with high oil prices, strong economic growth, and relative stability in both economic and political spheres.

In December 2001, the heads of the GCC met in Muscat and signed an agreement to enhance the GCC Unified Economic Agreement of November 1981, which prepared the ground for the economic relationship between member states and established the GCC Free Trade Zone (Gulf News 2005). The agreement of 1981 was signed a few months after the establishment of the GCC. It reflected the economic conditions prevailing at that time. The 2001 agreement was also a reflection of the prevailing economic, social, and political conditions. It, however, was expected to develop the objectives of the 1981 agreement, which included enhancement of economic ties among member countries and harmonization of their economic, financial, monetary, commercial, and industrial policies (ibid.).

A review of the 2001 agreement shows that it has provided for a customs union, common market, economic and monetary union, development integration, human resources development and cooperation in the research and development of communications, infrastructure and communications. Furthermore, the agreement added the following three issues: (1) economic integration among member countries through specific programs and, hopefully, workable mechanisms; (2) establishing a mechanism for implementation and follow-up; and (3) establishing a mechanism for the settlement of disputes that might arise during implementation.

One of the major issues that was discussed at the end of the 2001 meeting was to deepen economic integration by using a common currency—pepped to the U.S. dollar—by 2010 (IMF 2003b). The introduction of a single currency by 2010 in the six member countries is an objective that is supported by several factors including (1) the region's common history, culture, and language; (2) the relative homogeneity of its political systems; and (3) the similarity of economic structures among the member countries (Sturm and Siegfried 2005). The objective of the monetary union is to broaden the economic integration process. Some of the conditions for shifting to a common currency will be easy to satisfy. There is little difference between interest rates and inflation across the GCC. The principal advantage of a common currency would include (1) savings in transaction costs across the GCC and (2) stimulation of growth in trade among the Gulf countries. This aspect is of growing importance as the financial markets of the Gulf become more integrated (Anonymous 2005b).

However, before introducing the single currency in the Gulf countries, the following issues should receive the highest priority: (1) maintenance of a strong fiscal position and (2) adoption of a common code of fiscal conduct consisting of fiscal convergence criteria, a common accounting framework for public accounting, and adequate budgetary procedures (IMF 2003a).

The Impact on Multinational Companies

American and other foreign multinational companies continue to focus their expansion in the Gulf region as the market potential here is huge. The key factor is that most Gulf countries and local organizations do not always have the resources or know-how to cope with the increasingly complex global environment.

Among the Gulf countries, Bahrain's economy is one of the fastest growing economies and its excellent infrastructure makes the country an attractive choice for most multinational companies who have set up operations or subsidiaries in the Gulf area. Kuwait where the oil reserves increased by 2.5 billion barrels (3 percent), Qatar, Oman, and Saudi Arabia where higher oil reserve estimates were reported by the U.S. department of energy; their oil reserves increased by 4.9 billion barrels (2 percent) in 2006. Finally, the United Arab Emirates is considered as one of the best choices for investment for MNCs because it combines *a modern economy with traditional values*. Moreover, the UAE is seeking to diversify its economy and move away from its reliance on oil, which means that it is increasingly reaching out to businesses and investment from the rest of the world. Another important factor is the fact that the UAE is a Middle Eastern country and is one of the more liberal countries in the Gulf region, even though it is surrounded by very conservative countries such as Iran and Saudi Arabia.

The activities of multinationals and their economic significance have continued to grow in the 1980s despite a slowing down of world economic growth, increasing instability in foreign exchange rates, inflation and interest rates, and growing tendencies toward protection of local or national products. MNCs have been major forces toward change. New forms of business relationships have emerged, including international joint ventures among MNCs and subcontracting arrangements between MNCs and host countries' corporations in Middle East countries.

The relative importance of MNCs from different home countries has changed. The importance of U.S. MNCs has declined in the 1980s whereas that of Japanese and Western European multinationals have increased. Japanese MNCs have established themselves as manufacturers in the United States and Western Europe, and Western European MNCs have also made large investments in the United States. On the other hand, foreign investment by U.S. multinationals has expanded at a much slower pace than in the past, with more concentration on Egypt and Israel (Gray 1989).

Although the large MNCs account for a large share of the world economy, smaller companies are now just as likely as large ones to invest abroad. However, the 600 largest MNCs still account for a fifth of the world's total value added in manufacturing and agriculture. MNCs account for well over three-quarters of their home country's trade flows. However, half of all the world's companies investing abroad are small- and medium sized. The 1980s have also seen an increasing number of MNCs from developing countries, involved mainly in the extractive and mineral-processing industries, and from centrally planned socialist countries with state corporations expanding into services and especially marketing and trade (Gray 1989).

Multinationals have responded to the slow growth and uncertain economic conditions in the 1980s by developing global strategies to strengthen their position both in their home markets and in the major developed market economies, especially the United States. More specifically, there has been a trend toward concentrating on core and related business activities and toward diversifying geographically. Product consolidation has thus been preferred to product diversification. As a major part of this strategy, there has been a dramatic wave of international mergers, acquisitions, strategic alliances, joint ventures with corresponding divestment, and management buy-outs (UN 1988). Most of this activity has involved MNCs of both the United States and United Kingdom, but Japanese MNCs are now taking an increasing interest. In addition, there has been a growing trend toward cooperative arrangements with respect to both research and development and the implementation of new technology (Gray 1989).

In developing countries, with very small and limited securities markets, government policy makers need to watch and control economic and business activities of business firms to design and implement certain public policies; constituencies other than foreign investors, such as government, trade unions, and public-interest groups, seem to have a great interest in the affairs of MNCs. These groups can make decisions and actions, which might significantly affect the way MNCs operate their businesses in the country.

In the Gulf countries, MNCs have reacted to the general worsening of economic conditions and the instability of such countries by reducing foreign investment and increasingly preferring non-equity arrangements. In doing so, MNCs used different techniques including licensing agreements; management contracts; franchising; international subcontracting; and joint ventures to reduce their exposure to business and political risks.

MNCs, in general, are interested in maximizing their overall benefits and profits from total global operations; the priority interest of their host countries is to maximize national economic benefits. A potential conflict of interest exists between an MNC and the country in which it operates (Rahman 1990). Gulf countries need to design and implement certain policies to control MNCs' activities and make sure they are generating benefits compatible with their national goals.

Political groups often attack MNCs on the basis of allegations that they take out of the country more than what they invest in it. MNCs can avoid this kind of political risk by showing their contributions to the host economy. Preparing a local social responsibility (or accountability) statement as a supplementary report to the conventional financial statements can help achieve this. This statement provides valuable information about the activities that generate added value and the activities among which the added value is distributed.

The social responsibility statement would be useful to many groups of a Middle East country including government policy makers, local employees, trade unions, political groups, and other social groups. The distribution of this social responsibility statements will allow MNCs to reduce conflicts with host countries and thereby to receive favorable treatment from the political groups whose decisions might affect their business operations (Rahman 1990: 96).

American Business Council of the Gulf Countries

In 1989, the American Business Council of the Gulf Countries (ABCGC) was established to foster improved economic relations between the United States and the GCC countries through trade, investment, cross-cultural exchange, and mutual understanding. It is an affiliate of the U.S. Chamber of Commerce and made up of eight American Chambers of Commerce operating in the Gulf region (ABCGC 2007). In the six Gulf countries, American businessmen and businesswomen promote the U.S. exports in the face of intensive international competition, generate goods and services of the U.S. sales exceeding $20 billion each year, and create more than half a million jobs in the United States. The GCC is considered the fifth largest worldwide trading partner of the United States based on the American export of goods and services to the six Gulf countries and it comprises by far the largest market in the Near East and North Africa (ibid.).

Moreover, the ABCGC represents more than 700 American multinational companies operating in the Gulf countries by fostering American business activities and actively encouraging U.S. Government policies with respect to promoting America's commercial interests in the Gulf countries. The ABCGC is actually one of four regional groups; the other three are in Latin America, Asia, and Europe.

However, the Gulf market is more important than any other area in the world and it is a very competitive market for American multinational companies due to its location that houses two-thirds of the world's proven oil reserves and also due to the following two main reasons: (1) all the Gulf countries rely heavily on a wide range of imported goods and services and (2) most of the sales in the Gulf countries are traditionally paid in cash.

The ABCGC is actually an affiliate that is made up of eight American Chambers of Commerce operating in the Gulf countries. They serve as a critical commercial link by performing the following six activities (ABCGC 2007):

1. Holding important events with host-country government officials, Chamber of Commerce, and business leaders by serving as a bridge for closer business communication, cooperation, exchange of ideas and viewpoints;
2. Providing an important network for American business executives working in the Gulf countries, including helping new American companies looking for opportunities of new business in the area;
3. Encouraging American companies to explore opportunities in the Gulf region and hosting their group teams when they come to visit and providing them with advice about the local market conditions;

4. Holding periodical meetings with prominent American-based speakers by providing them with a forum to address the American community in the Gulf region;
5. Cooperating with the U.S. embassies in the Gulf region and their commercial officers with respect to the mutual needs of the American community and the U.S. Government; and
6. Providing briefings and presentations to all business groups, government officials, educational organizations, and all others in both the Gulf countries and the United States.

Financial Stock Markets in the Gulf Countries

Accounting is a technology that is practiced within different political, legal, economic, and social conditions. These have always been international as well as national, but since at least the last quarter of the twentieth century, the globalization of accounting standards and practices has become so important that national accounting and financial reporting standards can no longer be sustained. The important interrelated environmental issues, affecting the accounting standards and practices, including financial reporting, are as follows (Nobes and Parker 2006):

1. Major political issues, such as the control and influence of the U.S. government and multinational companies and the expansion of the European union;
2. Economic globalization, including the reformation of and significant increases in international trade and foreign direct investment;
3. The emergence of global financial stock markets in Europe, Asia, and the Gulf countries;
4. Patterns of share ownership, including the privatization of most of state-owned businesses especially in the developing countries, including the Gulf region;
5. The new changes in the international monetary system, including the use of the Euro as one common currency for most of the European countries; and
6. The growth, merger, and acquisitions of multinational enterprises.

The internationalization of capital markets is another important factor that has significant contribution toward the interest in global accounting standards among investors, accounting standard setters, corporate executive officers, and securities market regulators (Choi and Meek 2005). From 1995 to 1999, the dollar volume of cross-border equity offerings almost tripled. International offerings in bonds, syndicated loans, and other debt tools also grew significantly during the 1990s. In the early years of the current century, these trends were in steep decline due to the slowdown of world economy. However, global business activity is now on the upswing and these trends are expected to continue during the remainder of this decade (ibid.).

There are several international organizations involved in the harmonization of accounting standards either regionally (such as the GCC countries) or globally (such as the United Nations). At the global level, the most important one involved in this effort has been the International Accounting Standards Board. The International Organization of Securities Commissions and the International Federation of Accountants have also contributed toward the harmonization of accounting standards at the global level (Doupnik and Perera 2007).

At the level of international financial markets, there have been significant efforts to harmonize several accounting and tax issues that are considered barriers to the globalization of securities markets. These issues include differences in tax rules and regulations, foreign currency exchange restrictions, official restrictions in some Gulf countries on foreign investments, and financial reporting and disclosure requirements. Definitely, there are many advantages of harmonizing financial reporting rules and standards. If all countries implemented and used the same rules or standards to construct their accounting standards and practices, it would greatly enhance objective comparability. Financial analysts and potential investors would be able to compare the financial statements of companies in different Gulf countries without the need to make complex adjustments for the differences in accounting standards.

At the same time that international trade and foreign direct investments have increased, capital markets have been on the rise at the global level. This has been made possible by the deregulation of the leading national financial markets (e.g., the "Big Bang" on the London Stock Exchange in 1986); the speed of the innovation of financial tools (involving new trading techniques and new financial instruments); dramatic advances in the computer technology of communications; and growing links between domestic and global financial markets (Nobes and Parker 2006).

In the twenty-first century, the economies of the Gulf countries are more and more adopting market-based activities, and the role of the government is declining while the role of the private businesses is evolving. The demand for equity investments is increasing correspondingly to the growth in the number and size of Gulf and foreign multinational companies. This has given rise to the development of securities markets where the raising of investment and finance could be facilitated. Another trend is the growth of emerging markets in Europe and the Gulf countries, such as the EC market and the GCC. Securities markets are fundamental elements of the transition to a global economy, including the privatization of government-owned business entities and the need to attract foreign investments.

A key factor influencing accounting systems and practices in the Gulf countries was the emergence of securities markets, and the need for reliable and relevant financial information to help investors and creditors in making right decisions. The expansion of securities markets is well recognized by Gulf countries as one of the major keys in economic growth and development. Therefore, international accounting harmonization is a major step for the success of any newly developed securities market.

Historically, the attacks of September 11, 2001, in the United States are seen as the catalyst for a period of fear, war, and economic worry. However, in the oil-rich Gulf countries, September 11 is increasingly viewed as the event that kicked off a galloping economic boom, when Arabs divested from America and reinvested at home. Investors of Arab and Muslim countries pulled tens of billions of dollars out of the United States. They were angered by perceived American hostility toward Arabs and Muslims. They worried that their assets would be frozen by U.S. counterterror measures (Anonymous 2005c). Many Gulf citizens cited anger at U.S.-led wars and Middle East policy, and general hostility toward Arabs and Muslims as another reason for the divesting in the United States or Western Europe.

Most Arab investments that were pulled out of the United States were redirected into stocks and real estate in the Gulf region, laying the ground for a boom that accelerated as the price of oil shot skyward. Oil money is now bankrolling more than $100 billion in construction in the Gulf this year alone, according to the Washington-based Institute of International Finance (ibid.). For example, the Morgan Stanley Capital International Arabian Markets stock index (excluding Saudi Arabia) is up 3.3 percent in dollar terms since the start of year 2007. In contrast, the MSCI Emerging Markets Index has risen by 2.7 percent in the same period while the Dow Jones Industrial Average is essentially flat (Slater 2007).

The results have been amazing since September 2001; economies in the Gulf countries have soared, with stock markets up by a collective 400 percent. Over the same period, the Standard & Poor's 500 rose 24 percent (Anonymous 2005c). Most of the credit for the wealth influx in the Gulf area is because of the near-tripling of oil prices since 2001 to current levels of more than $67 a barrel (Anonymous 2005c). The boom is changing the face of Gulf countries. Building cranes line the horizon in the UAE, Qatar, and Bahrain. New highways are cutting through the empty deserts, and the use of imported laborers are establishing hospitals, universities, and entire districts of shimmering high-rise apartment towers—even artificial islands covered in luxury villas (Anonymous 2005). It may be argued by investors and economists that the jump in oil revenues is the biggest factor for the boom. However, the shift in strategy that led Gulf Arabs to divert funds from U.S. investments to home markets laid the groundwork (ibid).

At the end of 2007, the economies of the Gulf countries are expected to achieve sizable growth rates despite the sharp decline in their stock markets and the rise in short-run interest rates over the past year. The sharp increase in oil revenues will help the governments to increase their spending to carry out giant infrastructure projects, which in turn will give a strong push to the activities of the private sector (Azzam 2007).

In the Gulf countries, the overall trend is toward greater openness in the region, both in terms of what companies disclose and where foreigners can invest. The most important limitation is that foreigners are not permitted to buy shares in Saudi Arabia, the region's largest market, though they can invest in some Saudi mutual funds. Certain stocks in the UAE also are subject to restrictions on foreign investment (Slater 2007).

In 2007, the GDP of the Gulf countries is expected to be at 5 percent growth rate at fixed prices, compared with 8.5 percent in 2003, 5.9 percent in 2004, 6.8 percent in 2005 and 6 percent (estimated) in 2006. The UAE had the highest economic growth rates at fixed prices in 2006, standing at 10.2 percent, Qatar was the second highest of 7.5 percent, Kuwait at 6.5 percent, Saudi Arabia at 6.2 percent and both of Bahrain and Oman had the lowest rate of 5 percent (Azzam 2007). In the Gulf countries, inflation rate was 4 percent in 2006, compared with 2.7 percent in 2005, 1.8 percent in 2004, 1.3 percent in 2003, and 0.8 percent in 2002. Inflation rates are expected to decline in 2007, especially in the UAE and Qatar, because of the decline in the expected surplus demand in the housing markets of these countries after the construction of thousands of new housing units and residential buildings (ibid.).

In the Gulf countries, the important question is does the release of corporate annual financial reports have any effect on securities markets activities? The answer depends on the size and efficiency of the securities markets. In small securities markets, such as the one in Bahrain, Kuwait, Qatar, the UAE, or Saudi Arabia, the effect of the release of financial reports might not be significant. However, in major stock markets, such as the NYSE and TSE, the release of corporate annual financial reports causes a change in investor expectations, thus significantly changing trading volume.

Exact measures of the internationalization of the stock markets are hard to construct. Two basic measures are cross-border listing and the extent to which companies translate their annual reports into other languages for the benefit of foreign investors. In conclusive terms, the largest number of foreign listings is on the New York exchange (the world's largest); in percentage terms, Switzerland has the most foreign listing. The lack of foreign listings in Tokyo (the world's second largest stock exchange) and Toronto is very apparent (Nobes and Parker 2006). Between September 2001 and January 2006, the stock markets in the Gulf countries have grown tremendously in terms of market capitalization and trading turnover and the combined stock markets of the six Gulf countries are now larger than the Hong Kong Stock Exchange and nearly one-third the size of the London Stock Exchange market (Anonymous 2006a). The stock market capitalization in the six Gulf countries has increased by more than 950 percent, from $112 billion at the end of 2000 to approximately $1,061 billion at the end of October 2005 (ibid.).

In the volatile world of stock exchanges, the Gulf countries have become the latest "emerging markets" after the September 11 environment. This trend has become so clear that the Gulf-based investors have switched their focus on a massive scale from the West to the Gulf region (Anonymous 2006a). In Saudi Arabia, many of the large private companies are family-owned businesses. There are around 11,000 family businesses, of which only 126 are joint stock companies. For Saudi Arabia to move toward globalization, and for these companies to continue to exist, they will have to be publicly listed as trading companies; ownership and management should also be separated (Taher 2003). According to past international experiences, large institutions could collapse in a few generations if they do not widen the base of ownership, and this could lead to mass destruction in the national Saudi economy. If they are publicly listed and their shares are to be traded in the stock exchange, they have to implement adequate corporate governance to protect the right of their shareholders (ibid.).

However, on Wednesday November 15, 2006, the Saudi Stock market index stood at 8,187.74, having lost almost 25 percent of its value in 10 trading days to November 11, 2006 (Anonymous 2006b). The stock market contraction in Saudi Arabia and the UAE amounted to a significant emerging-market crash. The Saudi stock market had lost more than half its volume on November 2006 since reaching its peak in February 2006, with shrinkage amounting to approximately $400 billion (ibid.). Despite the stock market crash in November 2006, the recession has led to a healthy weeding out of junk stocks, especially of smaller companies. In contrast, large Gulf business firms have by and large delivered healthy profits. Consider the example of Saudi Telecome, Saudi Basic Industries, and the UAE's Emaar and Etisalat—these companies have improved their third-quarter results compared to the previous year (ibid.).

With respect to financial institutions, the GCC designed a financial system to unify banking and monetary regulations and laws, as well as to increase coordination between monetary agencies and central banks, including the initiation of one currency in order to further economic integration.

In concluding this section, the following major issues may have significant effect on the effectiveness of securities markets in the Gulf region:

1. Major political issues, such as the catalyst of September 11, 2001 in the United States and the significant increase in oil prices;
2. The impact of the patterns of share ownership or joint ventures, including the transition from state-owned business to private ownership;
3. The impact and importance of international financial accounting and reporting criteria and standards in securities markets of Gulf countries;
4. The link to other major international stock markets, such as NYSE and TSE;
5. Major global economic issues, such as the reformation of and significant increases in international trade and foreign direct investment;
6. The emergence of global financial stock markets in Europe, Asia, and the Gulf countries; and
7. The new changes in the international monetary system, including the use of the Euro as one common currency for most of the European countries and the intention of the GCC to establish a common currency for the Gulf countries by the year 2010.

The Effect of Environmental Variables on Accounting in the Gulf Countries

Like other human social activities and disciplines, accounting is a product of its social, economic, political, and legal environment. Accounting plays a significant role in measuring and communicating the results of the economic, social, and managerial performance of a business firm. Every day, it provides corporate executive and financial officers, managers, employees, shareholders, governments, the public, and professional organizations information for the reevaluation of financial, economic, social, and political objectives and activities.

In the industrialized countries such as the United States, Germany, United Kingdom, and Japan, the accounting function is responsive to environmental changes and will continue to be flexible and dynamic. However, in Gulf countries, such as Bahrain, Kuwait, Qatar, and Saudi Arabia, accounting and auditing systems and practices are very slow in responding to economic, social, or political changes in the local environment.

Significant changes in environmental factors affecting national economic, human cultural and behavioral differences have created new global challenges for international accounting and auditing systems and practices. In particular, the significant growth of market globalization and corporations coupled with the stimulus for economic integration and development in Europe and the Gulf countries create many important issues and problems that have yet to be resolved. As MNCs compete for a bigger market share of the Gulf region, they try to focus on the following two major issues: (1) the lowest production costs and the best-selling markets and (2) higher-quality products and higher customer satisfaction. In doing so, their CEO and CFO rely on both accounting and nonaccounting quantitative and qualitative information in making their strategic investment and financial decisions.

Financial statements and reports of local or foreign-owned companies should include a better set of indicators of the contributions of these firms to the economy of the host country. It will encourage new investors to get interested in the Gulf countries and will ensure that operating policies of managing their investments are not contradicting the objectives of the economy of the host country. However, financial statements of MNCs of Bahrain, Kuwait, Qatar, Saudi Arabia, and the UAE, for example, are not directly comparable because of the use of different accounting practices and principles. There are key differences in accounting principles among Gulf countries. If accounting principles and practices were the only differences among Gulf countries, then straightforward conversion of the accounting information of one country's principle to another would be sufficient to make financial statements of different Gulf countries comparable.

Now, it is obvious that Gulf countries have social, economic, political, and legal differences that prevent accounting results from being interpreted uniformly even if these were generated using the same accounting concepts and principles. These differences make international harmonization of accounting for Gulf countries neither practical nor valuable.

On May 20, 2001, the GCC established the Gulf Cooperation Council Accounting and Auditing Organization (GCCAAO) to organize and develop the accounting and auditing profession in the Gulf countries. Its main objective is to review, develop, and approve professional accounting and auditing standards including the codes of ethics for professional accountants, taking into consideration the international standards and practices of other countries. The GCCAAO has started to develop and unify all the rules and regulations of the accounting profession of the Gulf countries, including the conceptual framework of financial accounting; financial accounting standards; auditing standards; code of ethics and professional conduct, Certified Practitioner Accountant (CPA) examination, training and CPE programs; and quality review in the Gulf countries (www.gccaao.org). In the following sections, the accounting standards as developed by the GCCAAO are compared against both LASs and IASs.

Summary and Conclusions

This chapter summarizes the historical and general background of the economic, political, and common characteristics of the Gulf countries. It discusses and emphasizes the importance for accountants, CEOs, CFOs, managers to understand the environmental factors so that an effective global strategy can be formulated by the MNCs. This chapter also examined the international forces and organizations that have made significant economic and cultural changes in the Gulf region, such as the EEC, OECD, GATT, and the GCC.

This essay also noted how MNCs react and respond to the economic and political changes in the Gulf countries. A conflict of interest exists between MNCs' global goals and host countries' national goals. It is suggested that MNCs may reduce their risk and alleviate the conflict with host countries by transforming the traditional income statement and balance sheet into social responsibility statements and by presenting their significant economic and social contributions to the host country in terms of value-added activities.

Moreover, accounting plays a significant role in measuring and communicating the results of economic, social, and managerial performance of a business entity in the Gulf countries. The GCC established the Gulf Cooperation Council and Accounting and Auditing Organization to organize and develop accounting and auditing standards and profession in the Gulf countries. The closer the developed standards and practices of the organization to the International Accounting Standards the more acceptable and usable they will be.

The Gulf countries should design their economic and financial policy reform to promote and support the demand for environmental accounting information. More emphasis and pressure should be placed on shaping the accounting profession to be relevant and flexible for reporting and disclosing the necessary financial and economic information to

3

Islamic Business Ethics and Its Impact on Accounting, Tax, and Finance

Athar Murtuza

This chapter seeks to briefly survey the business ethics enjoined by Islam on its followers. Given nearly 1.5 billion followers of Islam, Muslims, around the world and their history, which dates back to the birth of Islam, this chapter has space only to discuss some aspects of Islam's history and the behavior of Muslims. In recent years Islamic banking has been making news. In order to introduce readers to Islamic business ethics and how they impact Muslims' behavior, let us begin with an update on Islamic banking. This chapter then discusses other aspects of Islamic business ethics and its impact on accounting, tax, and finance.

Introduction

Islam is one of the most significant determinants of cultural values and practices throughout the nations that border the Persian Gulf. It has a growing impact on the trade and business practices, judging from the major growth in the availability of not only Islamic banking but various financial and investment products. Life for any individual, a worker, manager, or an officer, is often influenced by many variables, and for a majority of people in any Islamic country, including the Gulf countries, the influence of culture (especially Islam) is apparent in many of their personal and public activities, actions, decisions, and behavior. Therefore, a businessman or an MNC doing business in the Gulf countries will undoubtedly encounter this influence during interpersonal interactions with Muslim individuals both within and outside the workplace and a sensitivity to and an understanding of these influences and preferences may contribute to improved personal and business relations.

Unfortunately, Islam is largely misunderstood not only by non-Muslims but also by many Muslims themselves. Since September 11, 2001, such misunderstandings seem to have exponentially increased. But a great deal, if not all, of the negative views being spewed by the preachers, politicians, and media pundits is based on lies and stereotypes going back 1,200 years, rather than on facts. This can easily be explained by deciphering the words Islam and Allah. For the Islamphobes, both are evil and Satanic terms. Yet, Islam is an Arabic word, which means "peace," or "submission" and living in accordance with the commands of the One and Only One God, who has created the universe and every thing in it, things as lowly as insects and things as astounding as the galaxies. As may be gathered from phonetic attributes, Islamic Salaam is very similar to Jewish Shalom. Yet the venom directed at Islam is spared the Jewish term, even though they both mean the same thing. The Arabic word for the Creator is Allah and it is also a demonized word. What most people living in the West do not know is that the word Jesus used on the cross to call upon God was not father, or dad, or even God. Since he spoke Aramaic, he used a word that is virtually similar to what Muslims throughout the world use and have used for more than 1,400 years to refer to the One God, excepting the difference in regional accents. The Arabic word incidentally has neither a gender nor a plural form.

Islam is not just a religion but a way of life, and offers guidance not only for a spiritual relationship with his/her Creator, God, but also for a practical day-to-day living including their business practices, accounting ethics and decisions. The practice of Islam requires the performance of prayers (*Salat*) five times a day, sharing one's wealth (*Zakat*), performing the pilgrimage to Mecca (*Haj*) once in a lifetime if one can afford it, and fasting (*Sawm*) during the month of Ramadan. A Muslim is also forbidden to eat pork or drink wine or use other intoxicating substances. Modesty in behavior as well as dress is advised and, therefore, it is considered improper for a Muslim man or woman to look directly into the eyes of someone belonging to the opposite sex when talking to them; it is deemed more appropriate to look down or away. A non-Muslim may consider this impolite; hence the importance of understanding the reason for this behavior.

An Update on Islamic Banking

A telling development in Islamic banking is the emergence of the term Islamic Financial Services Industry to describe what used to be called

Islamic banking. The change in the term is symptomatic of the changes taking place in the industry and in activities that are being carried out not only by the Islamic banks indigenous to Islamic countries but also by the subsidiaries of major Western banks, such as Citi Bank and HSBC who have joined, what was for all intent and purpose, a niche market. That such major players are making efforts to be more attractive to their potential Muslim customers is an interesting new element. It certainly reflects the importance of faith to contemporary Muslims in matters involving their wealth given that it has motivated heavyweight banks to make special efforts to cater to their beliefs.

Recent visitors to Bahrain and other places in the Gulf will observe what is developing in the Islamic financial industry. Bahrain's desire to become the center for the global Islamic financial industry seems quite obvious and there are others who want to be part of the scene. One manifestation of this is the promotion of products, such as *takaful* (Islamic variation of insurance) via mega billboards on the streets of Bahrain. The message stated prominently that the products being advertised were Shari'ah compliant. A cursory reading of the business sections of the local newspapers shows that even topics such as adaptation of hedging and derivatives is being seriously looked at by banks and consultants in the industry. There are institutions in the Gulf countries promising special prizes via lottery to those subscribing to their financial offerings. This is a noticeable change since as late as 2003 there was a considerable amount of controversy when Al-Azhar's scholars ruled regarding the permissibility of fixed rates of return.

A brief article in *Newsweek* (Matthew, October 31, 2005) succinctly surveys what is perhaps the most significant development in the Islamic Financial Service Industry, the emergence of the international banks as major players. Since Citigroup set up a subsidiary to carry out Islamic banking in Bahrain in 1996, other International banks have joined the field: HSBC, Societe Generale, BNP PaRibas, Deutsche Bank, and Standard Chartered. Citibank's Islamic subsidiary has deposits of more than $6 billion while the Bahrain branch of Al Baraka has little more than half a billion. There are over 270 banks in the world.

Along with the international banks, accounting and consulting firms have arrived, among them Ernst & Young and KPMG. Such Western players in the financial service game are employing Islamic scholars to give themselves an aura of credibility and Shari'ah-compliance, a phrase very much in vogue in the Islamic Financial Services sector. In 1996 Dow Jones launched its index of Shari'ah-compliant stocks and since then others have followed suit around the world. This has allowed mutual funds to become a feature of the Islamic financial industry and to be made available to Muslim investors. The Islamic indexes now number more than 40.

Yet another development is the birth of the Islamic Financial Services Board (IFSB) with its offices in Kaula Lumpur, Malaysia. The birth of IFSB was the result of Central Banks of Islamic countries working with the International Monetary Fund (IMF). Its role is to develop prudent and transparent standards that are Shari'ah complaint and to deal with issues such as risk management, capital adequacy, corporate governance, transparency, market discipline, and supervisory roles. The IFSB is expected to bring about standardization in Islamic financial products and services through Muslim countries. Another organization involved with Islamic banking for some time has been the Accounting and Auditing Organization for Islamic Financial Institutions (AAOIFI) with its offices in Bahrain. They have issued over 50 standards involving accounting, auditing, governance, and Shari'ah. Most recently, they have initiated a professional certification called Certified Islamic Professional Accountant (CIPA). The Islamic Development Bank located in Jeddah, Saudi Arabia, has taken the lead in setting up the International Islamic Financial Market (IIFM) to promote and develop liquidity management instruments and markets. They have also set up the International Islamic Rating Agency (IIRA) aimed at providing credit rating as well as rating of corporate governance and Shari'ah compliance by the Islamic financial institutions.

The current spurt in Islamic finance started after 9/11 when wealthy Muslims brought their money back home to the Middle East fearing the seizure of their assets by American politicians seeking to please their voters and the supporters of Israel. This movement of capital seems to have reversed what took place in the aftermath of the First Gulf war, which led to the transfer to Swiss banks of a large proportion of the capital in Middle Eastern Banks.

Other Muslim and non-Muslim countries such as Malaysia and the United Kingdom are seeking to get these funds invested in their countries. The scope of these available funds could best be seen in the growth of what is described as Islamic bonds, *sukuk*. These are assets backed, which presumably makes them acceptable and allows large amounts to be raised. These have been used by governments and corporations in amounts that have reached billions. Citi and HSBC are the leading players in raising *sukuk*-related funds. They emerged in 2000 but their popularity soared after September 11, 2001. In 2004 the total worth of *sukuks* issued was \$6.7 billion, with Malaysia accounting for \$4.7 billion. The largest *sukuk* raised \$11.4 billion for Dubai Ports, Customs & Free Zone Corporation (PCFC), and it was oversubscribed. It is a convertible instrument allowing for redemption of up to 30 percent in the form of equity shares of PCFC if it were to go for a public equity offering within the next three years (Islamic Banking and Finance, Winter 2006, p. 5). PCFC, or its arm DP World, then went to bid for P&O, which in turn unleashed a tsunami of misplaced xenophobia in the United States of America.

Another element that has gained in popular acceptance is *takaful*, which means reciprocal guarantee. It is seen as an Islamic mode of insurance based on mutuality, where the participant contributes a certain amount of money to a common pool, which is then used to defray losses incurred by the contributing members. It has its similarity with insurance as it emerged during nineteenth-century Europe and as it is practiced today; however, the practice of mutually handling disasters that impact members of the group has been documented not only among the pre-Islamic Arabs but in other parts of the world as well. The difference between insurance and *takaful* in theory stems from the alleged elimination of *Riba* (interest), *Gharar* (uncertainty), and *Maisir* (gambling) from the latter; however, in practice one finds that the major difference may simply lie in the restrictions placed in order to insure that the *takaful* funds are invested in Shari'ah-complaint ventures by the firms. In other words, a *takaful* fund is most unlikely to be invested in gambling casinos, filming and distribution of pornographic movies, or in the manufacture of WMDs. Halliburton as an investment may not be entirely acceptable.

Even though one cannot as yet fully answer the question about the long-term viability of Islamic financial services, one can still say that there are developments taking place and many of them are positive. What is beyond doubt is the strong emphasis given to their religious beliefs by Muslims and their willingness to act in compliance to those beliefs. The emergence of Western banks as major players in the industry is a testimonial to the significant level of money involved. It is also a comment on the relative distrust of the indigenous banks on the part of the investors, which is to a large extent a fallout of the absence of effective regulatory oversight and accountable governance in Muslim countries.

Economic Pursuits in Islam

Economic activity such as the pursuit of wealth was not often mentioned in the works of early Western Christian writers such as Alcuin, St. Anselm, and Abelard but this was hardly the case with Muslims even in the Middle Ages. The assertion that human beings do not live by bread alone would not have been taken to imply a renunciation of the worldly pursuits for Muslims, who are told explicitly in the Qur'an: "And seek the other world in that which Allah bestows upon you in this world. But do not forsake your share in this world. Do good to others as Allah has done good to you. Do not seek corruption, or allow it to happen to earth. Allah does not love the corrupters" (28: 77). And again: "Will you consider the denier of all reckoning? He is the person who pushes away the orphan, who does not enjoin the feeding of the destitute" (107: 1–3). Influenced by such Qur'anic exhortations, Muslim writers tend to be more sympathetic to mercantile activity than those of early Christian Europe, and a great deal of early Islamic literature was, in fact, written in a mercantile environment. The differences in the outlook of Islam and Christianity in the Middle Ages with regard to the pursuit of wealth can be attributed to the encouragement, indeed the mandating, of economic activity by the Islamic faith and tradition.

The difference between the Christian and Islamic attitudes and its potential impact can be better appreciated with the help of the research done by Udovitch (1970), among others. Udovitch has reported on the discovery of a fifteenth-century commeda (also known as *Mudarbha*, which consists of a partnership where one partner provides capital and the other operates the business, while both share risks and returns) between a Venetian and an Arab merchant in Alexandria. Thus, the commenda and other partnership contracts were indigenous to the Arab-Islamic world and spread to Latin Europe through contacts and writings of Arab scholars and jurists. Similarly the emergence of various other instruments and institutions facilitated the development of commerce and trade in Europe, such as the bills of exchange (*siftajah*), letter of credit (*hawla*), specialized trading centers (*funduq*), and a kind of early private bank (*ma una*).

From an Islamic perspective, Allah has given human beings custody over nature as well as the abilities to control and use natural resources. Human beings share the world with others, according to the Qur'an: "No animal that creeps on earth or flies in the air but belongs to a species like you [and stands under the commandments of Allah]. Allah's imperatives are relevant to all beings, to all things without exception. All will ultimately have to reckon with Allah" (6: 38). That human beings are accountable to their Creator is central to Islamic beliefs. Such accountability extends to the pursuit of wealth on the part of human beings. Muslims believe that Allah has made human beings agents, Khalifa, who may "utilize what is actually owned by Allah" (Qur'an, 12: 18). Human beings thus hold in trust what really belongs to their Creator and they are accountable to Allah as to how they use His blessings and for how they look after what is entrusted to them.

The following verses from the Qur'an shed more light on the Islamic perceptions of the economic pursuits by human beings: "It is Allah who has subjected the sea to you that ships may sail through it by His command, that you may seek of His bounty, and that you may be grateful. And He has subjected to you, as from Him, all that is in heavens and on earth.

Behold, in that are signs indeed for those who reflect" (55: 12–13). The emphasis is on the fact that human control over what is in the oceans, heavens, and earth is, in fact, a bounty from the Creator (12: 2). It behooves human beings to use the Divine gifts with gratitude and to exercise control over the earthly resources with respect. Clearly, Divinely bestowed control over nature requires that human beings use rather than abuse that which has been entrusted to their control. The use and development of natural resources must not be without moral restraints nor should their use become an end in and of itself. Natural resources, furthermore, must not be monopolized in order to benefit a few while being denied to society at large. One could argue that the expropriation of coastlines and beachfronts by resort hotels, as is done in many of the resort towns around the world, would not be an acceptable practice according to Islam.

Private Ownership and Wealth

The Islamic notions of private ownership, public domain, and wealth are grounded in the notion of human custodianship described in the earlier section. The following ramifications may be extracted from it:

- Ownership of property implies a transferable right to develop and use natural resources.
- The right of ownership requires that natural resources be put to use and developed.
- Owners are encouraged to not hoard the wealth accruing from the economic development of natural resources.
- Not all natural resources can be handed over to private individuals. There are resources, such as rivers and ocean shores, that must be available to everyone in the community.
- The right to own property brings with it a requirement to respect the interests of others as well as the natural resources themselves.

Islam places considerable emphasis on showing respect for the natural environment. Islam enjoins human beings to refrain from destroying or wasting God-given resources. Abu Bakr, who upon the death of Muhammad [pbuh] became the first Caliph of the Islamic State, exhorted his designated army commander being sent to battle not to kill indiscriminately or to destroy vegetation or animal life, even in war and on enemy territory. The same follows for Muslims in peacetime as well as on home territory. For a true Muslim, using torture or environmental abuse and degradation is prohibited both in peace and war.

Islam does not prohibit the pursuit of economic wealth, but at the same time it has provided guidelines about its uses, particularly with regard to sharing one's wealth. Such guidelines ensure that one is using permissible means to acquire wealth and is not exploiting others in the course of such pursuits of wealth. Worldly success, such as that explicit in acquiring wealth, is not prohibited by Islam. One of the prayers recited after each of the five daily prayers by Muslims asks Allah to confer on the supplicant's blessings in this earthly existence and in the after-life.

According to Islamic beliefs, the production of wealth results when the natural resources furnished by God are subjected to the application of knowledge, talents, and labor by human beings individually and collectively. Islam enjoins its followers to realize that natural resources have been created and provided by God to humanity in order to facilitate human existence. Such resources are meant for human enjoyment and comfort. Islam allows private ownership over such resources but not monopolies within limitations. At the same time, three parties, stakeholders, are entitled to share the wealth generated through the development of natural resources: the investors providing the capital, the workers helping in the production, and the community at large. The pursuit of wealth should not become an end in itself nor should it be earned through exploitation of other human beings. One of the very important tenets of Islam is the prohibition of economic exploitation and the misuse of wealth that Allah blesses human beings with. Nothing is as strongly condemned in the Qur'an as ill-gotten wealth acquired through human exploitation and nothing is more extolled and demanded from believers than reflection and thinking.

In addition to its emphasis on reflection and thinking, the Islamic scripture exhorts mankind to be governed by compassion and sharing rather than greed, gluttony, and exploitation of fellow human beings. The Qur'an exhorts people to share with others the Divine blessings bestowed on the wealthy and to acquire wealth in a righteous manner.

Repeatedly, the Qur'an urges Muslims to pay others what is owed to them since exploitation occurs when one does not pay one's obligation. It also condemns in the strongest terms those who cheat others through fraudulent means in commercial transactions. Bribes are perceived similarly judging from the sayings of the Prophet which refer to bribes and deception as *Riba* (Chapra 1983). The Islamic prohibition against cheating others is grounded in the same spirit as is the Islamic injunction against transactions involving usury. Both would encroach upon the basic right Islam, in effect, grants to all human beings, namely, the right to be free from economic exploitation. In the following section a brief survey of human rights as seen by Islam is discussed.

Sanctity of Human Life, Equality, and Property

In his last sermon, Prophet Muhammad placed freedom from exploitation on par with the sacredness of life and equality of all human beings irrespective of their ethnic and racial origins. In the same context, he insisted that males and females have rights and obligations toward each other. The principle that community has an obligation toward those who are poor was the hallmark of the so-called Charter of Medina, which was a covenant arrived at the birth of the Islamic State in Medina when Prophet Muhammad arrived there after fleeing the city of Mecca where those opposed to Islam had plotted to assassinate him. Medina contained Muslims, non-Muslims as well as Jews at that time, and the Charter was a formal agreement between all of them. In addition to establishing the obligation of the community to help the less fortunate among its ranks, the Charter also established the freedom of worship for those who did not convert to Islam. Some scholars have called this charter, dating back to 620s of the Christian era, the world's first written constitution, which subsequently guided for the most part the Muslim policy toward non-Muslims who lived amongst them.

Prohibition of *Riba*

To encourage economic activity while seeking to keep it from being exploitive as well as becoming an end in itself, Islam has exhorted its adherents to refrain from *Riba*, which translates literally as unlawful or exploitive gains. It must be equated with economic exploitation (Ibn al Qayyim quoted in Vogel and Hayes 1998), and the prohibition against it must not be construed as applying only to transactions involving usury or even interest. The prohibition against *Riba* is intended to promote ethical economic activities that do not exploit other human beings in order to create wealth for an individual.

All too often Muslim jurists and laity themselves have equated *Riba* only to the interest charged on loans. In doing so, however, they are ignoring the fact that the prohibition against *Riba* seeks not just to forbid loans involving usury, but all forms of activities that enrich one individual through the exploitation of others. As pointed out by Umer Chapra, the Sunnah of Prophet has also emphasized other aspects of *Riba* covering all forms of economic injustice, exploitation, and unearned income (other than that, like inheritance and genuine gifts, allowed by the Shari'ah). Accordingly it can be defined as all excess over what is justified by consideration. Chapra goes on to note Caliph Umer's injunction emphasizing that one should abstain from *Riba* as well as any income that has the semblance of *Riba* or that raises doubts in the mind about its rightfulness, thus covering all income derived from injustice to, or exploitation of, others (Chapra 1983).

Repeatedly, the Qur'an urges Muslims to pay others what is owed to them since exploitation occurs when one does not pay one's obligation. Such exhortations are very much a part of Islamic emphasis on social justice. In the same spirit, the prohibition against *Riba* must be construed as intended to ensure the freedom of human beings from being exploited by others. Islam prohibits exploitation of all sorts and in any form. Such prohibition extends to welfare fraud, Medicare over-charges, bribery, cheating, dealing in drugs, and environmental degradation, not just to the usurious interest charged on money loaned. The attitude implied in "buyers beware" is not quite Islamic—it is up to the sellers not to exploit, deceive, or extort!

Prophet Muhammad in his Farewell Sermon made one of the most significant of calls in all of human history directed to Muslims to prevent them from indulging in economic exploitation of others. The Prophet reminded his followers to be just in their dealings with others and made it unlawful to take something from others, unless it is given willingly (Armstrong 1992). In this sermon made centuries prior to the *Magna Carta* and the U.S. Bill of Rights, Prophet Muhammad issued what one internationally well-respected Hyderabadi scholar has described as "the charter of Humanity in Islam" (Hamidullah 1969). The sermon reasserts the basic elements of Islam: the belief in One God, prohibition against material or anthropomorphic representation of God, the equality of all Muslims, the outlawing of discrimination on account of race, gender, or class, and the insistence that one cannot claim superiority over another except by means of the individual excellence in the matter of piety and the fear of God. The sermon also makes clear the sacrosanct nature of the rights of each and every human being concerning his person, his property, and his honor. In addition to declaring the sacredness of property rights, the sermon sought to make this right tangible by issuing in strongest terms the prohibition on *Riba*. Through his last sermon, the Prophet sought to prevent the development of conditions that can facilitate economic exploitation among Muslims. He was underscoring what Qur'an itself (30: 39) and (2: 276) has proclaimed by condemning increase brought on through *Riba* while extolling *zakat* which is translated both as purification as well as increase, refers to sharing of one's wealth. This makes *Riba* the opposite of *Zakat*: both terms may be translated as increase, but they are opposite to each other with regard to how an increase in wealth is to be attained. One seeks increase in one's wealth through exploitation, while the other, through sharing, seeks to increase what should be called communal wealth. One's wealth will increase if those around him are also enjoying an increase in their wealth or spending power.

The Nature of *Zakat* (Taxes)

Muslims are religiously obligated to share their wealth with others; such religiously enjoined sharing is known as *Zakat*. There is some hesitation about calling it a tax as noted by Baydoun and Willet (1997); nonetheless, it has almost all the attributes one associates with tax, plus its religious sanction. For a large number of Muslims it is equated with giving to "charity" certain percentage of their wealth every year—but it is wrong to translate the word as charity, since it is much more than what charity connotes. In the Qur'an, in the sayings of the Prophets, and in the practices of the early days of Islam, it is also called *sadaqat* and *haqq*, and meant all sorts of taxes imposed by the Muslim State on its Muslim subjects: tax on agricultural produce, on subsoil exploitation, on commercial capital, on herds of domesticated animals grazing on public pastures, as well as on cash and personal wealth. In the beginning all these taxes were paid directly to the government, but later, during the time of the third Caliph Uthman it was decided that Muslims could directly give the *zakat* to its beneficiaries instead of letting the government collect and distribute it (Hamidullah 1974).

On account of such religious sanction, this requirement of Islamic belief becomes an exceptional mode of public finance, a levy individual Muslims are obliged to pay as a required part of the observance of their faith. Such sanctified redistribution of wealth is one of the five basic tenets of Islam. A large number of scholars see it as being ranked next to prayers in terms of its importance for Muslim believers. The importance of this religious obligation is seen in the fact that the first caliph, Abu Baker, upon succeeding the Prophet [pbuh] as the head of the Muslim State, made war upon those tribes who refused to pay it.

That the word *Zakat* literally means "that which purifies" and "that which fosters growth" leads Hamidullah to see Muslims' payment of a part of their wealth to the community as being intended to purify their wealth (1969). In addition to providing resources to meet the needs of the community, it also serves additional functions. It can curb human tendencies toward acquisitiveness and greed. It may also act as a reminder to the rich to share their wealth with those who are indigent. It serves as the instrument to help the community by meeting the social and economic needs of its members. Lastly, it serves to prevent the accumulation of wealth in few hands and allows it to be distributed to a large number of people.

The Qur'an uses additional terms to describe the nature of this financial obligation expected of Muslims. In Chapter 9, verse 60, the word *sadaqat* is used to describe this obligation. The term *sadaqat* means truth and charity. In the opinion of Hamidullah (1969), this implies that to be true to humanity, Muslims must be charitable toward the less fortunate than themselves. In Chapter 6, verse 141, the term *haqq*, meaning truth and right, is used to refer to this obligation. The three terms *sadaqaat*, *haqq*, and *Zakat* are used synonymously to describe what has been termed *ibadat maliyah*—worship through financial means and instruments (Hamidullah 1969).

Historical Background of Zakat *(Taxes)*

According to most contemporary Muslim economists, *Zakat* must be seen as the pivot and hub of the Islamic public finance. It was the primary source of revenue for the Islamic State during the time of Prophet Muhammad [pbuh] and the four caliphs who succeeded him, Abu Bakr, Umer, Uthman, and Ali, collectively known as the Pious Caliphs. Initially, in the Islamic State governed by the Prophet [pbuh] there were no "taxes" to provide revenue for the community's needs. The Qur'an exhorted and the Prophet [pbuh] encouraged Muslims to perform charitable acts and to spend for the sake of Allah. The early Muslims moved by such exhortations would often bring their charities to the Prophet [pbuh] himself and entrust him to spend as he liked. But such voluntary contributions proved inadequate for the needs of the community when a crisis was brought on through the murder of a Muslim ambassador sent to the then Byzantine territory, Syria, by the Prophet [pbuh]. Since the murder of an ambassador was considered to be a serious act of aggression, Prophet Muhammad in his role as the head of the Muslim State, sent a punitive expedition, 3,000 strong, but the enemy was 33 times more stronger in number at the battle of Mu'ta, and the Muslim army returned with significant losses (Hamidullah 1974). Thereupon Muslims prepared for what became the expedition of Tabuk through an army that numbered 30,000 soldiers. Voluntary contributions alone could not have supported such a large expenditure, and this led to voluntary contributions becoming institutionalized. Henceforth, specified amounts needed to be paid on various forms of wealth such as agricultural harvests, savings, commercial capitals, import and export, herds of cattle, and minerals extracted. In addition, a time was set for making such payments, and those who did not want to contribute "were constrained to submission by the use of force. It remained an act of piety, a part of religion obligations, yet it became a State tax. The original name *Zakat* was retained, yet it became an obligation, and no more a voluntary act on the part of those who were in a position to pay" (Hamidullah 1974).

Even while the institution was being changed from voluntary alms-giving to a formal tax due from the community to the state, the Prophet Muhammad and his family members were excluded from those described as being the beneficiaries of *Zakat*. According to Hamidullah (1969), "The Prophet [pbuh] formally declared that revenues of the Muslim State, coming from the Muslim taxpayers, were religiously forbidden to him and to all members of his tribe". This exclusion sets up the principle that the resources of the community are not to be treated as the personal wealth of the ruling family. Following the death of the Prophet [pbuh], the first caliph was allowed a state stipend in order to free him from earning a livelihood while also serving as the head of the Muslim State. Umer, who felt that the first caliph's time was better used if it was directed toward serving the needs of the state rather than making a living, suggested this stipend.

Prescribed Uses of Zakat *(Taxes)*

The Qur'an itself is virtually silent on the subject of the property and wealth objects to be taxed. The rates of *Zakat* due on various forms of property and the manner in which it is collected owe their origin to Prophet and the Pious Caliphs and not the Qur'an itself. At the same time Qur'an gives quite specific details as to its uses and its beneficiaries. Such precise specification for its uses is a special feature of this religious requirement expected of Muslims. Hamidullah (1974) also construes such Qur'anic treatment of *Zakat* to imply that the actual rate of taxation is left to the representatives of the people to decide according to the specific needs at a given point in time.

The Qur'anic verse dealing with the disbursement and the beneficiaries of *Zakat* reads as follow:

> The proceeds are only for the poor (among the Muslims) and the destitute (among the non-Muslims), and those who work for these (revenues), and those whose hearts are to be reconciled, and for freeing the necks (of prisoners and slaves), and those heavily charged, and in the path of God, and for the wayfarers; a duty imposed by Allah, Allah being knower, wise. (9: 60)

These eight categories are, in fact, very comprehensive and are seen by a number of contemporary scholars as defining the social responsibilities of a Muslim State.

The first two categories refer to the needy. According to one school of thought the first, *fu'qara*, refers to the Muslim indigents, and the second, *masakin*, are the poor among the non-Muslim inhabitants in the Muslim State. On the other hand, the Muslim jurist, Ibn Taymiya, sees the two categories as referring to the needy—the difference between them being that one begs and lets his needs be known, while the other does not inform others of his needs (Islahi 1998). The third category, referring to those who work for its collection and the subsequent disbursement, according to Hamidullah (1969), may include not only those directly involved, such as "the collectors, accountants, those in charge of the expenditure, controllers and auditors," but may, in fact, "practically embrace the entire administration, both civil and military, of the State in view of the fact that the beneficiaries of these revenues include practically all departments of administration." The next category, "those whose hearts are to be won," is seen by Hamidullah as representing first, those who need encouragement for coming to the aid of the Muslim community; second, those whose who are to be induced to abstain from doing harm to Muslims; third, those who are attracted toward Islam; and fourth, those whose conversion to Islam may lead others to do the same. Hamidullah (1969) adds: "It is lawful to benefit each and every one of these categories" and whether those included in these categories profess Islam is immaterial. Muslim jurists from the early centuries of Islam, Abu Yusuf and Abu Ya'la, have written that non-Muslims could be the beneficiaries of *Zakat* disbursements (Hamidullah 1993). In the contemporary context, one could use *Zakat* for educating the public about the meaning of Islam through setting up think tanks and for informing the general public about Islam.

The next category, referred to by the term "freeing the necks," has generally been seen as alluding to the emancipation of slaves and the ransoming of those taken as prisoners of war by an enemy. Even though Islam did not forbid slavery outright, back in the seventh century everyone who could owned them; nonetheless, Islam was the first of the world religions to have paid specific attention to improving the condition of the slaves. Qur'an (20: 33) orders that if a well-behaving slave is prepared to pay off his value to his master, his master cannot refuse the offer; in fact, he should be required by Islamic law to grant his slave opportunities to earn and save the necessary amount for obtaining his freedom.

The object of permitting slavery in Islam, according to Hamidullah was not the exploitation of an unfortunate fellow being. Far from that, its aim was first to provide shelter to the prisoners of war who had lost everything, and for some reason or other are not repatriated; and second, to educate them and give them the opportunity of acquiring culture in Islamic surroundings, under the government of God. Slaves were to be obtained only in legitimate war, waged by a government. Private *razzias*, kidnapping, or even sale of infants by their parents have no legal sanction whatsoever"

(Hamidullah 1969). The fact that a portion of *Zakat* was earmarked for freeing the slaves certainly demonstrates that Islam sought to prevent and certainly contain the abuses connected with slavery that were commonly practiced at that time.

One must not limit the two Qur'anic phrases "those whose hearts are to be won" and "freeing the necks" to their literal sense. Indeed the figures of speech used by the Qur'an would have one interpret them as metaphorical. Clearly human beings can be enslaved in many ways and winning the hearts could be accomplished by appealing to human minds. Through specifying such uses of the *Zakat* funds side by side with the needs of the needy and indigent, the Qur'an is seeking to extend the uses of *Zakat* beyond meeting the basic needs of food, clothing, and shelter of the indigents. *Zakat* is, therefore, not an act of charity; rather it is an instrument for enriching a community not only through an eradication of poverty but its underlying causes as well. It may be also used to protect the community from external threats and to help meet calamities that could beset members of the community, natural and financial. It is thus an instrument for preventing conditions, which make economic exploitation of human beings more likely. That *Zakat* not only is meant to serve as a comprehensive safety net but also to help promote community growth and prevent economic exploitation is seen in the remaining three uses specified for it—helping those heavily indebted, for promoting the cause of Allah, and helping travelers.

The injunction to use it to help those who are heavily indebted can be taken to mean helping those who have encountered hardships or natural disasters. In the days of Caliph Umer, the state provided interest-free loans to individuals to help them get back on their feet after they encountered hardships. One must see the injunction to help those heavily indebted to mean not only providing disaster relief to those stricken by natural calamities but also those whose "indebtedness" is due to the systemic forms of poverty that add to the economic hardships of individuals in poor communities.

In present-day America, one is familiar with disaster-relief funding as well as the concept of enterprise zone to rebuild urban pockets of poverty. Small business loans are also familiar means of promoting economic enterprise. Other variations of "indebtedness" that prevent individuals from an optimum realization of their God-given abilities come to mind, such as poor farmers who had to borrow from moneylenders money that they are unable to pay back due to bad crops or natural disasters. The role of *Zakat* as a safety net aimed at eradicating the potential for exploitation can also be construed to mean eradication of the disparities obvious in the educational opportunities available to community members, such as the disparity of school funding in different districts within a state, such as New Jersey, which leads to major disparities in the quality of education being imparted to children in different parts of the state. One must interpret broadly the nature of "indebtedness" just as we should the phrases "those whose hearts are to be won" and "freeing the necks." The seventh use of *Zakat* signified by the phrase "in the path of God," according to Hamidullah (1969), "includes every charitable cause; and the jurists have not hesitated to start with military equipment for the defense of Islam." This category has also been taken to mean building religious centers, hospitals, schools, libraries, and sponsoring religious outreach and missionary work.

The last category, the "wayfarers," literally means that one should use *Zakat* to help travelers by providing them hospitality. But helping travelers can also imply building highways and maintaining a transportation system, an infrastructure that will ensure security of routes and permit measures that will provide for the well-being of those who have to travel through the land. Such facilities should be available to every one irrespective of their faith and national origin. Indeed, transportation of goods and the ability to travel are indispensable for the well-being and growth of a community, to raise its standard of living, and most important, to prevent economic exploitations. In short, the uses of this Islamic pillar of faith make it a much more than an act of simple charity. The prescribed uses make it a resource for eradicating conditions that promote exploitation of human beings.

Islamic Rationale for Taxes

The requirement that Muslims as an expression of their faith pay *Zakat* is meant to help fulfill the community responsibility to take care of its members' needs. Making sure that the needs of the community are met with the help of such assessments is an absolute imperative, according to Yusuf (1990): "The obligation is absolute and preferential in the sense that if the collection at the normal rate is inadequate for the purpose, the state is compelled to supplement the same by resorting to borrowing (of course, without interest) and/or taxation to the extent and till such time as is required by the needs of the situation."

The revenues from *Zakat* are to serve as a religiously sanctioned safety net for community members. If the fund is not utilized, the surplus will go on accumulating and be reserved in the state treasury—Bait al-Mal. It is expressly prohibited that the *Zakat* fund (Yusuf 1990) be diverted to any other head of expenditure—however, as discussed earlier, the eight categories that the Qur'an specifies are rather broad and do allow considerable latitude in spending it. A very persuasive case can be made to argue that the basic justification underlying this religious requirement imposed on

Muslims is aimed at ensuring that the basic needs of all members of the community are met. But, at the same time, the eight specified uses of *Zakat* are not limited to providing food and shelter for the indigent members of the community (Hamidullah 1993). As noted earlier, the funds collected are also designed for community building through uses that are meant to equalize opportunities, further trade and commerce, help build highways, aid in promotion of enterprise on the part of community members, allow for disaster relief, provide for military defense, and even help provide incentive to potential friends of the community. While prohibiting its use for the personal enrichment and gratification of the head of the state and his family, a provision is made for expenses incurred in administering the disbursement and collection. To ensure that such administrative overheads would not consume most of the funds collected, Islamic jurists have argued that the salaries of those involved with civil, military, and judicial functions of the state must be from other sources of revenues accruing to the state—such as *Kharaj* (Yusuf 1990).

The institution of *Zakat* indicates that Islam permits the state to tax its citizen specifically for the discharge of the obligations laid upon the state. Making taxation an act of pious belief does not totally abolish tax evasion, yet it can serve to minimize the problem of tax evasion. To further ensure tax payments, even while making such fiscal sharing a form of worship and a requirement for belief, Islam emphasizes control over the uses of such contributions. Research has shown that citizens have a greater willingness to pay taxes as long as the funds are used properly.

Islam has had its share of "Boston tea parties." There have been disagreements over what to tax and to what extent. In fact, the efforts of Saladin against the Crusaders almost failed on account of his hesitation to levy taxes that were not in keeping with *Fiqh*. In this context, one could cite the ordeal underwent by Muslim jurists in resisting the innovation of taxes, allegedly unrecognized by Islam and imposed by rulers seeking to meet their budgets. One of the more notable examples is that of al-Sarakhsi, the famous scholar of what is now Central Asia. He exhorted the people to stop payment of taxes that were not sanctioned by Islam and for which he was imprisoned in a well from where he dictated his voluminous books to the pupils sitting on the periphery of the well. The point is that the imposition of a new tax "constitutes a serious violation of the Shar'ia; it is not just a matter of ingenuity on the part of a minister and his advisors" (Yusuf 1990).

Taxes are hardly the cherished symbol of the allegiance citizens owe to their states. Throughout the world, professional tax experts seek to aid citizens in avoiding or at least minimizing taxes. Tax avoidance through legal and illegal means is and has been a global reality. Such desires to

With the arrival of Western colonialism and the simultaneous eclipse of Islamic political strength, most of the Muslim institutions underwent a drastic decline. The institution of *Hisba* also declined in effectiveness and virtually disappeared. Both the Prophet [pbuh] himself and the Caliph Umer appointed women as *Muhtasib*. Only in later centuries, the position was reserved for men only.

The Nature of the Institution of Hisba

The duties performed by a *Muhtasib* were of three categories. First of these consisted of those relating to (rights of) God. These covered religious activities such as punctuality of prayers, organization of Jum'a and `Id congregations, and maintenance of mosques. The second category consisted of those duties relating to rights and obligations of people and these related to community affairs and behavior in the market, such as accuracy of weights and measures and honesty in dealings. The third category was related to both: affairs connected to municipal administration such as keeping the roads and streets clean and lit at night and preventing the building of a factory or dwelling place that could damage the community interests.

The *Muhtasib* could appoint others, such as technically qualified experts to investigate matters pertaining to different crafts and trades. He received complaints from the public but could also initiate an investigation on his own. He had wide powers, but was required to use them sensibly. The powers assigned to him to carry out his functions included simple advice, reprimand, rebuke, obstruction by forces, threat, imprisonment, and expulsion from the town. The *Muhtasib* was required to choose a stronger punishment only if a milder one was either ineffective or seemed to carry no weight with the person being admonished. The code of conduct for a *Muhtasib* provided a system of checks and balances. For example, he could not doubt a prima facie approved behavior nor could he engage in secret probing into a doubtful affair. The behavior of a person should be obviously against the injunctions of the Shari'ah before a *Muhtasib* could intervene. Similarly he could not issue new edicts involving interpretations of the rules—to punish people; instead he could forbid them from only those actions on which there existed a consensus among the community. He was expected to act with wisdom and foresight and not overzealously. His actions ought not to bring about a greater mischief than the one he sought to stop—he was to think through the consequences of his activities. On questions of social practices, the *Muhtasib* was expected to invite community participation and refrain from imposing his personal opinions and standards on the majority. In summary, the office of *Muhtasib* was only a logical necessity of the Islamic State to perpetuate and preserve its social norms. It was not merely a secular office to regulate markets and administer municipal services (Khan 1997).

Essence of Hisba

The literature on the institution of *Hisba* relates it to "*amr bil ma `ruf wa-n-nahi `anil munkar*" (promote good and prevent evil) enjoined on all Muslims. From this the following may be established: first, it was the *Muthasib's* responsibility to ensure that the community as a whole had proper organization and facilities for performance of worship, `Ibadat. Second, the *Muhtasib* paid special heed to various municipal services, especially with regard to the hygienic conditions in the town. In effect he acted as a municipal officer in the Muslim society. He would look into the entire municipal administration such as street lighting, removal of garbage, architectural designs of buildings, water supply, and antipollution sanctions. Third, the *Muhtasib* was concerned with the implementation of `*adl* (justice) in the society. He would try to enforce fair play among different economic factors to minimize possibilities of exploitation from the economy. Consequently, he would be involved with inspection of weights and measures, metallic content of coins, and quality of food products. Similarly the *Muhtasib* would check manipulation of prices, supplies and production, monopolistic collisions, cheating, fraud, and any other form of inter-sectorial inequity. In brief, he had to intervene wherever the economic flows were manipulated by the economically powerful individual or groups to meet their selfish ends.

It would appear that the need to regulate business so that public interest is protected is a notion that goes back in history. It is no surprise that it was a part of Islamic civil society for well over 1,200 years. Its effectiveness depended on the individuals performing the job as well as the governance of which they formed a part. Just like the modern public auditor's performance as a defender of public interest has been uneven, one may assume the performance of the *Muhtasibs* varied through the ages.

Conclusion

One way to conclude the chapter would be to ask the obviously relevant question at this point in human history: Why are the injunctions of the Qur'an with regard to the use of reason and ethical pursuit of wealth so different from the practices and environment that characterize much of the Muslim world. Among countries known for endemic corruption and abysmal unaccountable governance, Muslim countries occupy a very prominent place. Nor do they seem very inclined to practice reflection and reasoning.

The correct answer to the question posed earlier would in fact be that it is not sufficient to just proclaim the ideals—which the Qur'an and other Scriptures, the corporate ethical codes and legislations such as Foreign Corrupt Practices Act as well as Sarbanes-Oxley seek to accomplish. Unless there are constant attempts to insure good and just governance, which accountants would label as control, to see that the ideals are implemented, *Homo sapiens*, being human, would fall prey to greed and gluttony. That the ideals of the Qur'an do not get practiced in the contemporary Muslim world has a great deal to do with the absence of good governance, which in turn breeds corruption, ignorance, and exploitation of the powerless.

Muslim countries are not the only places where greed and gluttony seems to overpower justice and compassion. The developed world has its problems stemming from the ability of the vested interests to get away with earning maximization and corruption—the recent corporate scandals in the United States and Europe demonstrate the problem well enough (Clarke, Dean, and Oliver 1998). Those seeking to promote good ethical business in accounting, tax, and finance must remember that it is not automatically engendered—MNCs need constant nourishments, exhortations, and good governance if they are to become successful companies. Furthermore, the environment where the good companies are located must also be free of corruption and subject to the rule of law and justice. In other words, economic Goodness requires not just lip service to ideals, but willingness and ability to insure that ideals are implemented and practiced. Making sure that the ideals are not violated or rendered ineffective by the vested interests requires vigilance by all members of a civil society, especially against those seeking hegemonic collusion and consolidation of the economic resource for the benefits of the rich and powerful through unjust laws, monopolies, cartels, and price manipulations. This was something Jesus made obvious when he harshly dealt with the money changers carrying out their business in the temple. The potential for a variance between mere belief and actual behavior, the gap between what is professed and what is practiced has been commented upon by none other than Jesus himself: "Why do you keep calling me 'Lord, Lord' and never do what I tell you" (Luke 6: 46). Mercy and Forgiveness, attributes of the Deity would be rendered obsolete if there were to be no sinners!

References

Armstrong, K. 1992. *Muhammad, A Biography.* Harper Collins: New York.

Baydoun, N. and R. Willet. 1997. "Islam and Accounting: Ethical Issues in the Presentation of Financial Information." *Accounting, Commerce & Finance: The Islamic Perspective* 1 (1): 1-25.

Chapra M.U. 1983. "Comments on CII Report on Elimination of Interest." In *Money and Banking in Islam.* Ed. Ziauddin Ahmed et al, Institute of Policy Studies: Islamabad, Pakistan: 212–223.

Cook, Michael. 2000. *Commanding Right and Forbidding Wrong in Islamic Thought.* Cambridge University Press: Cambridge, United Kingdom.

Hamidullah, M. 1969. *Introduction to Islam.* 3rd edition, Centre Culturel Islamique: Paris, France.

———. 1974. *Muhammad [pbuh] Rasulullah.* Centre Culturel Islamique: Paris, France.

Islahi, A.A. 1998. *Economic Concepts of Ibn Taimiyah.* The Islamic Foundation: Leicester, United Kingdom.

Udovitch, Abraham L. 1970. *Partnership and Profit in Medieval Islam.* Princeton University Press: Princeton, New Jersey.

Vogel, Frank and Samuel Hayes, III. 1998. *Islamic Law and Finance: Religion, Risk, and Return.* Kluwer: Hague.

Part II

Accounting and Auditing of the Gulf Countries

4

Accounting Standards and Practices of the Gulf Countries

Wagdy M. Abdallah

This chapter examines differences and similarities in accounting between Accounting Standards of the Gulf countries and International Accounting Standards (IASs). First, several economic and financial factors that are unique to Gulf countries are discussed. Second, several key accounting issues such as inventory, investment, asset valuation, consolidation, and foreign currency translation, and transactions are analyzed in terms of the similarities and discrepancies between the Local Accounting Standards (LASs) with the International Accounting Standards (IASs). Third, general guidelines and recommendations on the accounting quality of accounting systems and practices of the Gulf countries, to help investors and creditors in making their investing and financing decisions in the Gulf countries, are presented.

Background

Comparable accounting information is essential to ensure the free flow of capital across international borders. In recent years, the growth of cross-border financial transactions has led a number of organizations to work toward harmonizing accounting rules and practices. Among these groups seeking to harmonize global accounting practices is the International Accounting Standards Board (IASB). The IASB has been the most active, but not the only one. The efforts of the IASB and others have led to the adoption of internationally accepted standards in many countries; however, such acceptance varies from one country to another.

With respect to the Gulf countries, if the accounting systems and practices of Bahrain, Kuwait, Oman, Qatar, Saudi Arabia, and the United Arab Emirates (UAE) were identical, there would be no problem for international investors, creditors, and capital market regulators in understanding the published financial statements of domestic and multinational companies (MNCs) operating in any one of the six countries. Unfortunately, this is not the case here. For economic and social developments, Gulf countries require accounting systems and practices tailored to their needs. The development of accounting should be able to match the high rates of economic and social growth and to provide them with relevant, timely, and reliable information to help entrepreneurs, investors, and MNCs to make right decisions. Given the lack of accounting comparability and harmonization between accounting systems of Gulf countries, it is not surprising, then, that the investing and financing decisions tend to be risky.

In an attempt to attract higher levels of foreign investment, Gulf countries should be responding with several tools; they include the following (1) increasing the flow of economic information to investors, (2) broadening the use of international accounting standards, and (3) improving the efficiency of their capital markets. Due to the fact that the quality of financial disclosure influences the quality of decisions made by the investors and creditors, it is essential for foreign investors and creditors to understand the accounting systems and practices of Gulf countries. The reasons include (1) to compare the financial reports of MNCs operating in Gulf countries, (2) to analyze the differences in financial reporting systems and auditing standards and practices of Gulf countries, (3) to know the effect of accounting differences on asset valuation and income determination of local or joint ventures operating in Gulf countries, (4) to decide where to invest at a high rate of return and a low rate of political risk, and (5) to look for the possibility of designing the appropriate harmonized financial reporting systems and practices of the Gulf countries.

Success in implementing the right International Financial Reporting Standards (IFRSs) in the Gulf countries, as in many European Union listed companies, depends on to what extent and how quick the listed firms in the Gulf countries are responding to the global financial community convergence. By looking at the situation from an investor's viewpoint, Gulf countries can turn the process around to their best interests and to the companies' advantage and get the needed strategic foreign investments into their countries to help them in expediting economic reforms and, at the same time, making it attractive destinations for investors.

The environmental variables of Gulf countries and their implications on the development of local accounting and auditing standards were discussed in chapter one. This chapter examines first the similarities and differences of five key accounting issues between LAS of the Gulf countries and IASs issued and revised by the IASB. The key accounting issues including inventory, investment, asset valuation, foreign currency translation and transactions, and consolidation are discussed in detail. Finally, general guidelines and major recommendations on the implementation of IFRSs, to help investors and creditors in making their strategic investing and financing decisions, in the Gulf countries, are presented.

Comparisons of LASs and IASs

Accounting is considered as the measurement and communication of relevant economic information about a business entity to decision makers International accounting researchers have been examining two important questions; they are (1) What differences and similarities exist across national accounting systems? and (2) What environmental factors explain these differences and similarities? (Doupnik and Salter 1995). Unfortunately, there have been limited efforts in research to develop theories to explain how different environmental variables affect national accounting systems and practices.

In general, accounting systems and financial reporting have been closely interrelated with the economic, legal, and political changes in several countries. Until now, the accounting profession in Gulf countries has not responded adequately to these environmental developments for several reasons (Farag 1991)

1. The nature of business entities was basically in production and services, especially for commodities of the agriculture and mineral sectors. Manufacturing, marketing, and finance functions were not among priorities for local investors;
2. Large public and private ownership of most economic resources were concentrated in the hands of few entities or individuals;
3. Capital securities markets are either not functioning at all, are very small-scale activities, are not affected much by annual corporate financial reporting, or do not exist; and
4. Economic or political unexpected negative movements or actions may deteriorate the confidence of local investors and the link between savings and investments. Most rich Gulf citizens have been investing all their savings abroad; however, foreign investors finance most local projects and enterprises.

In the following sections, the accounting standards as developed by the GCCAAO are compared against both LASs and IASs. In order to achieve this objective first, an attempt has been made in this essay to highlight, briefly, the GAAP of each Gulf country included in this study. Then the LAS and practices of five important accounting issues in the six Gulf countries are compared with both IAS and GCCAAO standards. Finally, the conclusions and future research directions are presented.

Bahrain

Bahrain is a member of the International Federation of Accountants (IFAC). It is officially required of all business firms to keep their financial accounting reporting to be according to IASs (Ernst & Young 2003). The accounting firms or the CPAs practicing in Bahrain are also required to use International Auditing Standards issued by the IFAC.

Since 1992 financial year-end, the Bahraini Monetary Agency (BMA) required all banks to produce statements in accordance with IASs. Thereafter, they referred to International Standards on auditing and IASs. Further, locally incorporated and publicly quoted banks have been required to publish financial statements on a quarterly basis. These statements need not be audited, but should be reviewed by external auditors and published within eight weeks of the end of the quarter (Hussain et al. 2002). Financial statements are prepared under the historical cost convention, modified in the case of some banks by the revaluation of premises and equipment with respect to certain subsidiaries.

Kuwait

The accounting profession in Kuwait developed tangibly in the early 1950s. Driven by need, the Kuwait government passed legislation that required public firms to report audited financial statements. However, there was no stipulation in those early regulations as to what accounting standards were to be followed. The stock market crash of 1982 had a lot to do with a lack of accounting, accountability, and professionally credible auditing. Unlike Saudi Arabia, Kuwait does not have accounting standards of its own. Compliance with the IAS promulgated by the IASB is mandatory for shareholding- and limited-liability companies for accounting periods starting on or after January 1, 1991.

The Kuwaiti Association of Accountants and Auditors is the only local professional body of accounting. Law No. 5 of 1981, in setting legal rules governing the auditing profession, requires that registered auditors should be persons of Kuwaiti nationality. To practice accounting, members have to pass an exam similar to the CPA exam in United States. The Kuwaiti Association is a member of the IFAC. In Kuwait, all business firms are required to keep adequate financial records and books. They do not have to be maintained in Arabic. All books and records of foreign companies, operating in Kuwait are subject to the provisions of the Tax Decree of official Ministerial order. The books and records that should be maintained include a general journal, inventory sheets, a general ledger, an expenses analysis journal, and a stock record.

Law No. 6 of 1962-Practice of Audit of Accounts, amended by Law No. 5 of 1981, was the first law enacted by the Kuwaiti government to regulate the accounting profession. It covers the rights and obligations of auditors and requires that the auditor shall complete his work according to generally acceptable auditing and accounting standards that are specified by the technical committee (Shuaib 1985).

Starting from January 1, 1991, shareholding- and limited-liability companies are required to use the IAS. Three rules of IASs have had a significant impact on accounting and financial reporting in Kuwait; these are (1) IAS No. 24, "Related Party Transactions," which affected the reporting of related party transactions and the quantification of such transactions; (2) IAS No. 27, "Consolidated Financial Statements and Accounting for Investments in Subsidiaries," which was introduced for the first time in Kuwait to the large family trading groups; and (3) IAS No. 30, "Disclosures in Financial Statements of Banks and Similar Financial Institutions," which improved significantly the disclosures of Kuwaiti banks' financial statements. Audited balance sheet and income statements of both public shareholding- and limited-liability companies are required to have an annual audit. The auditor must be independent and registered with the Ministry of Commerce and Industry. Audited financial statements must be submitted to the Ministry of Commerce and Industry within 10 days of the annual general meeting. In general, the financial statements of Kuwaiti firms are also required to follow IASs.

Oman

Oman is not a member of IFAC but Law 53 of 1996 requires enterprises to follow IASs. However, the law requires that audits be performed by an authorized independent auditor. Auditors must be independent of the company being audited and need not provide technical, administrative, and consulting services to the company on a regular basis (Ernst & Young 2003).

Qatar

Qatar contains the third largest natural gas reserves in the world. Qatar is also emerging as a major exporter of liquefied natural gas. An OPEC member, Qatar exported slightly less than 900,000 barrels per day of oil during the first 10 months of 2003 (EIA 2003). Since the middle of the 1990s, the Ministry of Media and Information has started the privatization program and the creation of the national stock market. The authorities are further debating the possibility of establishing a national association of accountants with the responsibility of issuing accounting standards (Al-Katar and Naser 2003).

In Qatar, the economic development coincided with an increase in the number of companies operating in the GCC region. Consequently, national stock exchanges have been established and now all GCC countries have stock exchange markets. However, the creation of stock exchanges was not matched by development in the accounting and auditing systems. A gap exists between the degree of economic development and the development of the accounting and auditing systems and practices within the GCC countries. The main problem that faces Qatar is the lack of specific accounting standards that govern the activities of companies. Although GCC countries, such as Bahrain, Kuwait, UAE, and Oman, have adopted the IASs, and Saudi Arabia has attempted to develop its own accounting standards, until now Qatar has neither developed its own standards nor has it adopted the IASs. However, most large companies operating in Qatar are using the IASs promulgated by the IASB (Al-Katar and Naser 2003).

Saudi Arabia

The Saudi accounting profession is controlled by the Ministry of Commerce (MOC). The MOC, the official agency of the profession, is responsible for issuing public accountant certificates and exercise a discipline role. The Saudi accounting profession was given a formal standing by a Royal Decree in August 1974. The decree was titled *Nazam Al Muhasibean*, which translates as "Rules and Regulation for Public Accountants." This was followed by the formation of The High Commission of Public Accountants composed of representatives from the Ministry of Commerce, General Public Accounting Office, representatives from the academia, and the accountant profession.

In 1986, the MOC approved the financial accounting objectives and concepts as a conceptual framework and a basis for financial accounting standards. In the same year, the MOC issued two publications: (1) Accounting Objectives and Concepts, which presents the Saudi Arabian Standards of General Presentation and Disclosure in the financial statements; and

(2) Auditing Standards, which emphasizes the professional qualification of auditors, including the discussion of independence, due care and documentation of auditors' working papers. Both the Accounting Objectives and the Auditing Standards may be considered the source of guidelines for the accounting profession of the private sector. The Saudi concepts and standards are similar to the accounting principles issued by the American Institute of Certified Public Accountants (AICPA). However, compliance with the new concepts and standards is not currently enforced by an independent government agency or a private organization. The Saudi Accounting Association (SAA), through its special technical committee comprising Saudi and non-Saudi accountants, in coordination with the MoC, is in the process of formulating new accounting standards in the kingdom.

The Saudi GAAP (SGAAP) issued to-date pertain to the requirements of general presentation and disclosure in the financial statements of profit-oriented entities and consolidated financial statements; provide pro-forma examples of presentation; and determine the treatment of accounting changes and contingent gains or losses. The SGAAP require financial statements to include a profit-and-loss statement, a statement of appropriation of profits, a balance sheet, and an auditor's report. The statement of source and uses of funds are included but are not mandatory. No specific presentation format is imposed except for banks. A joint venture, with its auditor, can establish its own format.

Currently, there are several Saudi standards dealing with important issues; these are listed in table 4.1. In general, the Saudi GAAP asks for

Table 4.1 The Saudi accounting standards

Standard No.	*Standard*	*Date of Issue*
1	Presentation and general disclosure	Updated 1996
2	Foreign currency	1997
3	Inventory	1997
4	Related parties' transactions	1997
5	Consolidation and mergers	1997
6	Revenue recognition	1998
7	General and administrative expenses, and sale and distribution expenses	1998
8	Research and development expenses	1998
9	Investment in equity securities	1998
10	Interim reports	1999
11	*Zakat* and income tax	1999

much more detailed disclosure than other Gulf countries, even though the additional detail is not mandatory. The Accounting Standards Committee conducted a comprehensive study on previously issued standards and determined the topics that are considered as significant to be covered by accounting standards, and consequently commenced preparing 20 standards.

The CPA certificates are only given to public accountants on the basis of an approved degree in accounting and sufficient practical experience in accounting or auditing. Saudi public accounting titles are usually granted to Saudi nationals only. All large international accounting firms are associated with local accountants and operate under a Saudi name.

United Arab Emirates (UAE)

In 1999, a federal law passed requires that all banks and financial institutions prepare their financial statements according to the IASs. Federal law No. 22 of 1995 organizes the auditing profession. Like other GCC states' commercial laws, it determines the requirement of registration, licensing, the responsibility and duties of auditors, the penalties and disciplinary acts, and the general rules. Article 6 states that auditors, as in other GCC countries, are not allowed to be employees in other organizations. However, in UAE, academics are exempt from this requirement (Al-Qahtani 2005). The central bank has made it mandatory for all commercial banks in the UAE to prepare their accounts based on IASs from 1999 onward. Few banks began to use IASs well before it was required to do so. Locally incorporated banks must submit their audited consolidated accounts no later than March 31 of each year (Hussain et al. 2002).

Comparison of Five Key Accounting Issues

This section includes key accounting differences and similarities of the six Gulf countries as compared with the IAS and the GCCAAO standards. The following accounting principles are used for comparison between Gulf countries and IASs, as can be seen from table 4.2: investments, inventory, asset valuation, foreign currency translation, and consolidation. For Qatar and Oman, their GAAP for two or more of the five accounting issues either do not exist or are in the very early stages and they allow foreign firms and joint ventures to use IASs. Therefore, in the analysis that follows, the concentration is mainly on IASs, Bahrain, and Saudi Arabia. UAE and Kuwaiti GAAP are only discussed in terms of the issues in which they either differ from IASs or in which they use different concepts than that of other Gulf countries.

Table 4.2 Local accounting differences compared with IAS/IFRS and GCCAAO

Accounting Differences	*Investment*	*Inventory*	*Asset Valuation*	*FC Translation*	*Consolidation*
IAS/IFRS	ST-CA-LCM LT-cost revalued amount	FIFO/WA benchmark- LIFO allowed/LCM	CA-NRV/LCM NCA-cost	Local currency-functional/ CR US$-functional-use temporal	More than 50%— For acquisitions-pooling or purchase method
GCCAAO	ST at cost LT at FMV	Similar assets at WA; LIFO and FIFO allowed but disclose the differences	HC, systematic decline in value-FMV, losses recognized-same year	A and L at Spot Rate R and E at WA Translation adjustments in OE section	Only purchase method allowed; GW amortized over 20 years
Bahrain	At cost with provision for permanent decline	Compliance with IAS	HC with revaluation in certain cases	CR, FE G/L in IS	Compliance with IAS
Kuwait	ST/LT at cost	Compliance with IAS	CA-NRV/LCM NCA-cost	CR-FE G/L treated in different ways	Compliance with IAS
Oman	LT-cost, provisions for any decline ST at LCM	Compliance with IAS	HC but may be revalued	CR, FE G/L in IS but Banks use IAS	GW amortized over 5 years or written off immediately
Qatar	At cost-a provision for any decline	Compliance with IAS	Compliance with IAS	CR, FE G/L in IS	Compliance with IAS
Saudi Arabia	ST-LCM LT-cost	FIFO/WA-LCM	CA-LCM NCA-cost	Compliance with IAS	Required but seldom prepared
UAE	ST-MV, LT at cost	Compliance with IAS	HC	CR and G/L in IS	Compliance with IAS

Note: BS = Balance Sheet, CA = Current Assets, FMV = Fair Market Value, IS = Income Statement, LCM = Lower of Cost or Market Value, LT = Long Term, MV = Market Value, NCA =Net Current Assets, NRV = Net Realizable Value, CF = Cash Flow Statement, P&L = Profit and Loss Statement, SH = Shareholders, ST = Short Term, CC = Current Cost, CF = Cash Flow Statement, CR = Current Rate Method, FE G/L = Foreign Exchange Rate Gains or Losses, OE = Owners' Equity, RE = Retained Earnings, WA = Weighted Average method.

Investments

Internationally, three IASs address several related issues of accounting for investments. These include IAS No. 25, IAS No. 28, and IAS No. 31. IAS No. 25 covers the general topic of investment in the debt and equity securities of other business entities, for those situations where the investor does not have significant influence over the investee. In this case, investments may be treated using different methods, depending on whether the investments are for a short- or a long term. Short-term investments should be carried at market value or LCM and long-term investments should be carried at a cost-revalued amount, applied on a portfolio basis (Epstein and Mirza 1999). IAS No. 28, which addresses investments in associates, is covered under the equity method. IAS No. 31, which concerns the accounting by an investor for its interest in a joint-venture arrangement, is outside the scope of this book.

Under the GCCAA guidelines, long-term investment in securities should be measured at cost in the Statement of Financial Position (Para. 10) Short-term investment in securities should be measured at fair market value in the Statement of Financial Position. Any unrealized holding gains and losses for trading securities should be included in the current year income (Para. 11).

In Bahrain, investment securities are stated at cost, with provision being made for any permanent decline in value (Hussain et al. 2002). In Oman, long-term investments are stated at cost, with fewer provisions for any decline in value other than of a temporary nature. Treasury bills are stated at face value. Short-term investments are stated at the lower value of cost and market value (Hussain et al. 2002). In Kuwait, the dominant basis for valuing investments is the cost basis applied in varying ways. For quoted securities, the lower value of cost or market value is considered; for unquoted securities, the evaluation is done at cost value, and if the cost exceeds market value, a provision is established. In some companies, investments in domestic securities are valued at their costs, which is less than their market value on the stock market (Hassan 1985). In Oman, trading investments, whether quoted on the Doha securities market or unquoted, are stated at cost value with a provision for any decline in value on the basis of the aggregate portfolio of investments and not for each investment individually (Hussain et al. 2002).

In Saudi Arabia, current assets are segregated into main groups in the Statement of financial position according to their nature. For significant items of each group, a segregation should be made between the monetary and nonmonetary items in the statement of financial position or the related notes. Financial statements are prepared using the historical cost basis. Some current assets, such as marketable securities, are carried at the lower value of cost or market value. Any value above the cost, such as current value or market value, is seldom used. For banks, trading securities must be valued at cost upon acquisition and thereafter be marked to market value at the date of each financial period. Profit or loss realized from trading in securities and revaluation differences must be included in the income statement. Investment securities must be valued at cost, with any differences between cost and the nominal value of a security being recorded as premium or discount and amortized over the remaining life of the security. Temporary changes in market value must be ignored and only permanent changes in the value of a security must be reflected in the income statement (Hussain et al. 2002).

In the UAE, there is no uniform accounting treatment for investments. Most major banks value trading account securities at market price, while investment securities held with the intention of being retained until maturity are stated at cost adjusted for any premiums and discounts amortized on a straight-line basis. Many banks now state the market value of their securities. Investments in companies not exceeding 20 percent of their paid-up capital are stated at the lower value of cost or fair market value, whereas investments in companies of over 20 percent and below 50 percent of their paid-up capital are accounted by applying the equity method. The accounts of companies in which a bank directly owns more than 50 percent of paid-up capital are consolidated with those of the parent. Goodwill arising on consolidation is amortized over 25 years or, alternatively, written off at the time of acquisition (Hussain et al. 2002).

Inventory

Internationally, IAS No. 2 "Valuation and Presentation of Inventories in the Context of the Historical Cost System"—the first-in-first-out (FIFO) and weighted average cost methods are defined as benchmark treatments, while the last-in-first-out (LIFO) method is an allowed alternative method. Lower value of cost or net realizable value is used.

Under the GCCAA guidelines the cost of the inventory of similar products is calculated based on the weighted average. If this method has proved to be inappropriate due to the nature of the operations, the firm can use either the FIFO or the LIFO methods and it should indicate the reasons for using such a method. In such a case, the firm should disclose the difference between the cost of costs sold and the inventory cost calculated based on the method used and the weighted average method. The value of ending inventory is measured by the lower value of cost or market value.

exchange gains and losses are taken to the equity. All assets and liabilities are translated at the closing (current) rate, and all income and expenses items should be translated using the average exchange rate.

Under the GCCAA guidelines, assets and liabilities should be translated using the spot rate at the date of the financial statements. Income Statement items (revenues, expenses, gains, and losses) should normally be translated using the spot rate at the date of the transaction; however, due to practical conditions, the weighted average exchange rate during the period should be used to translate these items, except for significant gains and losses, which should be translated using the spot rate at the date of the event. Translation adjustments should be reported in a separate item in owners' equity until the foreign entity is disposed of through sale or liquidation. At that time it should be accounted for in the "Investment in the Foreign Entity" account.

In Bahrain, the foreign currency translations are translated to the currency of the firm's balance sheet at rates prevailing on transaction dates. Assets and liabilities denominated in foreign currencies are translated at rates prevailing at year-end and any resulting gains or losses are taken to income (Hussain et al. 2002). However, by law, companies are required to maintain the accounting books and records necessary to reflect properly both the company's operations and its financial position, and to prepare its annual financial statements in full compliance with IASs.

In Kuwait, companies translate assets and liabilities at the year-end rates of foreign exchange. In practice, foreign exchange translation gains or losses are treated in different ways (Hassan 1985). These include (1) the establishment of a special provision for translation losses and it is presented on the balance sheet in the owners' equity section, whereas unrealized profits on translation appear on a separate account on the balance sheet; (2) losses are charged directly to the profit and loss account; and (3) realized or unrealized losses on translation are treated as in (2). If losses on translation are small amounts, they should be treated as in (2). In Oman, the banks translate transactions in foreign currencies into the local currency at the exchange rates prevailing on the transaction dates. Assets and liabilities denominated in foreign currencies are translated into Omani currency at the exchange rates prevailing on the balance sheet date. Differences on exchange are included in the profit and loss account as they arise (Hussain et al. 2002). Omani banks that have foreign branches are required to translate their assets, liabilities, and income statements into Omani currency at the rates of exchange on the balance sheet date. In accordance with IASs, any differences between opening and closing net assets arising from changes in exchange rates are taken directly to reserves (ibid.).

In Qatar, transactions during the year in foreign currencies are translated into Qatari currency at the rates of exchange prevailing on the transaction date. Assets and liabilities denominated in foreign currencies on the balance sheet date are translated into Qatari riyals at rates prevailing at year-end. Exchange gains and losses are included in the statement of income (Hussain et al. 2002). Under the Saudi GAAP, foreign currency transactions denominated in foreign currencies are recorded in Saudi currency at the current exchange rates prevailing on the date of the transaction. FX-denominated assets and liabilities are converted at the rate of exchange as of balance sheet date. All resulting realized and unrealized gains and losses are recorded in the income statement as income from major operations, except those from equity investments in subsidiaries and affiliates, which are equity accounted. Assets and liabilities held by foreign subsidiaries must be translated to local currency by applying the spot rate of exchange. Revenues, expenses, gains, and losses must be translated using the weighted average exchange rate. Exchange differences resulting from the translation of financial statements should be taken to special equity reserves (Hussain et al. 2002). In practice, however, the Saudi multinational companies use International Accounting Standard (IAS) No. 21, "The Effect of Changes in Foreign Exchange Rates."

In the UAE, assets and liabilities denominated in foreign currencies are translated into UAE currency at current rates on balance sheet date, whereas foreign exchange transactions are translated at rates prevailing on transaction dates. Gains or losses arising from normal activities are charged or credited accordingly in the profit and loss. Exchange differences arising from the retranslation of the opening net investments in overseas operations are taken directly to reserves (Hussain et al. 2002).

Consolidation

Consolidated financial statements are prepared to reflect the operations and financial positions of a parent company that owns a share from 51 to 100 percent and it is presumed to have control over its wholly- or majority-owned subsidiaries. Internationally, when the acquired business entity is merged into the acquiring business entity or when both entities are consolidated into a new business entity, all assets and liabilities are recorded directly on the books of the surviving or new business entity. Depending on whether the conditions stated by the original IAS 22, "Accounting for Business Combinations," are met, the transaction will be treated as either a pooling of interest or as a purchase method. Either purchase or the pooling of interest method is allowed. Goodwill may be amortized on a systematic basis over its useful life not exceeding 20 years from the initial recognition. However, IAS 22 was superseded by IFRS 3 on Business Combinations, issued in March 2004. This standard includes requirements relating to the treatment of business combinations and accounting for goodwill. The revised standard tightened up the criteria for the pooling of interest method and required that the goodwill factor must be recognized as an asset and must be amortized against revenues on a systematic basis over its useful life (not to exceed 20 years). The method of immediate write-off against reserves was eliminated by the IASB.

Under the GCCAA guidelines, assets and liabilities of a purchased subsidiary should be valued at fair values on the date of purchase. These values should also be used to prepare the consolidated financial statements at the date of acquisition and later dates (Para. 14). When a firm is acquired at a cost that exceeds the fair value of net assets at the date of acquisition, the difference between the acquisition cost and fair value of net assets should be accounted for as goodwill in the consolidated financial statements (Para. 15). Goodwill arising from acquisition through purchase should be amortized over its expected useful life or 20 years, whichever is shorter (Para. 17).

In Kuwait, consolidated financial statements and accounting for investments in subsidiaries defines subsidiary ownership on the basis of control; requires consolidated financial statements from all groups except wholly owned, foreign and domestic subsidiaries; and provides guidelines for line-by-line consolidation and disclosure in a parent separate financial statement of its inventory in a subsidiary. Kuwait's companies use the following policies regarding the basis of consolidation of accounts: (1) holding shares or securities of less than 20 percent of the company's shares—considered as a "commercial investment"; (2) associated companies that hold 20–50 percent of the company's shares; and (3) subsidiaries holding more than 50 percent of its shares. Holdings, commercial or in associated companies, are valued on the basis of the net assets of these companies and the proportion of holdings. For commercial investments, the resulting difference between valuation and cost is considered as unrealized gains or losses, except for a continuous decline in value that should be considered as a realized loss. In associated companies, they are regarded as realized gains or losses (Hassan 1985). In Oman, under consolidation, goodwill is recognized as an asset and amortized on a systematic basis over its useful life. This period may not exceed five years, unless a longer useful life can be justified and explained in the financial statements. Goodwill may also be written off immediately against shareholders' equity (Hussain et al. 2002).

Under Saudi GAAP, consolidated financial statements are required to comply with the standard of general presentation and disclosure issued by the Ministry of Commerce. However, consolidated financial statements are seldom prepared. The cost method is generally used to account for investments in voting stock of other companies. The Saudi standard defines the requirements of disclosing minority rights, reciprocal ownership of shares and differences in the financial periods of the holding company, and the subsidiary or subsidiaries. However, the standard does not define the requirements of preparing consolidated financial statements nor the circumstances under which these statements should be prepared. It also does not address the circumstances that are necessary for the preparation of consolidated financial statements. In general, business entities either follow the U.S., U.K., or international accounting standards for accounting purposes.

Summary and Conclusions

After the five accounting issues have been discussed using the LAS for the six Gulf countries as compared with the IASs and GCCAAO, it is helpful to make a comparative analysis of these differences and similarities across the countries. Table 4.2 summarizes these similarities and differences. In the case of accounting treatment of investments, Kuwait, Oman, Qatar, and Saudi Arabia are in compliance with IASs; GCCAAO is using the fair market value for long-term investments, and accounting treatment for inventory: all Gulf countries follow IFRSs. IFRS is using the LIFO as an alternative to be permitted. In the case of asset valuation, U.S. GAAP and IASs are similar, and all selected Gulf countries using the same method. All selected Gulf countries follow the same pattern as the IASs, except Saudi Arabia, which uses the cost method for financial reporting. In the case of foreign currency translation, Kuwait, Oman, and Qatar are consistent with the IASs. The GAAP of both Saudi Arabia and UAE do not cover the foreign currency translation; however, foreign firms and joint ventures are allowed to use IFRSs. With respect to consolidation, in all selected countries, financial statements are consolidated if the voting controls 50 percent or more of subsidiaries. Recently, FASB has decided to use only the purchase method for consolidated financial statements. IFRS still gives the option of choosing between the purchase method and the pooling of interest method.

References

Abdallah, Wagdy. 1999. "American Joint Ventures in the Middle East: The Case of Amoco-Egypt-Managerial, Financial, and Tax Implications." *Middle East Business Review* 1 (3): 49–64.

Abdallah, Wagdy. 1997. "Accounting Standards in Saudi Arabia and International Accounting Standards." *International Review of Accounting* 2 (1): 27–41.

AlHashim, Dhia D. 1977. "Social Accounting in Egypt." *The International Journal of Accounting Education and Research* 12 (Spring): 127–142.

Al-Khatar, Khalid and Kamal Naser. 2003. "User's Perceptions of Corporate Social Responsibility and Accountability: Evidence from an Emerging Economy." *Managerial Auditing Journal* 18 (6/7): 538–549.

Al-Qahtani, Abdulla K. 2005. "The Development of Accounting Regulation in the GCC." *Managerial Auditing Journal* 20 (3): 217–226.

Briston, Richard J. and Ahmed A. El-Ashker. 1984. "The Egyptian Accounting System: A Case Study in Western Influence." *International Journal of Accounting Education & Research* (Spring): 129–155.

Crossborder Monitor. 1997. "Middle East and North Africa Outlook," New York, January 15.

Doupnik, Timothy S. and Stephen B. Salter. 1995. "External Environment, Culture, and Accounting Practice: A : Preliminary Test of a General Model of International Accounting Development," *The International Journal of Accounting* 30: 189–207.

Energy Information Administration (EIA). 2005. "Country Analysis Briefs-Oman." January. http://www.eia.doe.gov/emeu/cabs/oman.html.

Ernest & Young. 1993. *Doing Business in Saudi Arabia.* New York: Ernst & Young International.

———. 2003. *Doing Business in Bahrain.* Ernst and Young Global, New York. www.ey.com.

Epstein, Barry J. and Abbas Ali Mirza. 1999. *IAS 99-Interpretation and Application of International Accounting Standards.* New York: John Wiley & Sons, Inc.

Farag, Shawki M. 1991. "Accounting in the 1990s: An International Perspective," *The International Journal of Accounting* 26: 243–251.

Financial Accounting Standards Board. 1976. *Financial Reporting for Segments of a Business Enterprise.* Statement of Financial Accounting Standards No. 14. Stamford, CT: FASB.

Gulf Cooperation Council Accounting and Auditing Organization. 2007. http://www.gccaao.org/en/index.html.

Hassan, Naim. 1985. "International Accounting Standards: Desirable as a Short-Term Solution in the Case of the Arab Gulf States." In V.K. Zimmermaan, ed., *The Recent Accounting and Economic Developments in the Middle East.* Urbana-Champaign, IL: University of Illinois, Center for International Education and Research in Accounting, 69–100.

Hussain, Mostaque, Mazhar M. Islam, A. Gunasekaran, and Kooros Maskooki. 2002. "Accounting Standards and Practices of Financial Institutions in GCC Countries." *Managerial Auditing Journal* 17 (7): 350–368.

International Accounting Standards Committee. 1999. *International Accounting Standards*. London.

Jahmani, Yousef, Ahmad Al-Omari, and Anwar Y. Salimi. 1996. "The Development of Financial Reporting in Jordan." Working Paper presented at the IABD.

Khanna, Nitin. 1999. "A Commercial Hub for the Middle East?" *Accountancy*, London, February 1.

Saudi Organization for Certified Public Accountants. 2005. SOCPA. http://www.socpa.org.sa.

Shuaib A. Shuaib. 1985. "Auditing Standards in Kuwait." In *Comparative International Auditing Standards*. American Accounting Association, 95–102.

Wallace, R.S.O. 1990. "Survival Strategies of a Global Organization: The Case of International Accounting Standards Committee." *Accounting Horizon*, American Accounting Association 4 (2) (June): 1–22, esp. 11.

cultural differences and the process of establishing rules, in every country, that specify how to prepare, report, and present financial statements; or those generally accepted accounting principles (GAAP) that determine the type of information that financial statements should contain and how that information should be prepared and presented (ibid.). If standardization eliminates any alternative of accounting rules to measure economic activities, harmonization means the reduction of alternatives while retaining a high degree of flexibility in accounting practices (Doupnik and Perera 2007). In other words, harmonization of accounting principles means that the differences among nations should be kept at a minimum.

In the global capital market, it may be acceptable to have alternative accounting principles of different countries as long as they are in "harmony" with each other and reconciliation of the differences is acceptable (Iqbal 2002). The main reason for developing harmonized international accounting standards has been to achieve a degree of comparability to help investors make their decisions while reducing the costs of MNCs in preparing multiple sets of accounting books and reports. However, comparability of financial statements is a more clear-cut concept than harmonization (Choi and Meek 2005). For example, this is the case when two sets of financial statements of two different companies of two different countries produced under two different accounting systems (such as Bahrani and Saudi), they are only comparable if they are similar in enough ways that the foreign or local investor can compare them with each other with no need to be ultimately familiar with more than one system of the two.

The importance of harmonization of accounting standards was emphasized by Graham Ward (2005), the president of the International Federation of Accountants (IFAC), at the first World Accounting Summit in Dubai, when he stated that having a multiplicity of accounting standards around the world is against the public interest, creates confusion, encourages error, and facilitates fraud, and the only solution for these problems is to have one single set of international accounting standards set by an international expert organization (Anonymous 2005).

Several international organizations have been concerned with harmonization of accounting standards. However, the most important key players in setting international accounting standards and promoting harmonization of accounting standards are International Accounting Standards Board (IASB), International Organization of Securities Commissions (IOSCO), Financial Accounting Standards Board (FASB), Commission of the European Union (EU), and International Federation of Accountants (IFAC).

The purpose of this chapter is to discuss the harmonization of accounting standards and the use of the International Financial Reporting Standards

(IFRSs) issued by the IASB and supported and recognized by both of the ISOCO, FASB, and IFAC. The chapter is divided into four sections. The first section covers the history and the role of the IASB and its effect on the harmonization of accounting systems and practices in the Gulf countries. In the next section, the question of the need of the Gulf countries to adopt international financial reporting standards is discussed. The next section looks at the efforts of the global constituents who have been involved in the development of international accounting standards, including FASB, SEC, IOSCO, IFAC, and other professional organizations. Finally, the question of relevance of the IFRSs for the Gulf countries is analyzed and discussed, and whether new regional standards are needed, and, if so, how they can be developed and implemented in the Gulf countries.

International Accounting Standards Board (IASB)

From 1973 until a comprehensive reorganization in 2000, the structure for setting International Accounting Standards (IASs) was known as the International Accounting Standards Committee. There was no actual "committee" of that name. The standard-setting board was known as the IASC Board. The IASC was formed by an agreement of the leading professional accounting bodies of nine countries such as Australia, Canada, France, Germany, Japan, Mexico, the Netherlands, the United Kingdom and Ireland, and the United States. Since 1983, the members of the IASC have included all the professional accountancy bodies that are members of the International Federation of Accountants (IFAC). The International Accounting Standards Board (IASB) was formed in 2001 to replace the IASC. The IASB is an independent, private-sector body that develops and approves International Financial Reporting Standards (IFRSs). The IASB operates under the oversight of the International Accounting Standards Committee Foundation (www.iasb.org).

The International Accounting Standards Board (IASB) is based in London, and was restructured in 2001. The government of IASB was vested in a board of trustees, with a new standards board empowered to make decisions on IASs. Contributions are usually collected from several groups including its Trustees, the IASC Foundation, from the major accounting firms, private financial institutions and industrial companies throughout the world, central and development banks, and other international and professional organizations to fund the operations of the IASB. The 14 Board members (12 of whom are full-time) are drawn from nine countries and have wide international experience and a variety of functional backgrounds.

3. Consulting the Standards Advisory Council about the advisability of adding the topic to the IASB's agenda;
4. Formation of an advisory group (a "working group") to advise the IASB and its staff on the project;
5. Publishing a discussion document for public comment;
6. Publishing, for public comment, an Exposure Draft approved by at least nine votes of the IASB, including any dissenting opinions held by IASB members;
7. Publishing within an Exposure Draft a basis for conclusions;
8. Considering all comments received within the comment period on discussion documents and Exposure Drafts;
9. Considering the desirability of holding a public hearing and of the desirability of conducting field tests;
10. Approving of a standard by at least nine votes of the IASB and inclusion in the published standard of any dissenting opinions; and
11. Publishing within a standard a basis for conclusions.

It is very important to note that the IASB has sole responsibility for establishing International Financial Reporting Standards (IFRSs). The IASC Foundation oversees the work of the IASB, the structure, and strategy, and is responsible for fund-raising. However, the International Financial Reporting Interpretations Committee (IFRIC) develops interpretations for approval by the IASB. A list of the revised IASs and the recently issued IFRSs is shown as tables 5.1 and 5.2, respectively. Even though the IASB does not have the authority to enforce IASs and/or IFRSs, since compliance is voluntary, many countries, including the Gulf countries, have based their national standards on IASs.

In September 2002, both the FASB and IASB signed the Norwalk Agreement, a memorandum of understanding that formalized their commitment to converge U.S. GAAP and IFRSs. The two boards agreed to use their best efforts to remove existing differences between the standards and to coordinate their future standard-setting agendas and work on major issues together. In February 2006, the FASB and the IASB have published a Memorandum of Understanding (MOU) that reaffirms the Boards' shared objective of developing high-quality, common accounting standards for use in the world's capital markets. The MOU is a further elaboration of the objectives and principles first described in an MOU published in 2002. While the new document does not represent a change in the Boards' convergence work program, it does reflect the context of the SEC's "roadmap" for the removal of the reconciliation requirement for

Table 5.1 A list of revised IAS

Revised International Accounting Standards		*Revised*	*Effective Date*
IAS 1	Presentation of financial statements added disclosures about an entity's capital	2005	Annual periods beginning on or after January 1, 2007
IAS 1	Presentation of financial statements	2003	Annual periods beginning on or after January 1, 2005
IAS 2	Inventories	2003	Annual periods beginning on or after January 1, 2005
IAS 8	Accounting policies, changes in accounting estimates and errors	2003	Annual periods beginning on or after January 1, 2005
IAS 10	Events after the balance sheet date	2003	Annual periods beginning on or after January 1, 2005
IAS 15	Information reflecting the effects of changing prices	2003	Withdrawn effective January 1, 2005
IAS 16	Property, plant and equipment	2003	Annual periods beginning on or after January 1, 2005
IAS 17	Leases	2003	Annual periods beginning on or after January 1, 2005
IAS 19	Employee benefits Option to recognize actuarial gains and losses in full, outside profit or loss, in a statement of changes in equity	2004	Annual periods beginning on or after January 1, 2006
IAS 21	The effects of changes in foreign exchange rates	2003	The effects of changes in foreign exchange rates
IAS 21	The effects of changes in foreign exchange rates	Minor amendment issued November 2005	Annual periods beginning on or after January 1, 2005
IAS 23	Borrowing costs	2007	Borrowing costs relating to qualifying assets for which the commencement date for capitalization is on or after January 1, 2009
IAS 24	Related party disclosures	2003	Annual periods beginning on or after January 1, 2005
IAS 27	Consolidated and separate financial statements	2003	Annual periods beginning on or after January 1, 2005
IAS 28	Investments in associates	2003	Annual periods beginning on or after January 1, 2005
IAS 31	Interests in joint ventures	2003	Annual periods beginning on or after January 1, 2005

Continued

Table 5.1 Continued

Revised International Accounting Standards		*Revised*	*Effective Date*
IAS 32	Financial instruments: disclosure and presentation	2003	Annual periods beginning on or after January 1, 2005
IAS 33	Earnings per share	2003	Annual periods beginning on or after January 1, 2005
IAS 36	Impairment of assets	2004	Business combinations after March 31, 2004
IAS 38	Intangible assets	2004	Business combinations after March 31, 2004
IAS 39	Financial instruments: recognition and measurement comprehensive revisions	2003	Annual periods beginning on or after January 1, 2005
IAS 39	Financial instruments: recognition and measurement amendment for macro hedging	2004	Annual periods beginning on or after January 1, 2005
IAS 39	Financial instruments: recognition and measurement amendment for day 1 gain/loss transition	2004	Annual periods beginning on or after January 1, 2005
IAS 39	Financial instruments: recognition and measurement amendment for hedges of forecast intragroup transactions	2004	Annual periods beginning on or after January 1, 2006
IAS 39	Financial instruments: recognition and measurement amendment for fair value option	2005	Annual periods beginning on or after January 1, 2006
IAS 39	Financial instruments: recognition and measurement amendment for financial guarantee contracts	2005	Annual periods beginning on or after January 1, 2006
IAS 40	Investment property	2003	Annual periods beginning on or after January 1, 2005

Source: www.IASplus.com; July 2007.

non-U.S. companies that use IFRSs and that are registered in the United States. It also reflects the work undertaken by the Committee of European Securities Regulators (CESR) to identify areas for improvement of accounting standards (IASplus.com).

Table 5.2 A list of recently issued IFRS

New International Financial Reporting Standards		*Issued*	*Effective Date*
IFRS 1	First-time adoption of International Financial Reporting Standards	2003	First IFRS financial statements for a period beginning on or after January 1, 2004
IFRS 1	First-time adoption of International Financial Reporting Standards Amendment relating to IFRS 6	2005	Annual periods beginning on or after January 1, 2006
IFRS 2	Share-based payment	2004	Annual periods beginning on or after January 1, 2005
IFRS 3	Business combinations	2004	Business combinations after 31 March, 2004
IFRS 4	Insurance contracts	2004	Annual periods beginning on or after January 1, 2005
IFRS 4	Insurance contracts amendment for financial guarantee contracts	2005	Annual periods beginning on or after January 1, 2006
IFRS 5	Non-current assets held for sale and discontinued operations	2004	Annual periods beginning on or after January 1, 2005
IFRS 6	Exploration for and evaluation of mineral assets	2004	Annual periods beginning on or after January 1, 2006
IFRS 7	Financial instruments: disclosures	2005	Annual periods beginning on or after January 1, 2007
IFRS 8	Operating segments	2006	Annual periods beginning on or after January 1, 2009

Source: www.IASplus.com; July 2007.

The Structure of the IASB

The IASC formed a Strategy Working Party (SWP) to consider the strategy and structure after completing the core standards work program. In December 1998, the SWP issued a discussion proposal entitled "Shaping IASC for the future." The proposal had a completely different structure and process for the development of international accounting standards. In December 1999, the IASC Board approved the proposals unanimously, and the IASC member bodies did the same in May 2000. A new IASB Constitution took effect on July 1, 2000. The standards-setting body was renamed the International Accounting Standards Board (IASB). It would operate under a new International Accounting Standards Committee Foundation (IASCF), which is an independent organization having two main bodies: the trustees and the IASB.

On April 1, 2001, the restructured IASB took over from the IASC the responsibility for setting IASs. The IASB structure has the following main bodies (www.iasb.org):

Trustees

The IASC Foundation Trustees appoint the IASB members, exercise oversight, and raise the funds needed, but the IASB has sole responsibility for setting accounting standards. The IASB has 22 trustees, as of August 2007: 6 from North America, 6 from Europe, 6 from the Asia/Oceania region, and 4 from any area ("subject to establishing overall geographical balance") (www.iasb.irg). The trustees' responsibilities include appointing the members of the Board, appointing members of the Standing IFRIC and the SAC, reviewing the strategy of the IASB and its effectiveness, establishing operating procedures for the Board, and approving the annual budget of the IASB among several other responsibilities as stated in the constitution of the IASB. However, they are not involved in the technical issues relating to accounting standards. The trustees act by simple majority vote except in the case of amendments to the constitution, which requires a three-fourths majority.

The IASB Board

The Board consists of 14 members: 12 full-time and 2 part-time members. Members are appointed for a 5-year term, which can be renewed once. Under the new structure, the IASB has sole responsibility for establishing, preparing, and approving IFRSs. Trustees should make sure that the IASB is not dominated by any particular constituency or geographical interest. Moreover, the IASB should consist of an appropriate mix of recent practical experience including auditors, preparers, users, and academics.

The Standard Advisory Council (SAC)
The Standard Advisory Council (SAC) is appointed by the trustees, has approximately 40 members, and advises the IASB on its agenda and priorities. The members are from a diverse group of geographical and professional backgrounds and are appointed for renewable terms of three years. The chair of the IASB is also the chair of the SAC.

The International Financial Reporting Interpretation Committee (IFRIC)
The IFRIC consists of 12 members appointed by the trustees for terms of 3 years. The main responsibilities of the IFRIC are (1) to develop

interpretations of the application of IASs and IFRSs in the context of the IASB's Framework for approval by the IASB; and (2) to provide guidance on financial reporting issues that are not specifically addressed in any IASs or IFRSs.

Working Groups

The IASB may form working groups or other types of specialist advisory groups to give advice on major projects. So far, the IASB has formed working groups on Accounting Standards for Small- and Medium-Sized Entities; Financial Instruments, Insurance, Joint International Group on Performance Reporting (joint IASB-FASB working group), and Employee Benefits Working Group.

Recognition and Support for the IASB

Today, the support and interest shown in the IFRSs of the IASB by global organizations has been increasing and the use and application of IFRSs are widely and internationally recognized. Several multinational companies (MNCs) and international financial institutions prepare their financial reports in accordance with IFRSs. Moreover, many companies of many countries, including the Gulf region, endorse IFRSs as their own either without amendment or else with minor additions or deletions. Many stock exchanges accept IFRSs for cross-border listing purposes. The IASB works closely with the national standard-setting bodies, securities regulatory agencies, and stock exchanges in individual countries that accept IFRSs for cross-border listing purpose, intergovernmental organizations (such as the International Organization of Securities Commissions-IOSCO, European Union, the OECD, and the United Nations), and development agencies such as the World Bank.

In October 2002, the FASB and the IASB issued a memorandum of understanding, also known as "the Norwalk Agreement." This marked a significant step toward formalizing the commitment to the convergence of U.S. and international accounting standards (Financial Accounting Standards Board, News Release, 2002). Under this agreement, the FASB and IASB agree to

1. Undertake a short-term project aimed at removing a variety of individual differences between U.S. GAAP and the IFRSs;
2. Remove other differences between IFRSs and U.S. GAAP that will remain at January 1, 2005 through coordination of their future work programs;

3. Continue progress on the joint projects that they are currently undertaking; and
4. Encourage their respective interpretative bodies to coordinate their activities.

It is important to note that this agreement does not mean that the FASB will always try to move toward the direction of IASB standards to reduce or eliminate existing differences; the opposite is also expected to occur. However, both organizations have agreed to work together on future issues to try to come up with common grounds or solutions for existing accounting issues.

The AICPA organization considers the IASB as an independent standard-setting body unaffiliated with any professional organization, country, or national standard-setter. The AICPA supports the IASC in its efforts to improve its structure and agrees with the IASC that its primary objective should be to develop high-quality accounting standards that provide transparency and comparability of information useful to investors and lenders in making economic decisions (AICPA 1999).

While the SEC still requires reconciliation with U.S. GAAP nonnational companies, there is some pressure to allow international companies to report using only IFRSs. However, in June 2007, the SEC issued a "proposing release" that would eliminate the requirements to reconcile financial statements with U.S. GAAP if the financial statements are in full compliance with the IFRSs. This proposed approach would give foreign private MNCs a choice of using IFRSs without reconciliation with U.S. GAAP in preparing financial statements that are filed with the SEC either in a registration statement or in an annual report. The changes would apply starting with their 2008 annual reports, which would be filed in 2009 (IASplus.com).

Moreover, in August 2007, the SEC has published a Concept Release to obtain information about the extent and nature of the public's interest in allowing U.S. issuers, including investment companies subject to the Investment Company Act of 1940, to prepare financial statements in accordance with IFRSs for purposes of complying with the rules and regulations of the SEC. U.S. issuers presently prepare their financial statements in accordance with U.S. GAAP. The release includes 35 specific questions to which the SEC seeks responses (ibid.).

A EU regulation requires all EU-listed companies to produce consolidated financial statements under IFRSs by 2005 at the latest. The EU has adopted a regulation that requires publicly traded companies to follow IFRSs, which have been approved in an EU endorsement process, for their consolidated accounts starting January 2005, which will affect approximately 7,000 publicly traded companies in Europe. Unlisted corporations in Europe are expected to eventually follow IFRSs (ibid.). Many other countries from Africa and Asia, such as China, Philippines, and other countries in Southeast Asia, have started the policy of converging their national standards with IFRSs to be part of the global financial market.

In Japan, the Accounting Standards Board of Japan (ASBJ) and the IASB have agreed to accelerate convergence between Japanese GAAP and IFRSs, a process that was started in March 2005. By 2008, the two boards will seek to eliminate major differences between Japanese GAAP and IFRSs, with the remaining differences being removed on or before June 30, 2011 (ibid.).

The Relevance of the IFRSs for Gulf Countries

Now, an important question about the relevance of the IFRSs for the Gulf countries needs an honest answer. The question has several dimensions: Are Gulf countries similar to each other in their cultural, economic, political, legal, and educational environmental variables? Do Gulf countries have different cultural, political, legal, and educational environmental factors than European, South Asian, or other countries? If the answer is yes, will the IFRSs be relevant for Gulf countries' needs? However, if the answer is no, do Gulf countries need a different IFRSs to be more relevant to their environment? Are the differences between Gulf countries and other countries, currently using IFRSs, so big to not justify the use of IFRSs for their financial reporting systems? Is the U.S. GAAP more relevant to Gulf countries than IFRSs?

If we take a closer look at the Gulf countries, it may be true that accounting systems and practices in certain Gulf countries have been significantly influenced by several Islamic cultural values, with the religion being the most significant one. It may not be acceptable by these countries to use the IFRSs as a substitute for their national accounting standards. If the national cultural values of Islamic society shape and reinforce both accounting systems and practices, it is suggested that it will be a rational decision to harmonize the accounting standards of those countries as one subgroup of the international community. With more brief investigation of the cultural values and accounting systems and practices of Gulf countries it may be possible to come up with a reasonable solution. An understanding of how Gulf cultural values affect cross-national accounting diversity can be useful in efforts to answer the aforementioned question and to reduce this diversity and enhance the comparability of accounting information worldwide.

Accounting systems and reporting practices usually arise from the need to inform the interested groups in the society in which they are developed.

Therefore, in every society of every Gulf country, accounting systems and practices are expected to be a function of the environmental factors that influence business practices in that society. Financial reports are also expected to reflect the outcome of these Middle East environmental factors.

An accounting "standard" is a model, example, or criterion that outlines how certain accounting items or transactions on financial statements or reports should be measured and presented, and what information should be disclosed for the interested users. The three accounting standards that are applicable to our analysis include: (1) the local standards, established by the national standard-setting body; (2) the U.S. standards, as set by the FASB; (3) the IFRSs, established by the IASB.

If every Gulf country decides on using one standard versus another, it will result in the creation of different financial statements, depending on the circumstances. An MNC, such as Dell or Proctor & Gamble whose organizations wish to acquire a major factory in Bahrain or start a joint venture in the UAE, may need to be familiar with all local accounting standards. The dilemma of different standards raises even more questions. What accounting standard should they use to prepare their financial statements for review? Which accounting standard should be adopted by the MNCs and local capital markets of the Gulf countries? The answers to these questions create challenges for the IASB and national standard-setting organizations in the Gulf and around the world. The solution, and the standards agreed upon, affects global financing and investing in the integrated world economy. The decision also affects the viability and procedures of standard-setting groups in every Gulf country (Sturge 1998).

To harmonize national accounting standards with IFRSs means that the differences between IFRSs and national standards should be kept at a minimum. Harmonization has many advantages; they include the comparability of international financial information. One advantage of harmonization is that Omani or Saudi companies' financial statements may become comparable to that of British, Japanese, or Singaporean companies. This will help to alleviate the current misunderstanding about the reliability of non-U.S. MNCs' financial statements. Another advantage is the reduction of the cost of consolidating divergent financial statements.

However, harmonization might entail imposing Western accounting principles upon Gulf countries whose business and accounting practices are thought to be less developed than that of the West (Hamid, Graig, and Clarke 1993). It also ignores the fact that accounting is considered as a socio-technical activity, in any country, including human, nonhuman, financial and nonfinancial resources or techniques, as well as interaction between the two. Moreover, Hamid and colleagues (1993) suggested that cultural inputs, such as religion, should not be ignored because it is a confounding element in harmonizing the IFRSs.

If we take a look at the history, we will find out that local accounting standards of the Gulf countries were originally developed when world market was not as global as it is today. Those standards in individual Gulf countries were based on their unique social, legal, and educational environmental variables, with little regard for standards in other countries. Moreover, the increasing integration of the global economy has created the need for international standards. Financial organizations and professionals at all levels are finding it increasingly more challenging to analyze statements that are produced with such a wide variety of different standards. At the present time, all European and many other countries have participated, recognized, adapted, and supported the work and objectives of the IASB.

In the Gulf region, there are conflicting groups of culture: Arabs and Israel. The Gulf countries have many things in common, although they may perceive themselves from time to time as having different political and economic aims. The three main common characteristics of the Gulf citizens are concentrated in their cultural values; they are basic values, basic religious attitudes, and basic self-perceptions (Nydell 1996). Notwithstanding the fact that some of them are very rich, they are all developing countries attempting to build a modern business infrastructure within the limited social and physical resources. However, Gulf countries represent the largest, most diverse, and most politically influential Muslim ethnic group in the world (Bethany 1997a). However, historical link between Arabs and the Islamic religion is still very strong.

Gulf or Arab cultures are more heavily influenced by institutions such as family, religion, and government, which interact to shape the value systems of individuals and groups than the Americans. These cultural differences have been directly linked to differences in managerial practices and accounting systems and practices that have been evidenced in these two cultures (Yasin, Green, and Zimmerer 1992). A good illustration of how Gulf countries' financial reporting works is the stock market in both Gulf countries. In the Gulf countries, stock markets may be inefficient in terms of valuation, especially compared to those of the United States and Europe. Investors and financial institutions need to pay more attention to the countries with better growth prospects, and to firms whose shares are currently undervalued but that have a market niche that would help support their profitability and growth.

The Gulf countries' stock markets are small, representing almost 9 percent of the total market capitalization of the 38 emerging markets in Asia, Latin America, Africa, and Eastern Europe in late 1990s (Azzam 1999). However, in 2007, Gulf companies are expected to raise $40 billion through debt issues, an increase of more than 100 percent compared to the previous year, according to projections by international credit rating agency Moodys Investors Services (Gulf News 2007). Seeking funds for mega projects, the UAE and other Gulf countries were actively pursuing the international debt market. According to Moodys estimates, project finance requirements of the Gulf region exceed $1.2 trillion due to the unexpected growth in key sectors such as real estate, infrastructure, telecommunications, and energy. With the regional equity markets yet to recover from the slump that began last year most of the funding requirements of Gulf companies are expected to be raised through debt issues. Moreover, the Gulf countries raised $18.2 billion through debt issues in 2006 with Islamic sector contributing almost 40 percent. The UAE accounted for 83 percent of the total corporate debt issuance, while Saudi Arabia, Kuwait, and Qatar had shares of 7, 6, and 4 percent, respectively (ibid.).

This has been attributed to a number of factors such as volatile stock markets, Gulf governments' policy of self-financing of public companies, the growing demand for refinancing short-term debts, and unprecedented growth in cross-border expansion in response to the growing demand for debt issues Debt issues are expected to keep up the increase of investment in new projects and to continue to fuel the growth in mergers and acquisitions in the region.

However, some believe that accounting standards and practices in the Gulf countries may be becoming increasingly diverse, with more and more companies following U.S.-style accounting practices. Kantor, Roberts, and Salter (1995) have concluded that the evidence from their study tends to contradict this assertion. Instead, it has been found that the accounting practices in the three Arab countries examined are remarkably similar. They also found out that, in general, differences in financial reporting practices are driven by differences in financing patterns. And it is expected that the Arab countries, in the near future, will move more toward adopting the accounting practices commonly followed in the United States as the typical pattern of financing corporation changes.

When we compare accounting practices and education of Gulf countries with American and European countries, we are bound to see a difference. Thus, Saudi Arabia and the UAE should differ from Western countries such as the United Kingdom, France, or the United States. In the latter countries, there is more emphasis on strict financial accounting and auditing, whereas in the former countries the emphasis is on information needed for economic planning at the macro level. Another difference is the relative emphasis on income measurement. In developed countries, income determination is one of the most important tools because the majority of businesses are privately owned. This is not the case in Gulf countries, because government and family ownership are far more dominant than public ownership (Kantor, Roberts, and Salter 1995).

A study by Kantor and colleagues (1995) examined 100 financial reporting practices and found out that only 3 practices were found to be significantly different across the 3 selected Gulf countries. Given the nature of these economies, these differences are relatively minor. In contrast to this finding that the three Gulf countries form a group with virtually identical financial reporting practices, substantial differences emerge between this group and the Western countries. Of the 100 issues examined, only 30 items did not differ between the Arab countries and at least 1 of the 3 Western countries.

Moreover, Kantor, Roberts, and Salter considered 3 Western countries individually, and found out that the least differences emerged between the Arab group and France, with only 21 of the 100 issues resulting in significant differences. This is in marked contrast to the position of either the United Kingdom, where 46 of the items resulted in significant differences, or the United States, where significant differences emerged for 59 items. The reasons for these findings may lie in the very different cultures of the societies and in the perceived role of financial reports and accounts. It is particularly noticeable that differences across the Arab countries and the United Kingdom and the United States emerge with regard to both measurement and disclosure issues (Kantor, Roberts, and Salter 1995).

In light of the move of all the world's major capital markets toward IFRSs, Gulf MNCs with good corporate governance should consider anticipating the move to IFRSs, which are considered as the best practice for corporate governance and should be the basis for measuring managements' performance and taking strategic decisions at the global level.

It can be argued that the adoption of IFRSs would benefit many users of accounting information in the Gulf region, who demand comparable and reliable information. In international business, divergence of national accounting standards and practices reduces the ability to understand foreign financial statements. Benefits from the adoption of IFRSs would include the exclusion of certain unfamiliar or misleading practices and the narrowing of the range of acceptable alternatives across the countries in the Gulf region.

In general, IFRSs are of great use for Gulf countries or other countries that do not have their own national standard-setting body or do not have the financial and nonfinancial resources to undertake the full process of preparing appropriate accounting standards to meet their needs. The preparation of accounting standards involves considerable cost and, quite apart from the advantages of uniformity, it would not be economical for each country to have a separate process and a separate set of standards. There are some Gulf companies that use the IFRSs for their financial statements to list their securities on the stock markets. Table 5.3 shows a summary of the information available of the six Gulf countries. It shows whether the IFRSs are permitted, required for some, required for all, or not permitted at all for reporting by domestic listed and unlisted companies of every one of the Gulf countries. As can be seen from table 5.3, Saudi Arabia is the only Gulf country that does not permit the use of IFRSs for both domestic listed and listed companies on the Saudi stock exchange market. While the UAE regulations requires only banks and companies trading at Dubai International Financial Center to use IFRSs, the other four Gulf countries (Bahrain, Kuwait, Oman, and Qatar) require all the listed and unlisted companies to use IFRSs.

The Gulf Countries Council (GCC) should establish an independent accounting organization to work on the roadmap for the convergence of all local GAAPs to the IFRSs. This would not only save companies from undertaking significant reconciliation procedures, which otherwise results in additional costs and the risk of being exposed to errors in

Table 5.3 Use of IFRS for reporting by domestic listed and unlisted companies in the Gulf countries

Country	*IFRS Not Permitted*	*IFRS Permitted*	*IFRS Required for Some Companies*	*IFRS Required for All Companies*	*Domestic Unlisted Companies*
Bahrain				Yes	IFRS required for all
Kuwait				Yes	IFRS required for all
Oman				Yes	IFRS required for all
Qatar				Yes	
Saudi Arabia	Not permitted				IFRS are not permitted
United Arab Emirates			Banks and companies trading at Dubai International Financial Center		

Sources: International Accounting Standards Board Internet Site: www.iasb.org.uk (August 2007).

reporting under the different accounting frameworks, but also significantly enhances the quality of financial reporting. The convergence to IFRSs will also greatly enhance the ability of Gulf countries to raise and attract foreign capital at low cost. It will also mean escape from multiple reports for Gulf companies that have to prepare their financial statements under multiple GAAPs.

Now, the time has come for the professional organizations of the Gulf countries to start training the preparers of the financial statements under IFRSs. Even though they may be from the home country, they would still be sought after by accounting firms and Gulf companies that converge toward IFRSs. With the world changing to IFRSs, international businesses in Gulf countries would have a massive requirement for IFRS resources, and Gulf IFRS literate resources could feed this appetite and provide a huge fillip to this sector. Could IFRS convergence be the next big thing for the international business in the Gulf countries? Gulf IFRS professionals will not only stoke the growth of the Gulf economy, but also of other economies. The opportunities are tempting, but they come with some huge challenges. The adoption of IFRSs in the Gulf countries would be a landmark achievement and a significant step toward global acceptability of Gulf corporations and professionals. However, every change brings along with it a degree of apprehension and, therefore, it needs to be ensured that these apprehensions are addressed early to ensure an effective and efficient transition period. New priorities of the IFRS's adoption by 2010 is expected to have a significant impact on all stakeholders, such as the GCC, chartered accountants, regulators, preparers of financial statements, analysts, users of financial information, and so on.

It is suggested that the Council of the Gulf countries (GCC) should adopt a new IAS regulation requiring listed Gulf companies, including banks and insurance companies, to prepare their consolidated accounts in accordance with IFRSs from 2008 onward. The goal of the new regulation should be to eliminate barriers to cross-border trading in securities by ensuring that the Gulf company accounts throughout the Gulf region are reliable, transparent, and comparable. The GCC should have the force of law without requiring transposition into national legislation. However, for GCC, to ensure appropriate political oversight, it should establish a new mechanism to assess IASs to give them legal endorsement before they can be used in the Gulf region or in other countries. Member states have the option of extending the requirements of the regulation to unlisted companies and to the production of individual accounts.

However, if Gulf countries are looking forward to having one regional standard-setter and one set of IFRSs, the following four principles are essential in achieving this ultimate goal:

1. All Gulf countries involved in global financial reporting must have a common mission or objective of financial accounting and reporting.
2. Gulf countries must have a process for developing financial reporting standards that is accepted and trusted by all constituents and one that assures that the mission of the standard-setter is fulfilled.
3. Gulf countries should develop standards that achieve high quality.
4. One regional standard-setting body should be formed and must have the power to enforce the use of the appropriate IFRSs upon all national companies listed on the Gulf stock exchange markets of all Gulf countries.

Under the threat of further financial crises, Gulf countries' governments, intergovernmental agencies, and global financial institutions now have a real fear that the crisis in Asia will be repeated elsewhere and on an even greater scale. Facing this threat, Gulf countries may have been forced to look for ways of securing greater economic stability for the future. And at last, after several years of largely unproductive debate, there is a growing trend of the urgency of enforcing a relevant set of IFRSs to ensure that the information upon which local and foreign investors and other stakeholders base their decisions is transparent, relevant, comprehensive, reliable, consistent, and internationally comparable. Moreover, the accounting profession organizations in Gulf countries should play an important role in this trend and participate in the implementation of the appropriate IFRSs for the Gulf countries, and to cooperate with accounting firms that serve the business community in the area in implementing these standards.

Summary and Conclusions

This chapter addresses the International Financial Reporting Standards (IFRSs) promulgated by the International Accounting Standards Board (IASB) and their effect on accounting standards of the Gulf countries. It discusses and emphasizes the importance of understanding the efforts of various constituents who are involved in the development of international accounting standards, including FASB, European Union, SEC, IOSCO, and other professional organizations. This chapter also covers the relevance of the IFRSs to the environment of Gulf countries, and whether the use of IFRSs is the only choice for Gulf companies, how can they be implemented and enforced upon the countries in the region.

There has been a growing recognition of the urgent need of enforcing one single set of high-quality international accounting standards in all countries around the world: (1) to provide investors, creditors, and other users with relevant, comprehensive, reliable, consistent, and internationally comparable information for their investing and financing decisions and (2) to facilitate the right flow of capital between markets and the pricing of capital within the markets. However, this depends upon the establishment of an internationally acceptable accounting standard-setting body. To date, the restructured IASB has held itself out as the international standard-setting body because of its broad-based membership and its two stated goals.

Today, the support and interest in the IFRSs of the IASB from the worldwide professional and governmental organizations have been increasing and the use and the application of the IFRSs are widely and internationally recognized. In 2002, the FASB and IASB came up with the Norwalk agreement as a significant step toward formalizing the commitment to the convergence of U.S. and IFRS accounting standards. In June 2007, the SEC issued a proposal to eliminate the requirements to reconcile financial statements of foreign firms listing their securities on the New York Stock Exchange market with U.S. GAAP if the financial statements are in full compliance with the IFRSs. Since January 2005, the EU regulation requires all EU-listed companies to prepare their consolidated financial statements using IFRSs issued by the IASB.

The Gulf countries to a large extent have welcomed the IASB and its IFRSs. Some countries consider these standards as a replacement for their domestic standards, while others accept IFRSs financial statements from foreign companies for listing purposes in their stock exchanges. The national standards of some countries are either based on or are similar to IFRSs even though they may not have adopted IFRSs. Only one of the six Gulf countries, Saudi Arabia, does not permit the use of the IFRSs for their listed and unlisted domestic companies.

The Gulf Countries Council (GCC) should establish an independent accounting organization to work on the roadmap for the convergence of all local GAAPs to the IFRSs. This would (1) save companies undertaking significant costly reconciliation procedures, (2) significantly enhance the quality of financial reporting, (3) greatly enhance the ability of Gulf countries to raise and attract foreign capital at low cost, and (4) help companies escape from multiple reports for Gulf companies that have to prepare their financial statements under multiple GAAPs.

It is suggested that the GCC should adopt a new IAS regulation requiring listed Gulf companies, including banks and insurance companies, to prepare their consolidated accounts in accordance with IFRSs from 2008 onward. The goal is to eliminate barriers to cross-border trading in securities by ensuring that the Gulf company accounts throughout the Gulf region are reliable, transparent, and comparable. The GCC should have the force of law without requiring transposition into national legislation by establishing a new mechanism to assess IASs to give them legal endorsement before they can be used. It is recommended that if Gulf countries are looking forward to have one single regional standard-setter and one set of international financial reporting standards, the following four principles are essential in achieving this ultimate goal:

1. All Gulf countries involved in global financial reporting must have a common mission or objective of financial accounting and reporting.
2. Gulf countries must have a process for implementing and adapting the IFRSs that are accepted and trusted by all constituents and one that assures that the mission of the standard-setter is fulfilled.
3. Gulf countries should establish a mechanism to assess IFRSs that achieve high quality.
4. Gulf countries should ensure establishing efficient corporate governance systems including financial disclosure and transparency for all listed domestic companies in Gulf stock exchange markets.

In conclusion, all Gulf governments, intergovernmental agencies, and global financial institutions now have to be forced to look for ways of securing greater economic stability for the future. Now, it is more important than before for Gulf countries to enforce the convergence of local and IFRSs to ensure that the information upon which investors and other stakeholders base their decisions is transparent, comprehensive, reliable, consistent, and internationally comparable. Currently, Gulf countries have no choice but to follow IFRSs starting by 2008. Moreover, the accounting profession in Gulf countries has to participate in the adaptation and the use of IFRSs for their financial statements for all listed and unlisted domestic companies to compete in the global market for the best use of resources in achieving their ultimate goals.

References

American Institute of Certified Public Accountants (AICPA). 1999. "AICPA Supports International Standards." *The Practical Accountant*, Boston, June: 12.

Anonymous 2005. "Transparency Key to Attracting Foreign Investment." *Al Bawaba*, London, June 7: 1.

Azzam, Henry T. 1999. "Arab Stock Markets: Country-by-Country Analysis and Review." *Middle East Executive Reports*, Washington, April.

Basoglu, Besalet and Ahmed Goma. 2002. "International Accounting Standards and Selected Middle East Stock Exchanges." *Middle Eastern and North African Economies Electronic Journal* 4 (September). http://www.luc.edu/orgs/mea.

Bethany World Prayer Center. 1997a. "The Unreached Peoples Prayer Profiles-The Diaspora Arabs." *The Internet.*

Choi, Frederick D.S. and Gary K. Meek. 2005. *International Accounting.* 5th Edition. Upper Saddle River, NJ: Pearson/Prentice-Hall.

Deloitte Touche Tohmatsu. 2007. "The IFRS and SEC." www.Iasplus.com.

Doupnik, Timothy and Hector Perera. 2007. *International Accounting.* New York: McGraw-Hill/Irwin.

Dzinkowski, Ramona. 2007. "Saying Goodby to U.S. GAAP." *Strategic Finance*, June, 47–49.

Financial Accounting Standards Board (FASB). 2002. "News Release: The Norwalk Agreement." September. Norwalk, CT: FASB.

Gulf News. 2007. "Stock Slump Fuels Gulf Debt Market." May 3, Gulfnews.com.

Hamid, Shaari, Russell Graig, and Frank Clarke. 1993. "Religion: A Confounding Cultural Element in the International Harmonization of Accounting." *ABACUS* 29 (2): 131–147.

Harding, Frank. 1999. "Corporate Credibility—Why a Harmonised Global Accountancy Framework Matters." *Accountancy Ireland*, Dublin, April: 16–17.

International Accounting Standards Board (IASB). 2007. http://www.iasc.org, August 14.

Iqbal, M. Zafar. 2002. *International Accounting: A Global Perspective.* 2nd edition. Cincinnati, OH: SouthWestern College Publishing.

Kantor, Jeffrey, Clare B. Roberts; and Stephen B. Salter. 1995. "Financial Reporting Practices in Selected Arab Countries: An Empirical Study of Egypt, Saudi Arabia, and the United Arab Emirates." *International Studies of Management & Organization* 25 (3) (Fall): 31–45.

Nydell, Margaret K. 1996. Understanding Arabs: A Guide for Westerners. Yarmouth, ME: Intercultural Press, Inc..

Sturge, Derrick. 1998. "Who Sets the Standard?" *CMA Management*, Hamilton, March: 3–4.

Yasin, Mahmoud M., Ronald F. Green, and Tom Zimmerer. 1992. "Executive Courage across Cultures: An Organizational Perspective," *International Journal of Commerce and Management* 2 (1 and 2): 75–87.

6

Evolution and Practices of the Auditing Profession in the Gulf Countries

Mohamed E. Ibrahim

This chapter reviews the historical development of the auditing profession and its practices in the Gulf countries. It shows that the necessary institutions and their infrastructures required for truly functional professions are still in the early developmental stage in some countries and do not exist at all in some others. In countries such as Saudi Arabia, a national profession body has been established to set accounting and auditing standards and monitor practices. In other countries such as the UAE and Sultanate of Oman, such national bodies do not exist. That is to say, the auditing profession is still a young one and it will be sometime before it achieves its professional status as in the Western societies.

Introduction

In the past few decades, the Gulf countries have witnessed rapid economic development, which is mainly financed by oil revenues and foreign investments. This economic development is being achieved through the increased number of economic and financial enterprises and institutions, a legal structure, and development of human resources. The accounting and auditing profession has also witnessed several changes in each country over the years.

This chapter starts by examining the general meaning of the concept "profession." This concept has evolved in the literature based on some sociologists' observation that people in some occupations resisted dominant trends in their workplace. These trends are usually referred to as bureaucracy. With many changes in the means and methods of doing business and transportation following the industrial revolution, many jobs and tasks have been broken down into small steps (a concept known as division of labor) to emphasize specialization. This direction in thinking and application shifted the determination of the conditions of entry into and exit from an occupation from the control of key knowledgeable people to the control of the organization. That is, job requirements, selection and removal criteria, and performance evaluation criteria fell into the hands of management of the organization.

Members of professional occupations, who rely on their knowledge and skills, resisted this new dominant trend of organizational control. As a result, an alternative trend emerged. This alternative trend was termed "professionalization of labor."

To strengthen the alternative trend and compete in the process of professionalization (to have a profession), many practicing members of occupations tended to form professional bodies that represent their collective power to organize and develop conditions and standards that govern the conduct of the members. According to Millerson (1964), a professional body has five primary functions and some other secondary functions. The primary functions are to organize, qualify, study specific issues that are of interest to the members and communicate the results to the intended users, register competent members, and promote and preserve high standards of professional conduct.

For the Gulf countries, each country had a professional body for the accounting and auditing profession. However, in the past few years, there has been a movement toward unifying the standards and practices in the Gulf countries through the establishment of the GCC Accounting and Auditing Organization. This organization was established to carry out activities that help organize and develop the accounting and the auditing profession in the GCC countries. It also enhances coordination and integration among these countries. The organization has a set of five primarily objectives; they are as follows (Accounting and Auditing 2005):

1. Prepare, review, develop, and approve professional standards, particularly accounting and auditing standards and codes of ethics and professional conduct, taking into consideration the international standards and experiences of other countries and professional organizations.
2. Develop and unify the means followed in organizing the profession including proposals for amending, developing, and unifying

existing laws and rules regulating the profession, and procedures followed to obtain practicing licenses.

3. Establish necessary rules for fellowship examination and conducting it, provided such rules cover professional, practical, and theoretical aspects of the accounting and auditing profession.
4. Prepare and conduct continuing professional education (CPE) programs related to the profession.
5. Establish an appropriate quality review program, which includes CPA field monitoring, follow-up, and professional performance evaluation.

In the following sections, the evolution and practices of accounting and auditing standards in each of the six Gulf countries are reviewed first. Then, the question of the need of either national standards or the use of the international acceptable auditing standards will be discussed.

Bahrain

The Kingdom of Bahrain has charted a leading role in the area of Islamic accounting and auditing for financial institutions. There is an independent international organization (not-for-profit organization) that develops rules relating to accounting, auditing, governance, and ethical standards based on the Islamic Law (Shari'ah) for Islamic financial institutions and the banking industry. It is called the Accounting and Auditing Organization for Islamic Financial Institutions (AAOIFI).

The organization was established according to an agreement signed by Islamic financial institutions in 1990. It issues accounting and auditing standards through a special accounting and auditing standards board. The issuance of these standards is done through a due process that incorporates consultations and feedback from experts and industry practitioners. Until today, the organization has issued 22 accounting standards and 5 auditing standards. These standards are currently adopted in the Kingdom of Bahrain, Dubai International Financial Centre, Jordan, Lebanon, Qatar, Sudan, and Syria. In addition, the relevant authorities in Australia, Indonesia, Malaysia, Pakistan, Kingdom of Saudi Arabia, and South Africa have issued guidelines that are based on the organization's standards and pronouncements (AAOIFI 2007).

The Organization's Accounting and Auditing Standards Board (AASB)

The organization's Accounting and Auditing Standards Board (AASB) is composed of 20 part-time members appointed by the Board of Trustees for a five-year term. Membership in the standards board is represented by different categories (e.g., regulatory bodies, Islamic financial institutions, Shari'ah supervisory boards, university professors, certified accountants, and users of the financial statements of Islamic financial institutions). The board has the following powers:

1. To prepare, adopt, and interpret accounting and auditing statements, standards, and guidelines for Islamic financial institutions.
2. To prepare and adopt code of ethics and educational standards related to the activities of Islamic financial institutions.
3. To review with the aim of making additions, deletions, or amendments to any accounting and auditing statements, standards, and guidelines.
4. To prepare and adopt the due process for the preparation of standards, as well as regulations and by-laws of the Standards Board.

The Standards Board meets at least twice every year and its resolutions are adopted by a simple majority vote.

For privately owned companies and organizations (other than Islamic financial institutions) in Bahrain, financial statements are audited by accounting firms in accordance with generally accepted auditing standards. There are no national set of standards developed in this regard. However, Joshi and Wakil (2004) have shown that companies in Bahrain have utilized the idea of an audit committee, which is an essential factor of a good corporate governance environment for external auditors to work in.

Kuwait

The basic power of setting accounting and auditing standards in Kuwait rests with the Ministry of Commerce and Industry. The historical development of the profession started with the State Law No. 5 of 1981, which organizes the auditing profession. It addressed auditors' registration, qualifications, and duties. The law in Kuwait differs from other Gulf States by limiting registration to holders of bachelor degrees. Lower degrees are not acceptable. In addition, a practicing auditing professional must be of Kuwait nationality. Only non-Kuwaitis who were in practice before the issuance of the law were allowed to practice for a period of three years that is renewable for another two years with the permission of the minister of commerce. This exception has now expired and is no longer applicable.

As of today, there is no national professional body that sets accounting and auditing standards in Kuwait. However, many large companies operating in Kuwait use the international accounting standards. Public accounting firms are offering their audit services according to the generally accepted auditing principles.

Oman

The accounting and auditing profession in Oman is considered at its early stage of development. There is no national professional body in charge of setting accounting and auditing standards. However, similar to most Gulf countries, many large companies operating in Oman use the international accounting standards because of the mandatory publications of audited financial statements. But there is no official mandate to apply the international accounting and auditing standards.

Based on the ministerial circular number 11 of 2002, a charter for organizing and managing corporations has been prepared to protect the interests of all parties involved. The charter also was based on the Companies' Law No. 4 of 1974 and its modifications. The main points of the charter that deals with the accounting and auditing profession are summarized as follows (Suliman 2005):

1. There must be an audit committee that acts as a link between the board of directors and external auditors.
2. An external auditor is to be appointed for a maximum period of four consecutive years. However, the same external auditor can be reappointed again in the future after the passage of a minimum of two financial years from the period of four years.
3. The external auditor must examine the reasonableness and effectiveness of the internal controls of the company.
4. The external auditor should report on the financial viability of the company and its ability to continue.
5. The external auditor is to report to the board of directors on any violations discovered during the audit and any suspected transactions. Material violations should also be reported to the concerned authorizes.

In Oman, all auditors are required to follow IASs in preparing the financial statements of companies and banks. The Central Bank of Oman (CBO) supervises all the accounting and auditing policies used by banks. From time to time, the CBO contacts an audit firm to conduct feasibility studies on specific regulations that are intended to be used in the future. Occasionally, it uses external auditors to inspect banks on its behalf;

however, these inspections are lengthy and detailed, and take up to two months (Islam 2003).

Qatar

The accounting and auditing profession in Qatar is at an early stage of its development as there is no national professional body to set the auditing standards. However, many large companies operating in Qatar use the international accounting standards because of the mandatory requirements to publish the audited financial statements. But there is no official mandate to apply the international accounting and auditing standards.

The historical development of the accounting and auditing profession in the state of Qatar goes back to 1974 when the State Law No. 7 was issued to organize the work of accountants and auditors. It basically addressed the procedures to register accountants and auditors and the minimum qualifications required. In 1981, the government issued the Companies Act number 11, which outlined the conditions and terms for companies operating in Qatar and the issuance of annual financial statements. The law was subsequently modified by Law No. 9 of 1998 and 2002. These new modifications specified the financial statements that should be audited and published, and the additional notes that should be included with the financial statements. The law also specified that the maximum period of time that a company can utilize the service of an auditor is five years, after which a rotation must take place.

Saudi Arabia

The basic power of setting accounting and auditing standards in Saudi Arabia rests with the Ministry of Commerce. However, the passage of the CPA law of 1991 called for the establishment of quasi self-regulatory professional body called the Saudi Organization for Certified Public Accountants (SOCPA). This professional body has the responsibly of developing the accounting profession in Saudi Arabia. Its basic responsibility entails organizing, regulating, and monitoring professional practices. Thus, the Ministry of Commerce is no longer involved in organizing and providing CPA licenses. It is there primarily to direct, monitor, define, and redefine professional actions and activities through the SOCPA (Al-Angari and Sherer 2001).

The SOCPA has been active in promulgating accounting and auditing standards based on the international trends and experience of other countries. It has also been a major player in the formation of GCC Accounting and Auditing Organization. Perhaps Saudi Arabia is considered the only Arab Gulf State that has established a framework for its accounting and auditing standards.

It is important to realize that the current practices of the auditing profession in Saudi Arabia have two main dimensions. With respect to the first one, for privately owned companies and institutions, registered accounting firms are licensed to audit the financial statements of these companies and institutions according to the standards set by the SOCPA. Second, public organizations (owned by government) and other governmental units are audited by the General Auditing Bureau (GAB), which was established in 1953 (Al-Nofaie 2003). According to Article 7, GAB is responsible for the execution of comprehensive post-auditing on the State's revenues, expenditures, current and fixed assets, and for exercising auditing control to ensure proper utilization and maintenance of these resources.

The UAE

The basic power of setting accounting and auditing standards in the UAE rests with the Ministry of Commerce and Economics. As the country tends to move in the direction of applying the international accounting and auditing standards (starting with the bank sector), the need for establishing a national professional body that is empowered to develop accounting and auditing standards is not justified. However, a group of national practicing accountants realized the need for an independent body or association to cater to the needs of the profession and to drive the national effort for the recognition of the profession.

The association's main roles have been limited to increased awareness of the profession, holding some meetings and training session for young practitioners. The association has no authority to set standards or to monitor the conduct of practitioners. The association was established in 1997, as one of the public associations, based on the ministerial decision no. 227 from the minister of labor and social affairs to cope with the overall economic development in the UAE, particularly in the field of commerce and industry, which is manifested in the issuance of all economic legislations such as business Law, Central Bank and Commercial Banks' Act, Insurance Companies Law, and Business Transaction Law.

The evolution of the accounting and auditing profession in the UAE started with the Federal Law No. 9 of 1975, which was the first law issued to organize the accounting and auditing profession. It addressed the issue of registering accountants and auditors, determining the qualifications required to be an accountant or auditor, and describing possible actions to be taken against accountants and auditors in cases of professional violations.

The law indicated that no one is allowed to engage in public practice unless he is registered. The law specified the following six conditions for the registration of an auditor:

1. The person holds the UAE nationality or a nationality of any of the Arab countries. However, the law made two exceptions regarding nationality:
   a. Those who were practicing before the issuance of the law
   b. Those who are certified accountants in foreign countries.
2. The person is of the legal age as recognized in the civil law.
3. The person has good behavior and reputation.
4. The person has no criminal records.
5. The person holds a bachelor degree or a diploma in accounting.
6. In the case of those who hold bachelor degrees, the person should have two years of practical training at a practicing professional firm. For those who hold a diploma, the minimum number of years for practical training is set as six years.

The Federal Law # 22 (1995) that dealt with the organization of the accounting and auditing profession modified the earlier Law No. 9 of 1975. This new Federal law mandated the recognition of an auditor to be made uniform across the country and encouraged the entry of more nationals into the profession. It also required higher level of proficiency in performing the audit. The law also stated the responsibilities and obligations of auditors and insured their independence.

With respect to banks in the UAE, auditing standards have varied widely and the banking industry has been dominated by the Big Four international accounting firms (Islam 2003). They audit most of the local commercial banks in the UAE. Most banks have not changed their auditing firm for several years, and the Central Bank does not require them to do so (ibid.).

Auditing Standards in the Gulf Countries

The only two Gulf countries that have established national bodies to set accounting and auditing standards are Bahrain and Saudi Arabia. However, the set of standards developed in Bahrain are designed primarily for Islamic financial institutions. On the other hand, the set of standards developed in Saudi Arabia by the SOCPA is more complete and echoes the international practice. These standards revolve around the following three dimensions.

The General Standards

The general standards set forth the qualifications of the person or persons who will perform the audit in terms of education and training. Most Arab Gulf countries now require a bachelor degree in accounting as a minimum educational requirement and two years of practical training. Thus, one can say that the general standards do exist even in the absence of a set of auditing standards. However, there is no mandate for passing a national professional examination to obtain a license to practice.

The Field Work Standards

The field work standards are the standards that organize the auditors' work in the field. These include planning the audit, supervision of assistants, if any, study of internal controls, and obtaining audit evidence. While these standards are stated for the Saudi auditors, they are not stated for other Gulf countries. However, all auditors apply such standards as generally accepted ones.

The Reporting Standards

The reporting standards set of standards outline what should be included in the audit report in terms of the nature and scope of the work, the financial statements that were subjected to the audit, the period covered, the accounting basis used to judge the fair presentation of financial statements, the reasonableness of disclosure and the auditor's opinion. While these standards are stated for the Saudi auditors, they are not stated for other Gulf countries. However, all auditors apply such standards as generally accepted ones.

It is expected that the formation of the GCC Accounting and Auditing Organization (GCCAAO) will lead to the development of a set of auditing standards to be used in all six Arab Gulf countries. The organization has formed its committee structure and the first outcome of such a formation was the adoption of uniform guidelines for quality control for practicing auditors.

Auditing Practices in the Gulf Countries

The practices of the auditing profession in the Arab Gulf countries have evolved in the past six decades tremendously. Early practices were limited to financial auditing. However, with the trend toward globalization and internationalization, many internationally well-known firms as well as national and local firms have opened offices in the Arab Gulf countries. These offices now offer all accounting, auditing, and system services that are offered in developed countries around the world.

Adoption of International Standards and the Need for National Professional Bodies

In the past two decades, there has been a strong trend in many countries toward adoption of the international accounting and auditing standards. This trend has been influenced by some factors that include the cost of developing standards, failure of the accounting and auditing standards in the United States to handle the case of "Enron," and the adoption of the international standards by the European Union.

Such a trend raised the question about the need for national professional bodies to set accounting and auditing standards in the Arab Gulf countries. The answer is not that simple given that many countries view national professional bodies to be a sign of national pride. However, the trend of globalization and the costs involved in setting meaningful standards would dictate the adoption of international accounting and auditing standards. It is the opinion of the author that there is no need to reinvent the wheel. The international accounting and auditing standards have been developed over the years in a way that is suitable to all nations. After all, some of the Arab Gulf countries are active participants in the process of developing such standards.

Summary and Conclusions

This chapter summarizes the historical and general background of the auditing standards, practices, and profession in the Gulf countries. Although some studies (e.g., Hussain et al. 2002 and Al-Gahtani 2005) have compared the standards and practices in some Gulf countries, this chapter discussed and emphasized the development of the auditing profession in the six Gulf countries and its trends and functions over the past three decades. The issue of a choice between the adoption of International Auditing Standards or developing the national standards of the Gulf countries was analyzed.

It was noted that Bahrain is the leading country in the area of Islamic accounting and auditing standards for financial institutions. In Kuwait, Oman, and Qatar, there are no professional organizations in charge of setting accounting and auditing standards. In Saudi Arabia, the Saudi Organization for Certified Public Accountants (SOCPA) is the professional body that has the responsibility of developing the accounting profession. Its basic responsibility entails organizing, regulating, and monitoring professional practices. The SOCPA has been active in promulgating accounting and auditing standards based on the international trends and experience of other countries. It has also been a major player in the formation of GCCAAO. Therefore, Saudi Arabia may be considered the only Gulf country that has established a framework for its accounting and auditing standards.

However, in the UAE, the basic power of setting accounting and auditing standards rests with the Ministry of Commerce and Economics and a national professional body that is empowered to develop accounting and auditing standards is not justified. The accounting and auditing association was established in 1997, as one of the public associations simply to promote the profession and its image among the public.

In conclusion, the actual practices and services of the auditing profession in the Gulf countries are not that different from the practices known in the Western societies in terms of service types, scope, and the qualifications of the individuals involved in performing such services. However, there is one unique culture-based characteristic of actual auditing practices in the Gulf countries that is less known in the Western society; that is, the auditing services related to the Islamic banking. The author considers the Kingdom of Bahrain to be the leading champion in this area, where a set of auditing standards have been developed and practiced.

References

Accounting and Auditing Organization for Islamic Financial Institutions. 2005. *Accounting, Auditing & Governance Standards for Islamic Financial Institutions*. Manama, Bahrain: Accounting and Auditing Organization for Islamic Financial Institutions (AAOIFI).

Al-Angari, H. and M. Sherer. 2001. "The Implementation of Quality Review Programmes on Audit Firms in Saudi Arabia." Working paper, University of Essex, United Kingdom.

Al-Nofaie, M. 2003. "Audit Profile: The General Auditing Bureau of the Kingdom of Saudi Arabia." *International Journal of Government Auditing* 30 (4): 22–24.

Al-Qahtani, A. 2005. "The Development of Accounting Regulation in the GCC: Western hegemony or Recognition of Peculiarity?" *Managerial Auditing Journal* 20 (3): 217–226.

Hussain, M., M. Islam, A. Gunasekaran, and K. Maskooki. 2002. "Accounting Standards and Practices of Financial Institutions in GCC Countries." *Managerial Auditing Journal* 17 (7): 350–362.

Islam, Mazhar M. 2003. "Development and Performance of Domestic and Foreign Bank in GCC Countries." *Managerial Finance* 29 (2/3): 42–73.

Joshi, P. and A. Wakil. 2004. "A Study of the Audit Committees' Functioning in Bahrain: Empirical Findings." *Managerial Auditing Journal* 19 (7): 832–858.

Millerson, G. 1964. *The Qualifying Association: A Study in Professionalization.* London, United Kingdom: Routledge & Kegan Paul.

Suliman, N. 2005. "The Charter for Organizing and Managing Corporations in Sultanate of Oman." *Accounting & Auditing* 4 (1): 19.

7

Accounting Profession and Accounting Education in the Gulf Countries

Sivakumar Velayutham and Sabri Al-Segini

Introduction

An increase in commercial activity and the development of joint stock companies have always been accompanied by a sharp demand for competent accountants. In this environment, a vibrant accounting profession and institutions providing quality accounting education is critical to the steady supply of competent accounting professionals. Professional bodies contribute to the steady supply of competent accountants, firstly through education, training, and examination of aspiring accountants. To this end, they support applied research and diffusion of knowledge through publications and conferences. Professional bodies also develop codes of ethics and professional standards to ensure that the work and services provided by accounting professionals are of a high standard and are ethical in their dealings. More recently professional bodies have made continuing professional education a compulsory requirement for membership, ensuring that the knowledge and skills of its members are current.

The Arabian Gulf countries have in recent times seen rapid economic growth as well as the furious expansion of the national stock markets. The aforementioned developments have contributed to a huge demand for accounting professionals, which has been mainly filled by an expatriate workforce. The six Gulf countries have recently invested heavily in education to ensure that their citizens are not left behind in the job market and are equipped to fill the growing demand for professionals.

The purpose of this chapter is to evaluate the development and contribution of accounting education and the accounting profession to the economic development of the Gulf countries. The chapter is mainly based on an analysis of professional requirements and curriculums of different institutions of higher education in the different Gulf countries. The findings of the study would provide directions for the strengthening of professional bodies and accounting education in Gulf countries so that they can play a positive role in the development of the economies of the Gulf countries.

The rest of the chapter is organized as follows. The first section reviews global developments in the accounting profession and accounting education. This section provides a framework to analyze the development of accounting professional bodies and accounting education in the GCC countries. The next section traces the development of professional bodies in the different GCC countries and evaluates their contribution to the development of accounting. The succeeding section consists of an evaluation of the development of accounting education followed by some concluding remarks in the final section.

Global Development in the Accounting Profession and Education

Both the accounting profession and accounting education have gone through considerable changes in the last 30 years. This section reviews the major developments in both the accounting profession and accounting education. The review provides both a framework and a benchmark to analyze and put in context the development of the accounting profession and education in the GCC countries.

The Transformation of the Accounting Profession and Professional Bodies

The concept of "profession" as a topic for serious study developed when sociologists found a number of occupations resisting the dominant trend in the workplace, which was referred to as bureaucratization. The resistance by a number of knowledge based occupations to the dominant trend (organizational control) in the workplace presented a significant difficulty to Weber's (1964) account of the bureaucratization of society. The resistance of organizational control by a number of occupations represented an alternative trend, which Foote (1953) termed "The Professionalization of labor." The formation of professional bodies is an essential part of the professionalization process.

The first professional accounting body (The Institute of Accountants in Edinburgh) was formed in 1853 in Scotland. While, many professional accounting bodies have been formed since, the general role and scope of the professional accounting body remained the same till the 1970s, although some of the roles may have become more prominent in comparison to others. Since its formation, it has remained a local or national body with a mutual association structure; its principal goal is improving the interest and status of accountants through occupational control or closure (Lee 1990) and self-regulation. This goal is similar to that of other professions such as medicine and law, and is based on the premise that a lack of control and direction in the market for audit services is not in the public interest (Brown 1905), and that this direction and control should be driven by an organization representing qualified practitioners. Not only has the professional accounting body remained relatively unchanged, there has also been little debate on the need for change. Most studies on the professional accounting body have been historical (Walker 1995; Chua and Pollaos 1998).

From the beginning, the objective of closure has been pursued through self-regulation in the following areas:

1. Setting exams to ensure that only properly qualified individuals are allowed to practice, and keeping members up-to-date on new developments, which has been transformed into compulsory continuing professional education (CPE);
2. Developing and enforcing a code of ethics to ensure that individuals of dubious character are prevented from practicing as accountants;
3. Regulating the quality of services provided by accountants. Initially this was an informal process, which has in recent times become a formal process through accounting, auditing, and quality-control standards;
4. Representing the views of the profession to the governmental legislative process and to society in general.

Since the 1970s, however, there have been major changes in the role of the professional accounting bodies. In 1973, the American accounting profession, following the Wheat Committee report, decided that accounting standard-setting should be made independent of the profession (Evans 2003). In the same year the accounting profession around the world felt a need for the global harmonization of accounting standards, leading to the formation of the International Accounting Standards Committee (IASC) (Evans 2003). The formation of securities market regulators and independent standard setters has reduced the role of professional accounting bodies in the regulation of accounting services. As long as the regulators were nationally based, the accounting bodies have played a major part in the regulatory process. In 2000, the IASC was restructured to be more independent of professional accounting bodies and to include national standard setters in its standard-setting process. The IASC was also renamed the International Accounting Standards Board (IASB). This contributed to a further reduction in the professional accounting body's role in regulation.

It is not only the independent standard setters that are threatening the accounting body's role in regulation but also the emergence of global accounting firms. The membership of the professional accounting body has comprised individuals and, therefore, its regulatory power extends over its individual members. In the accounting service environment today, it is not the individual but the firm that is the provider of accounting services, and, therefore, is responsible for the services provided. The partnership form of ownership of accounting firms has allowed the profession limited self-regulation of the provision of accounting services, by ensuring that ownership of accounting firms is limited to members of the profession. This ensures that the interest of the profession coincides with the interest of the firm (Velayutham 1996). This has, however, not stopped a few of the global accounting firms from questioning the capacity of professional accounting bodies to regulate them (Sikka and Willmott 1995).

More recently, the collapse of big companies such as Enron and World-Com in America led to the enactment of the Sarbenas-Oxley Act 2002. The Act established the Public Company Accounting Oversight Board to oversee (regulate) auditors of public companies, which includes the registration of public company auditors; development of auditing, quality-control, ethics, and independence standards; and enforcement standards. Similar bodies have been set up in other countries, for example, the Financial Reporting Council in the United Kingdom. The aforementioned developments have considerably reduced the role of the professional accounting body.

The professional accounting bodies have also been changing their outlook and role. They are becoming global (Velayutham 2000). Initially the extension of the professional accounting body beyond national boundaries happened by accident when accounting bodies in the United Kingdom admitted foreign nationals who completed their training in the United Kingdom. Later, the demand for U.K. professional qualifications led some accounting bodies, for example, the Association of Chartered Certified Accountant (ACCA) and the Chartered Institute of Management Accountants (CIMA) to promote their examinations overseas. While the bodies accepted members from overseas they did not make any effort to meet their post-qualification needs.

In the last decade, however, the bodies have actively promoted their qualifications overseas, opened branches overseas, organized conferences, provided CPE programs, and catered to local needs by developing courses in local tax and law. The shift in strategy can be attributed to a number of factors; first, there was a realization that overseas members can be a major source of revenue, and second, it can provide an opportunity to develop an international profile. Most recently, the ACCA has attempted to project itself as an international body.

In the aforementioned environment professional accounting bodies recognize that their main asset is recognition of the qualification they offer. The concept of the professional accounting body as an owner of a brand name, and permitting others to use that brand name, was most clearly enunciated in the Wheeler Campbell Report that became a blueprint for the reorganization of the New Zealand Society of Accountants (Velayutham 1998). The report recognized the regulatory role of a professional association, not in the context of a profession, but rather as an owner of a brand franchised to members:

> We propose a conceptual framework that suggests that Society membership signals information about the quality of the services the consumer can expect. The ACA in this context can be seen as a brand, and brand reputation is the primary component of the Chartered Accountant product. (Wheeler Campbell 1993: 3)

The brand, they pointed out, provides important information about a product or service, based on perceptions of performance or reputation earned in the market, and reduces marketing cost to providers of a service.

The relationship between the professional accounting body and its membership can be analyzed in terms of the characteristics of a franchise (Velayutham 2000). The accounting body is the owner of the names or designations, for example, "CA" or "CPA", and allows a member to use the name or designation and the goodwill associated with it for an annual fee.

The Evolution of Accounting Education

The formation of professional accounting bodies generated an interest in accounting education. The need for professional accounting bodies to differentiate their members from nonmembers led them to set professional exams for those aspiring to gain membership. Initially, preparation for these exams was through an apprenticeship program that focused on the mastery of procedural skills, for example, bookkeeping and auditing techniques (Langenderfer 1987). The desire to raise the image and status of accounting to that of other professions such as medicine and law led the professional accounting bodies to promote the development of accounting programs at universities. In the 1950s the professional accounting bodies in the United States began requiring aspiring members to complete an undergraduate degree prior to taking professional examinations. While an undergraduate degree has become standard policy of the AICPA, the Institute of Management Accountants (IMA), and the Institute of Internal Auditors (IIA) in the United States, it is not a standard policy of the professional accounting bodies in the United Kingdom.

The requirement of an undergraduate degree as a prerequisite for admission to the professional accounting bodies laid the groundwork for debates on the ideal undergraduate educational program. One of the earliest attempts to determine the knowledge that the CPA must have at the outset, in order to provide the public with service of minimum scope and quality, was the Roy and MacNeill Study entitled *Horizons for a Profession* published in 1967 (sponsored by the Carnegie Corporation and AICPA). The study also served as the foundation for subsequent AICPA models for undergraduate accounting programs (AICPA 1969, 1978, and 1988). Roy and MacNeill (1967) provided qualitative descriptions of recommended coverage in particular areas. A major contribution of this study was the identification of mathematics and computers as essential prerequisites for accounting graduates (Roy and MacNeill 1967). It was also the first study to recommend that new AICPA members must have completed 150 college-level semester hours.

A major departure from the aforementioned approach to accounting education was the report by the AAA Committee on the Future Structure, Content, and Scope of the Accounting Profession (the Bedford Committee) (AAA 1986), which concluded that "the accounting profession—in government, corporate and public practice—currently is in a state of flux, reflecting massive changes taking place in technology and social values."

The Committee observed that "professional accounting education . . . has remained substantially the same over the past 50 years . . ." (AAA 1986). Based on this observation, the AAA (1986) shifted their focus from knowledge obtained by accounting graduates to what the graduates are able to do with that knowledge. The Committee also suggested that the "primary classroom objective" of accounting education should be helping students learn how to learn (169). Further, it called for the expansion of the generalist, liberal arts and science components of the traditional undergraduate accounting curriculum, and the use of participatory teaching methods to replace those methods that force students to become "passive recipients of information" (AAA 1986: 185). The eight largest public accounting firms, in an independent report, reiterated the findings of the AAA (Arthur

Andersen et al. 1989). This report emphasized that the accounting profession must produce graduates with a broad array of skills and knowledge "which may be divided into three categories—communication skills, intellectual skills and interpersonal skills" (5).

In 2003, the International Federation of Accountants (IFAC), in an attempt to bring about harmonization of accounting education, issued a series of International Education Standards (IES) (IFAC 2003). IES 2–6 identify the knowledge, skills, and values to be developed through the educational process and the practical experience component, and provide guidance on the assessment of professional capabilities and competence.

The Gulf Countries' Professional Accounting Bodies

The structure of the accounting profession in the Gulf countries is quite unique because there is a regional professional body whose objectives appear to be similar and, therefore, is in competition with the national professional bodies. The region's professional body is the Gulf Cooperation Council Accounting and Auditing Organization (GCCAAO). In addition to the GCCAAO, each of the Gulf countries (with the exception of Qatar) has its own professional accounting bodies: in the UAE the Accountants and Auditors Association (AAA) formed in 1997; the Saudi Organization for Certified Public Accountants (SOCPA) in Saudi Arabia formed in 1991; the Kuwait Association of Accountants and Auditors in Kuwait (KAAA) formed in 1986; Bahrain Accountants Association (BAA) formed in 1985, and the Omani Association of Certified Accountants (OACA) formed in 2004. In Qatar there is no accounting society or an organized profession as of today. Of the one regional body and the five local bodies, three of them (BAA, KAAA, and SOCPA) are members of the IFAC. Table 7.1 provides a summary of the professional setting in Bahrain, Kuwait, and Saudi Arabia.

Unlike most professional accounting bodies in the United States and Europe, membership of the professional bodies is open to both individuals and firms. This is against the general focus of professionalization, which is the maintenance of professional autonomy over organizational control in the workplace. This could also contribute to conflict between pursuing the interest of an individual against his/her firm.

Other than SOCPA, membership of the other professional bodies is very small. SOCPA, in information submitted as part of member body compliance program, had 2,061 associates and 131 non-practitioners. In comparison to SOCPA, BAA had 150 associates and Velayutham and Segini (2002) found that AAA of the UAE had 200 members, which is a

Table 7.1 Professional setting in Bahrain, Kuwait, and Saudi Arabia

	Bahrain	*Kuwait*	*Saudi Arabia*
Name of member body	Bahrain Accountants Association (BAA)	Kuwait Association of Accountants and Auditors	Saudi Organization for Certified Public Accountants
Date member body became a member of IFAC	1986	1987	1993
Source of revenue	Member dues and conference and Seminar activities	N/A	Member dues, publication sales, continuing education programs, donation, exam fees, and investment
Membership categories	Certified or chartered accountants, accounting technicians, and audit firms	N/A	Certified or Chartered Accountants, Non-Practioners, and Associates
Act or code governing auditing and financial reporting	Bahrain Commercial Companies Law	Commercial Law	Companies Act
Enacting body	Ministry of Commerce	Ministry of Commerce	Ministry of Commerce and Industry
Name of body responsible for setting audit and other assurance standards	Directorate of Commerce and Company Affairs under the Ministry of Commerce	Ministry of Commerce	SOCPA Auditing Standards Committee
Name of body responsible for setting ethics standards	The Auditors Affairs Committee	Ministry of Commerce	SOCPA Ethics Committee
Requirements to obtain professional certification	Academic study and practical experience	Academic study, practical experience and licensing examination	Academic study, practical experience, and licensing examination
Name of body responsible for setting private sector accounting standards	Bahrain Commercial Companies Law, Auditors Affairs Committee	Company departmental	SOCPA Accounting Standards Committee

Continued

Table 7.1 Continued

	Bahrain	*Kuwait*	*Saudi Arabia*
Securities Market Regulatory Authority	Bahrain Central Bank	Kuwait Stock Exchange	Securities and Exchange Commission
Regulatory oversight of the accounting profession	Ministry of Commerce	No	SOCPA Quality Review Committee
Existence of any organization to monitor a program of quality assurance, and compliance with reporting and auditing requirements	N/A	N/A	N/A
Process for investigating and disciplining the accounting profession	No	No	The investigation committee, Ministry of Commerce and Industry

small proportion of the accountants eligible for membership. The KAAA in its submission to IFAC did not identify the number of members it has. Furthermore, other than GCCAAO, SOCPA, and AAA of the UAE the other accounting firms do not even have an official website to publicize themselves and their activities, and some do not have official premises.

The low membership of the professional accounting bodies could be explained by the fact that, with the exception of Saudi Arabia, the right to practice as an accountant is regulated by the Ministry of Commerce through the codes of commercial law in the respective countries. The Ministry of Commerce sets the educational and experience requirements, accounting, auditing and ethical standards, and registers the accountants in public practice. The standards as well as ethical rules are enforced by the ministries and violations are investigated by them; the accounting profession has no role in the process. In Bahrain, the Bahrain Audit Law of 1996 identifies the requirements for licensing of auditors In Qatar, the auditing profession is organized by both the commercial code No. 7, issued in 1974, and the Ministerial Order No. 25 issued in 1979. Article 3 of the commercial code No. 7 requires interested applicants to possess a higher degree in commerce and membership of accredited institutions or practical experience of at least five years, and Qatari citizenship. The Ministry of Trade and Industry, however, can grant exemptions.

Some Gulf countries have different educational requirements for citizens and expatriates. For example in the UAE, according to Federal Law 22 of 1995, a UAE national wanting to register as an auditor must (1) possess a Bachelor of Science in Accounting, (2) not have a criminal record, and (3) not be engaged in any other jobs (exception is made for staff members of universities). An expatriate must (1) possess a UAE residence permit, (2) have an audit partner who is a UAE national, and (3) hold membership of a foreign accounting body for not less than five years. In Kuwait those wishing to be registered as auditors have to pass an examination set by the Ministry of Commerce. Table 7.2 summarizes the professional setting in two GCC countries, Sultanate of Oman and the United Arab Emirates.

With respect to accounting and auditing standards, the Ministry of Commerce in the different countries have adopted IFRS's promulgated by the IASB and auditing standards issued by the International Auditing and Assurance Standards Board (IAASB) of IFAC.

In Saudi Arabia, anyone who wants to practice as an auditor is required to be listed on the Register of Certified Public Accountants with the Ministry of Commerce. To be registered, one must maintain full membership of SOCPA. Membership of SOCPA is only open to Saudi nationals and all members have to pass the SOCPA fellowship examination for which a Bachelor's degree in accounting is a prerequisite. In addition to the aforementioned educational requirements, aspiring members must also have completed three years of practical experience. In Saudi Arabia SOCPA is also responsible for the development of accounting, auditing, and ethics standards.

From the preceding discussion, one can observe that SOCPA is the only professional accounting body, in the Gulf countries, of a significant size, with some regulatory powers. SOCPA was established by Article 19 of Royal Decree No.M/12 dated 13/5/1412 (Islamic). According to the Decree, SOCPA works under the supervision of the Ministry of Trade, and the minister of trade chairs SOCPA's board of directors (BOD). The BOD consists of

- The minister of trade—the chairman.
- The undersecretary of the Ministry of Trade.
- The undersecretary of the Ministry of Finance.
- The vice president of the General Audit Bureau.
- Two Saudi academics of the accounting departments of the Saudi universities nominated by the minister of higher education and appointed by the minister of trade.
- A representative from the Chamber of Commerce and Industry nominated by the Chamber's BOD and appointed by the minister of trade.
- Six certified public Saudi accountants elected by the general assembly of SOCPA. They are to serve for a three-year term renewable for one more term.

Table 7.2 Professional setting in Sultanate of Oman and the United Arab Emirates

	United Arab Emirates	*Sultanate of Oman*
Name of member body	Accountants and Auditors Association (AAA)	Omani Association of Certified Accountants
Date member body became a member of IFAC	N/A	N/A
Source of revenue	Member dues and conference and seminar activities	N/A
Membership categories	Working, affiliate, and honorary	Associate
Act or code governing auditing and financial reporting	Organization of the audit profession	Companies Act
Enacting body	Ministry of Economy	Ministry of Commerce
Name of body responsible for setting audit and other assurance standards	Ministry of Economy	Ministry of Commerce
Name of body responsible for setting ethics standards	Ministry of Economy	Ministry of Commerce
Requirements to obtain professional certification	Academic study and practical experience	Academic study and practical experience
Name of body responsible for setting private sector accounting standards	Ministry of Economy	Ministry of Commerce
Securities market regulatory authority	Emirates Securities and Commodities Authority	Capital Markets Authority
Regulatory oversight of the accounting profession	N/A	N/A
Existence of any organization to monitor a program of quality assurance, and compliance with reporting and auditing requirements	N/A	N/A
Process for investigating and disciplining the accounting profession	N/A	N/A

The GCCAAO was formed on May 20, 2001 to organize and develop the accounting and auditing profession in the Gulf countries. This followed the decision of the GCC Supreme Council in 1982 to open the door for GCC professionals to practice certain professions, including accounting and auditing, within the GCC countries, provided that registration and license is similar to that required for their counterparts in the hosting country (www.gccaao.org/en/history_1.html). The five main objectives of the organization as identified in its constitution are as follows (www.gccaao.org/en/history_1.html):

- Development of (1) a conceptual framework of financial accounting, (2) accounting standards, (3) auditing standards, and (4) codes of ethics and professional conduct.
- Development of unified regulations for practicing the profession.
- Establishment of GCCAAO fellowship exams.
- Provision of continuing professional education (CPE) and training.
- Establishment of quality-control standards and quality-review programs.

The GCCAAO website highlights major progress in all its stated objectives within the short period from its formation to today. The organization has developed a conceptual framework; accounting standards on various issues including fixed assets, intangible assets, lease accounting, foreign currency, and consolidated financial statements; auditing standards on standards of integrity, objectivity and independence, due care, control, and documentation, and so forth; and a code of ethics and professional conduct. The GCCAAO has also proposed a set of unified regulations for practicing the profession, which it hopes will be adopted by the GCC Secretariat General. In other areas, the organization has developed general rules for fellowship examinations, which, however, have yet to be implemented. General rules for CPE and quality review are also included.

All the Gulf countries have also established independent regulators to regulate the securities markets. In Oman, the Capital Market Law establishing the Capital Market Authority was enacted in 1998. This was followed by the UAE enacting the Federal Law No. 4 in 2000, which established the Emirates Securities and Commodities Authority, followed by the establishment of the Securities and Exchange Commission in Saudi Arabia in 2003 and the issue of the Consultation Paper on Securities and Exchange Regulation in 2004. The Qatar Financial Markets Authority (QFMA) was created in 2005 through Law No. 33. Whilst the securities regulators are supposed to be independent, they are frequently chaired by the minister of commerce and the membership of the board heavily comprises government officials. For example, the Board of Directors of the Securities and Commodities Authority of the UAE consists of the minister of economy and commerce (chairman), two members from the Ministry of Commerce, two members from the Ministry of Finance and Industry, one member representing the Central Bank, and four members nominated by the minister of commerce.

The aforementioned review highlights a number of features of professional accounting bodies in the Gulf countries. The professional bodies are very weak and poorly developed in the Gulf region for a number of reasons. First, the government control over registration of accountants and auditors as well as the non-requirement of membership of the local body provides little incentive for accountants to be members of the local professional body. Due to this reason SOCPA is the only professional body in the Gulf countries that has a sizeable membership, because membership is a prerequisite for registration. In a question (to a member of AAA board) as to the most important support the AAA (UAE) would look for from the government, the member of the board identified making membership of the AAA compulsory for firms seeking to be licensed auditing firms (Velayutham and Al-Segini 2002). Furthermore it can be observed that even where membership of the professional body is a prerequisite for registration as in the case of Saudi Arabia, the government maintains strict control of the professional body through the appointment of government officials on the board of directors of SOCPA.

Second, many of the accountants in the GCC countries are expatriates and they are only admitted as affiliate members with no voting rights, and, therefore, having no influence over the management of the professional bodies and so no capacity to organize activities of interest to themselves. The articles of the bodies could be amended so that affiliate members could vote as a minority on the Board of Directors, or this class of membership would have a separate committee with its own budget, so that affiliate members have a say in the management of the bodies while control of the association remains with citizens of the country.

The regional professional body (GCCAAO) has also not been able to make much progress because the Ministry of Commerce, in the respective countries, does not recognize membership of GCCAAO as a prerequisite for registration.

The aforementioned features of the accounting profession in the GCC countries is consistent with Hofstede's (1980) predictions on the influence of culture on institutions and Gray's (1988) predictions on the influence of national culture on accounting systems. Hofstede (1983) found Arab countries to be collectivistic with large power distance societies having a strong desire for uncertainty avoidance (Hofstede 1980). It is observed that these societies tend to be highly rule oriented with laws, rules, regulation, and controls to reduce the amount of uncertainty. In these countries powers also tend to be concentrated in the state with little rule-making powers delegated to nongovernmental organizations such as professional bodies (http://www.geert-hofstede.com/hofstede_arab_world.shtml, 2007).

Gray (1988) hypothesized that the lower a country ranks in terms of individualism and the higher it ranks in terms of uncertainty avoidance and power distance then the more likely it is to rank highly in terms of statutory control rather than professionalism. The structure of the accounting profession in GCC countries as described earlier shows a bias toward statutory control rather than professionalism.

It has been pointed out earlier that in many countries where membership of the professional body is not compulsory for practice, or when their regulatory role has been reduced by the formation of state-sponsored oversight bodies, professional bodies have sought to differentiate its members from others in the marketplace. GCC accounting bodies do not appear to have much success in this area. This could be attributed to two reasons; first, they do not have a brand name at the moment in order to develop; second, the big accounting bodies from the United Kingdom, for example, the ACCA, are aggressively marketing themselves in the region. ACCA from the United Kingdom has set up branch offices in the different countries and are identifying local providers to offer their courses. The aforementioned activities are further squeezing the development of the indigenous local accounting bodies.

The lack of government recognition of membership of the professional bodies and their small membership severely limits their role in the professional development of accounting in the GCC countries. They have limited financial resources because of the small-sized membership. The main source of revenue for many of the bodies is the organization of seminars and conferences. They have little influence over accounting education, accounting standards, and auditing standards. Their ability to enforce their code of ethics is also very weak because expulsion from membership does not imply that the individual cannot practice as an accountant. Their main contribution appears to be a forum for accountants (principally nationals) to meet and socialize and the organization of a few conferences and workshops.

Accounting Education in the Gulf Countries

Accounting education in the Gulf countries has gone through a major revolution in recent years. University education for a long time (until 1997) was controlled by the government and was open only to citizens. A World Bank (1999) study asserted that since the 1960s central governments in the region assumed a dominant role in providing education services without direct costs to the recipients. The study also asserted that this resulted in crowding out of private delivery through a lack of demand. Prior to 1997, the United Arab Emirates, Oman, Kuwait, and Qatar had one university each; Bahrain had two universities; and Saudi Arabia had seven universities. Table 7.3 provides a list of the aforementioned universities and whether they offer an accounting program.

In most of the Gulf countries, children of expatriates normally go back to their home country or other Western countries such as America, the United Kingdom, and Australia for their university education. Others pursued further education in private vocational institutions in Gulf countries that prepared them for the examinations of professional bodies such as the

Table 7.3 Major national government funded universities in GCC countries

Country	*Name*	*Year Established*	*Accounting Program (Instruction Language)*	*Total Credit Hours*
Bahrain	University of Bahrain	1986	Yes (English)	126
	Arabian Gulf University	1980	Nil	
Qatar	University of Qatar	1973	Yes (English)	125
Oman	Sultan Qaboos University	1986	Yes (English)	124
Saudi Arabia	Islamic University of Imam Muhammad ibn Saud, Riyadh	1953	Yes (Arabic)	144
	Islamic University, Medina	1961	Nil	
	King Abdul Aziz University, Jeddah	1967	Yes (Arabic)	128
	King Fahad University of Petroleum and Minerals, Dhahran	1963	Yes (English)	118
	King Faisal University, Dammam	1975	Yes (Arabic)	136
	King Saud University, Riyadh	1957	Yes (Arabic)	N/A
	Umm Al-Qura University, Mecca	1979	Nil	
UAE	United Arab Emirates University	1976	Yes (English)	132
	Zayed University	1998	Yes (English)	127
	University of Sharjah	1997	Yes (English)	129
Kuwait	University of Kuwait	1962	Yes (English)	130

Association of Chartered Certified Accountants (ACCA) or the Chartered Institute of Management Accountants (CIMA).

Since then, however, most governments in the GCC countries have allowed local private universities as well as branches of foreign private universities to be established and to open their doors to both national and foreign students. This has been mainly due to the inability of national universities to meet the growing demand for higher education. The development of private universities has raised concerns about the quality of many of their programs. The Ministry of Higher Education in a number of Gulf countries, for example, the UAE and Sultanate of Oman have established accreditation schemes to ensure that the private universities follow good practices in the area of higher education. A more recent phenomenon within universities in the Gulf countries has been to pursue external accreditation by foreign accreditation bodies, for example, the AACSB International.

Generally, the national universities have adopted the American system of a 129-hour, 4-year bachelor degree program. The core accounting curriculum in most GCC universities (with a few variations) follows the traditional accounting curriculum in the United States, consisting of two introductory accounting courses in financial accounting and managerial accounting; followed by three financial accounting courses—intermediate accounting 1, intermediate accounting 2, and advanced financial accounting—; one course each in cost accounting, accounting information systems, and auditing. Taxation is frequently not a core accounting course because there is no income tax in many GCC countries. In addition to these core accounting courses, many universities have a number of elective courses (some of these are required courses at some universities) in accounting that includes international accounting, government accounting, accounting theory, financial statement analysis, advanced management accounting, advanced auditing, and petroleum accounting. Foreign universities provide the same program they offer in their home countries.

The textbooks used are also frequently American textbooks, and that has not changed much in the last 10 years. This could be attributed to three reasons: first the market for textbooks in individual GCC countries is small; second many universities feel the use of foreign textbooks adds credibility to their programs; and third it is felt that the use of foreign textbooks could facilitate foreign accreditation.

The World Bank (1999) study observed that very little is known about the quality of higher education in the Middle East and that many of the countries did not participate in international assessment studies. Similar observations were also made by Shaw (1993) and Heyneman (1997). The

World Bank (1999) study reported that what little is known about the quality of education in Middle Eastern countries is not encouraging. Two Gulf countries (Bahrain and Saudi Arabia) that participated in the Trends in International Mathematics and Science Study (TIMSS) 2003 were close to the bottom of the table in mathematics (37th and 43rd among 45 countries, respectively) (http://timss.bc.edu/timss2003i/mcgdm.html). The World Bank (1999) study also observed that education in the region does not effectively impart the higher-order cognitive skills such as flexibility, problem solving, and judgment needed by workers who will face frequently changing tasks and challenges in a competitive environment. Gollady et al. (1998) found that the education systems in the Middle Eastern countries teach students how to learn and retain answers to fairly fixed questions in problem situations with little or no meaningful contexts, and thus reward those who are skilled at being passive knowledge recipients.

The scarcity of research on the quality of higher education is also reflected in the quality of accounting education, and most studies are anecdotal studies. Al-Rashed (1994) observed that accounting education in the GCC countries faced various deficiencies including

1. A shortage of qualified accountants—those who have gone through a program of theoretical and practical education and training.
2. The lack of an adequate route to enable young Arab students to train and qualify by examination and thus gain a certificate recognized both within and outside the Arab world.
3. The lack of locally written textbooks and other relevant literature.
4. The lack of educational research oriented towards the profession.
5. The enrollment policies of most GCC universities that are normally based on quantitative judgments rather than qualitative standards.
6. Universities are under political and social pressures to accept large numbers of students, which often goes beyond their actual capacities.

The accounting programs in many of the GCC countries are focused on the mastery of knowledge rather than the mastery of skills. Learning is defined and measured strictly in terms of knowledge of principles, standards, concepts, facts, and procedures at a point in time. The mastery of mathematical skills is also weak due to the poor skills acquired within the high school system reflected in student performances in TIMSS. Mahdi (1997) pointed out that, particularly in the Gulf universities, in the study of culture, history, society, and the economy there coexists an uneasy dichotomy of scientific methodology on the one hand, and received wisdom on the other. He suggests that to some extent higher education has been called upon to reaffirm prevailing ideologies and institutions within a rapidly changing economic environment.

This can be attributed to a number of reasons. First, the dissemination of knowledge requires much less resources than the development of skills, which requires more resources and as Al-Rashed (1994) pointed out universities are under political and social pressures to accept large numbers—more than their actual capacities. Second, there is also a lack of impetus to change because of the lack of input and pressure from the local accounting profession, and many of the local accreditation schemes are focused on the mechanism in place to disseminate knowledge. Third, students coming from the local high schools as highlighted by Gollady et al. (1998) are also more familiar with the rote-learning system rather than with a critical-thinking environment. Furthermore, many of the faculty in the universities have a short-term orientation because they are on short-term contracts with no job security (Al-Suwaidi 1997).

A major problem with the focus on content rather than skills is that the curriculum does not offer a foundation for lifelong learning, which is now considered a fundamental objective of accounting education. International Federation of Accountants (IFAC) (2003) stresses that a program of accounting education and experience must emphasize a set of knowledge, skills, and professional values broad enough to enable adoption of change.

An important missing link in improving accounting education in the GCC countries is the absence of a strong accounting profession. The accounting programs offered by the universities are not accredited by the profession and so to a certain extent are divorced from real-world pressures. The absence of professional exams also reduces the pressure on university accounting programs to produce students capable of passing external examinations.

Many Gulf universities have also in place schemes to provide scholarships to bright local graduates to pursue postgraduate qualifications so as to replace the expatriate academics in Gulf universities. This is, however, a slow process.

Finally, research in accounting is a powerful source of improving accounting practice, teaching, and learning, and so is an important element of accounting education. Shaw (1997) observed that Gulf universities have until recently been teaching institutions, dedicated to providing the skilled personnel needed for rapidly developing economies. The Arab Human Development Report (2003) highlighted the general poor productivity of research in the Arab world. The poor productivity of accounting researchers can be attributed to a number of reasons that include a lack of resources, heavy teaching workloads, and the absence of a research culture in many universities. The aforementioned review highlights that accounting education in the GCC is still largely fixed on content rather than skills, which is the focus of accounting education in the global scenario that is driven by tenets set forth by the AAA (1986) and Arthur Andersen et al. (1989).

Summary and Conclusions

The purpose of this chapter was to evaluate the development and contribution of the accounting profession and accounting education to the economic development of GCC countries. It is highlighted that in the last 15 years the GCC economies have experienced high growth rates as well as high population growth, which has contributed to a huge demand for accounting professionals. Much of the demand has mainly been met by a growing expatriate workforce.

In the past five years, the higher education sector has gone through a major change, mainly the opening up of many private universities. While the opportunities for higher education in accounting has grown exponentially, the approach to accounting education has not changed much. The focus of accounting education has continued to be the mastery of knowledge rather than the mastery of skills. The cause for this is attributed to the weak state of the accounting profession as well as the little connection between the practice environment and the academic programs that are based on the traditional American accounting curriculum.

It is pointed out that a major reason for the weak and poorly developed accounting profession in GCC countries is the government control over registration of accountants and auditors and the non-requirement of membership of the local body provides little incentive for accountants to be members of the local professional body. The small size of the professional bodies and hence their limited financial resources does not allow them to carry out the normal activities of a professional body such as improving accounting education, funding research and knowledge development, developing and enforcing work standards and ethical standards, and quality control.

References

Al-Rashed, W. 1994. "Accounting Education Correlation with the Profession in Gulf Countries." *Journal of Economic and Administrative Sciences* (November) 10 (2): 58–67.

Al-Suwaidi, K.A. 1997. "Higher Education in the United Arab Emirates: History and Prospects." In K.E. Shaw, ed., *Higher Education in the Gulf: Problems and Prospects*. Exeter: University of Exeter Press.

American Accounting Association (AAA). 1986. Committee on the Future Structure, Content and Scope of Accounting Education. "Future Accounting Education: Preparing for the Expanding Profession." *Issues in Accounting Education* 1 (1): 168–195.

American Institute of Certified Public Accountants (AICPA). 1969. *Report of the Committee on Education and Education Requirements for CPAs*. New York: AICPA.

———. 1978. *Education Requirements for Entry into the Accounting Profession*. New York: AICPA.

———. 1988. *Education Requirements for Entry into the Accounting Profession, Revised*. New York: AICPA.

Arab Human Development Report. 2003. *Building a Knowledge Society*. UNDP.

Arthur Andersen & Co., Arthur Young, Coopers & Lybrand, Deloitte Haskins & Sells, Ernst & Whinney, Peat Marwick Main & Co., Price Waterhouse and Touche Ross. 1989. *Perspectives on Education: Capabilities for Success in the Accounting Profession*. New York: Managing Partners of the Big Eight Accounting Firms.

Brown, R. 1905. *A History of Accounting and Accountants*, T.C. and E.C. Jack Publications, Edinburgh.

Chua, W.F. and C. Poullaos. 1998. "The Dynamics of 'Closure' amidst the Construction of Market, Profession, Empire and Nationhood: A Historical Analysis of an Australian Accounting Association, 1886–1903." *Accounting, Organizations and Society* 23 (2): 155–87.

Evans, T.G. 2003. *Accounting Theory: Contemporary Accounting Issues*. Ohio: South-Western.

Foote, N.N. 1953. "The Professionalization of Labour in Detroit." *The American Journal of Sociology* 58 (3): 378–380.

Gollady, F.L., S.E. Berryman, J. Avins, and W. Laurence. 1998. "A Human Capital Strategy for Competing in World Markets." In N. Shafik, ed., *Prospects for Middle Eastern and North African Economies from Boom to Bust and Back*. London: Macmillan.

Gray, S.J. 1988. "Towards a Theory of Cultural Influences on the Development of Accounting Systems Internationally." *Abacus* 24 (1): 1–15.

Heyneman, S.P. 1997. "Quality of Education in the Middle East and North Africa." *International Journal of Educational Development* 17 (4): 449–466.

Hofstede, G. 1980. *Cultures Consequences*. Beverly Hills: Sage Publications.

———. 1983. "Dimensions of National Cultures in Fifty Countries and Three Regions." In J.B. Deregowski, S. Dziurawiec, and R.C. Annis, eds., *Expiscations in Cross Cultural Psychology*. New York: Swets and Zeitlinger, 335–355.

International Federation of Accountants (IFAC). 2003. *International Education Standards 1–6*. New York: IFAC.

Langenderfer, H.Q. 1987. "Accounting Education's History: A 100 Year Search for Identity." *Journal of Accountancy* 163 (5): 302–331.

Lee, T.A. 1990. *The Closure of the Accounting Profession*. New York: Garland.

Mahdi, K. 1997. "Some Economic Aspects of Higher Education in the Arab Gulf." In K.E. Shaw, ed., *Higher Education in the Gulf: Problems and Prospects*. Exeter: University of Exeter Press.

Roy, R.H. and J.H. MacNeill. 1967. *The Common Body of Knowledge for Certified Public Accountants, Horizons for a Profession*. New York: AICPA.
Shaw, K.E. 1993. "Research into Education in the Arab Gulf States." *International Journal of Educational Development* 13 (1): 21–31.
Sikka, P. and Willmott, H. 1995. "The Power of Independence: Defending and Extending the Jurisdiction of Accounting in the United Kingdom." *Accounting, Organizations and Society* 20: 547–581.
Velayutham, S. 1996. "Corporatization and the Regulation of Accounting Services." *British Accounting Review* 28: 351–368.
———. 1998. "The Chartered Accountant in New Zealand: From Professional Qualification to -Franchised Brand." *Accounting Forum* 22 (2): 107–128.
———. 2000. "The Professional Accounting Body in the 21st Century: The Global Franchise." *Pacific Accounting Review* 11 (2): 163–171.
Velayutham, S. and Al-Segini, S. 2002. "The Contribution of Professional Bodies to the Development of a Knowledge Economy in the United Arab Emirates: The Case of the Accountants and Auditors Association." Paper presented at the Fifth Annual CBE Conference at UAE University, Al Ain during March 24–25, 2002.
Walker, S.P. 1995. "The Genesis of Professional Organization in Scotland: A Contextual Analysis." *Accounting, Organizations and Society* 20 (3): 285–310.
Weber, M. 1964. *The Theory of Social and Economic Organization*. Trans. T.Parsons. New York: Free Press.
Wheeler Campbell Limited. 1993. *A New Strategy for the New Zealand Society of Accountants: A Discussion Paper*. NZSA: Wellington.
World Bank. 1999. *Education in the Middle East and North Africa: A Strategy towards Learning for Development*. New York: World Bank.

Part III

Corporate Governance, Tax Regulations, Stock Markets, and Financial Institutions in the Gulf Countries

8

Corporate Governance System in the Gulf Countries

Wagdy M. Abdallah

Introduction

In recent years, several events came to light regarding major business failures such as Enron Corporation, Dynergy, Tyco, Rite Aide, and Worldcom; most of the multinational companies (MNCs), including the ones working and operating in the developing countries, especially in the Gulf region, have recently been forced to ensure that goals of the management of the corporation are in line with the goals of the other major stakeholders through efficient corporate governance systems. In general, corporate governance systems vary all over the world; therefore, it is almost impossible to find one corporate governance system that fits all countries (Cruz 2006). For example, if the United Arab Emirates (UAE) or Kuwait adopts the American model, how will this affect the financial and nonfinancial performance of Saudi's, Qatar's, or Bahrani's owned companies? And what is the best practice of corporate governance systems that would better align the interests of the board of directors and management with the interest of long-term stockholders in the Gulf countries?

In the Gulf area, some countries do not have proper bankruptcy laws while others have no merger and acquisitions legal codes. Moreover, most companies in the Gulf countries are family owned, have weak protection for minority shareholders, have no effective audit committees as part of the function of their boards, and in cases where audit committees exist they are not independent. However, there is a growing awareness that global capital requires a business environment that is open, transparent, and that encourages accountability and pushes the issue of corporate governance to the forefront (Kaul 2005).

It is essential for every corporation in the United States, the United Kingdom, Japan, Malaysia, Kuwait, or Saudi Arabia to ensure that they have maintained an efficient corporate governance system in order to have access to capital, offer financing on better terms, and improve performance. On December 20, 2006, IBM, retailer GAP inc., recruiter Heidrick & Struggles International Inc., and food company Tyson Food Inc. have dropped the stock options—which are worthless unless a stock price rises—in favor of compensation involving cash, restricted stock or outright equity stakes that both rise and fall with the share price (Lublin and Bulkely 2006).

This chapter examines the most important corporate governance issues and financial reporting transparency of the companies in the Gulf countries. First, the definition of corporate governance, the recommendations by the Organization for Economic Co-operation and Development (OECD), the revised version of its Principles of Corporate Governance, the goals and components of the governance system are discussed. Second, importance of corporate governance systems and standards in the Gulf region are analyzed. Third, the practice of corporate governance and financial reporting transparency in the Gulf countries and the key drivers for the changes in corporate governance are examined. Fourth, the expected next steps to be taken in the Gulf countries are analyzed. Finally, guidelines and recommendation of how to make improvement in corporate governance in the Gulf countries are presented.

The Corporate Governance System: Its Goals and Components

In general, corporate governance may be defined as the structures, process, and guidelines for the direction and control of companies, the distribution of rights and responsibilities among the main participants in a corporation, and the rules and procedures for making decisions on corporate relationships. It may be defined as methods, laws and policies that direct, control, and administer important functions of a corporation (Anonymous 2006). Typically, corporate governance is managed by the principal stakeholders in a corporation including the shareholders, management, and board of directors. Corporate governance is also defined as methods, laws, and policies that direct, control, and administer important functions of a corporation and is managed by the principal stakeholders—the shareholders, management, and board of directors—in a corporation (ibid.).

As a matter of fact, the control of financial and nonfinancial resources in business entities is the main component of corporate governance. It is concerned with the institutions that influence how business corporations allocate their financial and nonfinancial resources and returns on investments. It is a system of corporate governance that determines (1) who makes investment and finance decisions, (2) what types of investments and finance are made, (3) what is the best city, state, or country for investment, and (4) how returns from world wide investments are distributed (Cruz 2006). A closer look at business community reveals that corporate governance is related to the internal measures by which a corporation is operated and controlled. It includes the responsibilities, accountability, and relationships among shareholders, board members, and managers intended to meet corporate objectives. Corporate governance issues include the rights and treatment of shareholders, the responsibilities of the board, disclosure and transparency, and the role of stakeholders.

However, besides existing shareholders, there are other stakeholders who are eager to know how the board of directors and the management of the company are taking into consideration the interests of employees, customers, minority shareholders and potential new investors as well as, the society at large. The far-sighted board of directors recognizes that dealing fairly with all groups is consistent with building long-term value for shareholders. Official governments and regulators, on the other hand, would like to have in place effective corporate governance that will make their domestic capital and stock markets more attractive to local and international investors (Azzam 2004).

One of the main goals of corporate governance is to ensure that the goals of the management of the corporation are in line with the goals of the other major stakeholders. This is important since those that manage a modern corporate organization are typically not the same people as the shareholders of a corporation. By ensuring that goals are aligned through a corporate governance system, other stakeholders are able to ensure that their rights are well protected and that the corporation is working toward maximizing shareholder value and fairness (Anonymous 2006).

In 2004, the Organization for Economic Cooperation and Development (OECD) approved a revised version of its Principles of Corporate Governance. The Principles emphasize the importance of a regulatory framework in corporate governance and they include ensuring the basis for an effective corporate governance framework; disclosure and transparency; the role of shareholders in corporate governance; the rights of shareholders and key ownership functions, the equitable treatment of shareholders and the responsibilities of the Board (OECD 2004). According to the OECD, "corporate governance involves a set of relationships between a company's management, its board, its shareholders and other stakeholders. ... [It] also provides the structure through which the objectives of the company are set, and the means of attaining those objectives and monitoring performance are determined" (OECD 2004).

From the aforementioned issues, the item on disclosure and transparency is relevant to corporate financial reporting, as can be seen from figure 8.1. Under the Principles of Corporate Governance, the framework should ensure that timely and accurate disclosure is made on all material matters regarding the company, including the following issues:

1. The financial and operating results of the company;
2. Company objectives;
3. Major share ownership and voting rights;
4. Remuneration policy for members of the board and key executives;
5. Related party transactions;
6. Foreseeable risk factors;
7. Issues regarding employees and other stakeholders; and
8. Governance structures and policies.

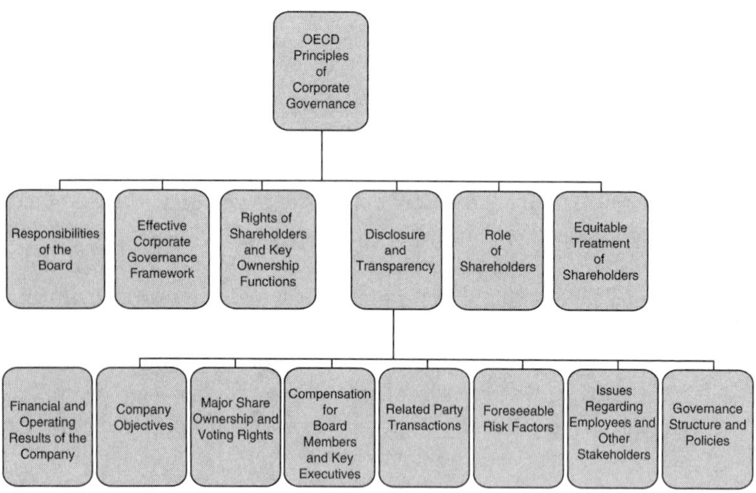

Figure 8.1 The principles of corporate governance issued by the Organization for Economic Co-operations and Development.

Source: OECD 2004.

The aforementioned recommendations by the OECD are designed to encourage national regulators to incorporate rules for disclosure and transparency in their national regulations and codes. Many countries now have codes of corporate governance. However, there are significant differences across countries in the degree of investor and minority ownership protection (La Porta, Lopez-de-Silanes, and Shleifer 1998). Countries that have a high concentration of equity ownership (and/or family controlled firms) within companies and with a lack of significant public equity markets might have low investor protection (ibid.).

For some countries, the corporate governance system may involve laws or regulations imposed by the official government; for others it may depend largely on private organization and market forces in a strong equity market (Robert, Weetman, and Gordon 2005). In general, equity investors have a strong appeal in seeing sound and high-quality corporate governance in companies in which they invest, and they are willing to pay more for a company that has a well-governed corporate system (McKensey 2000).

Recent corporate scandals and collapses, issues of executive compensation and legitimacy of the markets, resulting financial crises and breaches to financial market integrity, as well as expanded knowledge about the virtues of the corporate governance have enhanced interest in improving and updating the OECD corporate governance principles in several areas such as transparency and disclosure, shareholders rights, implementation, and enforcement. However, if corporate governance is related to the internal measures by which important functions of a corporation are controlled, accounting tools should help in establishing an efficient internal management system, an independent audit committee, and transparent financial reporting systems. In this case, the financial statements provided and information disclosed by accountants and management to all groups should be clear, reliable, timely, and prepared in a manner that users can easily understand and in formats they can easily analyze. Transparency includes all of these qualities.

Why Is Corporate Governance Important in the Gulf Region?

For global business community, corporate governance is essential for companies in developed as well as developing countries. A sound and high-quality corporate governance system is expected to improve access to capital, attract premium valuations, offer financing on better terms, and definitely improve the financial and nonfinancial performance of the company. Moreover, it may result in better leadership, oversight, and strategic direction, efficient information flows and work processes, and better compliance, accountability, and less conflict, all of which lead to better decision making and affect the long-term prosperity of companies.

Investors, in the Gulf countries, are concerned about corporate governance, as well-governed companies tend to outperform their competitors, safeguard and provide for higher returns on investment, protect shareholder rights, and provide assurance that management acts in the best interest of the company and all shareholders. On the other hand, governments of Gulf countries should care about corporate governance, as it develops the local capital markets, reduces vulnerability to financial crises, and improves a country's ability to organize, properly allocate, and monitor investments, all of which foster long-run economic growth. Therefore, it is necessary for every corporation in the Gulf region to ensure that they have and maintain a sound and high-quality corporate governance system in order to move forward.

In the Gulf countries, there is a growing awareness that global capital markets require an environment that is open, transparent, and that encourages accountability (Kaul 2005). Several key factors are the reasons for these changes in the Gulf countries. First, after September 11, 2001, majority of the Arab money used to go out into the West—especially European countries and the United States. Now, it is finding its way back into the Gulf region. These investors are coming back from the more developed markets and are used to a high quality of transparency and financial disclosure, and they expect the same quality of corporate governance back home (ibid.). Second, many Gulf countries have joined the World Trade Organization (WTO) and are opening up their financial markets, and they are obligated to implement and enforce more restricted regulatory rules for the financial sector. This will bring about more demanding regulators who will, in turn, ask for greater transparency and risk management norms.

Third, as regional markets look toward international investors to participate in their economic development plans, the Gulf countries have to use and comply with international standards and norms of corporate governance. In fact, as the number of stakeholders increases, and they find themselves in an increasingly competitive environment; they will try to improve corporate governance codes and practices in the region. In general, in the Gulf region, the corporate governance that works well and becomes an efficient system is expected to achieve the following goals:

1. Generating trust and creating the proper environment in which financial markets can operate in the Gulf countries,

2. Improving access to capital and offering financing on better terms,
3. Lowering capital costs,
4. Attracting foreign direct investment and deciding on the best place of investment,
5. Improving financial and nonfinancial performance,
6. Providing assurance that management acts in the best interest of the company and all stakeholders, and
7. Enforcing ethical standards.

Corporate Governance Practice and Financial Reporting Transparency in the Gulf Countries

Corporate governance is still evolving even in the United States of America. One of the big American multinational companies, IBM, announced that it no longer would grant outside directors stock options—which gives recipients the right to purchase company shares in the future at a set price. Instead, starting on January 1, 2007, these directors will get an annual $200,000 retainer, which they can take either in the form of IBM shares or partly in cash (Lublin and Bulkeley 2006). Stock options, used to be viewed by many companies as a vital tool for rewarding board members and aligning their interests with those of shareholders, are considered somewhat problematic and are falling out of favor as a perk amid scandal and accounting and legal changes (ibid.).

Recent events, especially those that came to light around major business failures such as Enron and Worldcom, have reinforced the need for greater corporate governance. Much of the drive for improved corporate governance is coming from stakeholders themselves to protect their investments, but some of these changes are coming about from federal regulations. In the Gulf countries, many of the biggest public companies still have large family shareholdings, family representatives among their senior management, and strong family representation on the board. There has also been no or weak protection of the rights of minority shareholders in the Gulf countries. This will definitely open the door for potential conflict of interest between the management of the companies and the controlling families (Azzam 2004). Moreover, only few corporations in the Gulf region have effective audit committees as part of the function of their boards, and when such committees do exist they are not formed of independent directors (ibid.).

It is the responsibility of the audit committees to ensure compliance with regulations, policies, plans, and procedures. They are the first line of defense against fraud, misconduct, and financial irregularities. If the audit committee is well managed, it should insure the reliability and integrity of the management and accuracy of financial reporting of their clients. Today, most members of audit committees of Gulf companies, especially those listed on the region's stock exchanges, tend to be major shareholders rather than independent professionals. It is important, therefore, for audit committee members to be both independent and financially literate and for the audit committees on which they serve to meet on a regular basis; such as four, five, or six times at least every and to allow its members to have unrestricted access to the company's financial records (ibid.). If the official regulatory authorities in the Gulf area do not introduce more effective corporate governance and enforce compliance with these rules, they will be encouraging foreign investors and market participants to look elsewhere for investment.

Financial statements and financial reporting structure of companies should reveal rather than hide all important information in order to be less risky and more valuable for investors. When financial statements are not transparent, investors can never be sure about a business entity's real value and true risk. Financial reporting transparency is assumed to improve local markets' efficiency, to enhance better corporate governance, and to ensure honesty of business firms. Local and business investors will only place their funds where they can reliably assess risk and return on the basis of standardized, comparable, and transparent financial information. Moreover, financial transparency makes it easier for auditors and managers to oversee the honesty and accuracy of the financial system, which in turn gives additional assurance and confidence to local and foreign investors.

Companies in the Gulf countries should consider investing in their infrastructure in the areas of financial reporting and disclosure, planning and analysis, and internal control. Transparency is considered as the best means to achieve better corporate governance (Bessire 2005). For financial institutions in the Gulf countries, it is a good start to embrace corporate governance norms; then they will also begin to push companies that they invest in toward better corporate governance practices. And this will provide the confidence and certainty that will definitely encourage and attract more local and foreign investors (Kaul 2005).

In Bahrain, the Monetary Agency—the Central Bank (BMA)—as a regulator, strongly believes in the importance of good corporate governance in its licensees, as well-run licensees are easier to supervise. However, more fundamentally, if licensees are not well run by their board of directors and management, then there is a limit to what the regulator can do to make up the shortfall. The BMA is currently working on upgrading its corporate governance requirements for bank licensees. In Bahrain, for insurance companies, corporate governance is also a key component of the new regulatory framework.

Recently, in Saudi Arabia, the Capital Markets Authority (CMA), in Saudi Arabia, has taken some important steps toward ensuring good corporate governance. It now requires companies to create and publish a "statement of ethics and business practices" that must be signed by the CEO, CFO, and all the directors. Definitely, this move was inspired by The Sarbanes-Oxley Act that was framed in the United States to toughen governance norms post-Enron collapse. The act requires companies to articulate and put down on paper a clear corporate governance framework that they intend to follow (Kaul 2005).

In the UAE, in July 2006, Hawkamah, the Institute for Corporate Governance in the region, and Emirates Securities and Commodities Authority (ESCA), have signed a groundbreaking memorandum of understanding (MoU) to develop the first ever corporate governance code for listed companies in the UAE (Anonymous 2006a). ESCA is the first capital market authority in the region that will develop and introduce corporate governance codes for listed companies consistent with international standards and best practice. The framework for the codes will include the principles of transparency, disclosure, protection of investors and shareholders rights, responsibilities of the board, and the importance of independent directors as well as financial reporting in accordance with international accounting and auditing standards. Introducing and implementing good corporate governance principles and practice will contribute to building investor confidence in financial markets and listed companies (ibid.).

The signing of the MOU aims to produce governance tools and procedures to develop sound practices where high performance will be achieved by companies in addition to credibility (ibid.). The three key roles of the MOU are as follows (Anonymous 2006a):

1. Highlighting of public awareness with regard to corporate governance in securities and commodities markets of UAE.
2. The exchange of information concerning corporate governance in such markets between the parties concerned.
3. Customizing training programs to accommodate the relevant cadres in the markets, brokerage companies, and listed companies in the field of corporate governance applications.

It is very important for ESCA to cooperate and work with Hawkamah on developing corporate governance codes for companies listed in the capital markets in the UAE. These codes will help build confidence in business organizations and its host economy and provide strong incentives for international trade and investment in both (Anonymous 2006a).

Signing of this MOU came into effect to combat current challenges met by both capital markets and regulating authorities. Furthermore, corporate governance is a complementary catalyst to the prevailing and existing regulations and legislations in compliance with international standards laid down by "IOSCO." This step will be a further tool to ensure justice and transparency in capital markets and it will also be the first step toward bridging the corporate governance gap between international and regional capital markets and moving toward economic and financial integration through the alignment and harmonization of corporate governance standards (Anonymous 2006a).

In the Gulf countries, several factors that might be the drivers for the changes in corporate governance should be considered for establishing sound and effective systems; these include lack of understanding; no proper regulation laws for bankruptcy; little protection for minority shareholders; weak enforcements; no effective audit committees; and relatively weak disclosure norms.

In the Gulf countries, corporate governance standards are improving and most institutions follow international accounting standards, but much more needs to be done to meet international corporate governance standards (Timewell 2006). Company laws in many countries in the region do define many things pertaining to good governance but it is not really well understood (Kaul 2005). This might be beginning to change now. For example, Oman is bringing out its own corporate governance code. In Qatar and Egypt, the central bank is pushing for change. It is imperative for investors to ensure that financial institutions that operate there can count on the highest standards of regulation and professionalism (ibid.).

In order to assist companies in the Gulf region listed on the Local Stock Exchange Corporation and the International securities Markets, to establish a sound corporate governance system, and to promote the integrity of the securities market, the financial and professional institutions should jointly issue "Corporate Governance Best-Practice Principles for Stock Market Listed Companies" to be followed by Stock Markets Listed companies.

What has been missing in the Gulf countries so far is the power and incentive to change the system. In countries, such as Egypt and Jordan, where knowledge of corporate governance issues are not priority items, the lack of understanding can be traced back to two sources: the region inherited French laws that tend to protect family owners at the expense of everybody else (as opposed to the Gulf countries, which inherited British laws). The Arabian culture, affected by family-owned businesses, is blamed because it teaches people to operate on their own rather than work as a team (Kaul 2005).

Moreover, some countries do not have proper legal bankruptcy laws while others have no takeover, liquidations, or merger and acquisitions corporate codes. The majority of firms have traditionally been family-owned and there was little or no protection for minority shareholders. Only a small proportion of shares are actually tradable. Even in the larger public companies, the shareholding is dominated by one or a few key rich shareholders (ibid.).

In most of the Gulf countries, the idea of independent directors is still alien. Although some countries do have regulations that mandate independent directors on the board, the enforcement is weak. Some of the more basic requirements, such as disclosure of conflict of interests or related-party transactions by directors, are often ignored. In practice, there is no independent process for selecting these directors. With respect to disclosure, norms are relatively weak in the Gulf countries in comparison to the more developed markets. For example, accounting, conflict of interest, directors' interests, risk analysis, concentration of exposures, disclosure of significant events are the areas that need to be properly addressed to all interested parties. The key issue is that the regulations, in this respect, are not strongly enforced by governments (ibid. 2005).

In general, corporate governance frameworks in the Gulf countries lag significantly behind corporate governance best practices (Timewell 2006). However, there is a great degree of variance among the corporate governance frameworks in the Gulf countries (ibid.). It is believed that Oman has the strongest corporate governance in the region with corporate governance requirements complying with about 70 percent of the international guidelines, followed by Kuwait and Saudi Arabia with about 50 percent compliance, and Bahrain and the UAE with 40 percent compliance with international governance standards (ibid.).

The scope of work of the audit committees includes as well the responsibility to identify suspected acts of fraud or conflict of interests involving the operation of the company. Nowadays, most members of audit committees of Gulf corporations are either major shareholders or represent strong shareholding interests. It is important, therefore, for committee members to be both independent and financially literate and to have unrestricted access to the company's financial records (Azzam 2004).

In general, Gulf companies, especially those listed on the region's stock exchanges, need stronger independent board members who devote proper attention to the audit committees they serve on. A well-functioning audit committee is needed, and so also separation of the responsibilities of the chairman of the board and the CEO. When the regulatory authorities in the Gulf region do not introduce more sound and effective corporate governance system and enforceable compliance with these rules, foreign and local investors may have no choice but to look elsewhere for investment. Capital will always go to those markets where the rules of investing are most transparent and where there is a sound system of corporate governance that protects the interest of minority shareholders and other stakeholders (Azzam 2004).

What Is Next for Corporate Governance in Gulf Countries?

The situation in most Gulf countries has its own specific features. The business environment may be distinguished from the Western-industrialized environment by being dominant by state-owned business entities, the large number of family-owned business entities, and the large number of small-scale enterprises (Saidi 2004). These characteristics are not in conflict with the practice of good corporate governance, but they may create problems for developing enforceable standards. Moreover, the companies in the Gulf countries tend to resist change, especially regarding the role and responsibility of the board of directors. However, as the economies of most Gulf countries integrate with the World Trade Organization (WTO), they will be forced to review the organization and structure of their financial institutions and organizations, including stock markets.

Nowadays, the Gulf economies are more and more adopting market strategies, and the role of the state is declining while the role of the private sector is evolving (Taher 2003). Corporate executive officers of Gulf region have started to consider good governance as one of the most important basic engines for economic growth, development, and prosperity because investors are ready to pay more for shares in firms that have an advanced culture and sound practice of good corporate governance systems. Sound corporate governance practices will attract new, much needed investment to the Gulf region because these improve management of firms and reduce risk.

Therefore, corporate governance has been considered as one of the important issues, with particular attention to disclosure, transparency, and accountability. Recently, a corporate governance movement has been far-reaching through the Gulf region. Practitioners from capital markets, banks, the public and private sectors, and other financial and nonfinancial community groups have recognized and accepted the need for establishing and maintaining sound and efficient corporate governance systems as one of the crucial issues affecting the international competitiveness, the investment environment, and the development of the capital markets of Gulf countries (Saidi 2004).

It is very obvious that many of the spectacular failures of corporate governance in recent years have been in the jurisdictions of the most advanced industrial countries. So a discussion of the principles of corporate governance can indeed yield lessons for all of us (Knight 2005). In the Gulf region, for corporate governance systems to be successful in generating trust and creating the proper environment in which financial markets can operate, the key factors or ingredients of the suggested model for a successful corporate governance system in the Gulf countries, as can be seen from figure 8.2, are (1) establishing enforceable strong standards for transparency, accountability, and responsibility; (2) establishing and implementing guidelines of ethical standards for people on whom corporate success or failure depends, as has been strongly evident from the recent corporate scandals in different countries, including the shareholders, the board of directors, and the management; and (3) covering the important issues in the corporate governance system such as transparency and financial reporting, independent auditing and audit committee, avoidance of conflicts of interest, ethics, protection of minority shareholders' rights provides a solid foundation for meaningful and more trusted economies and financial institutions in the Gulf countries.

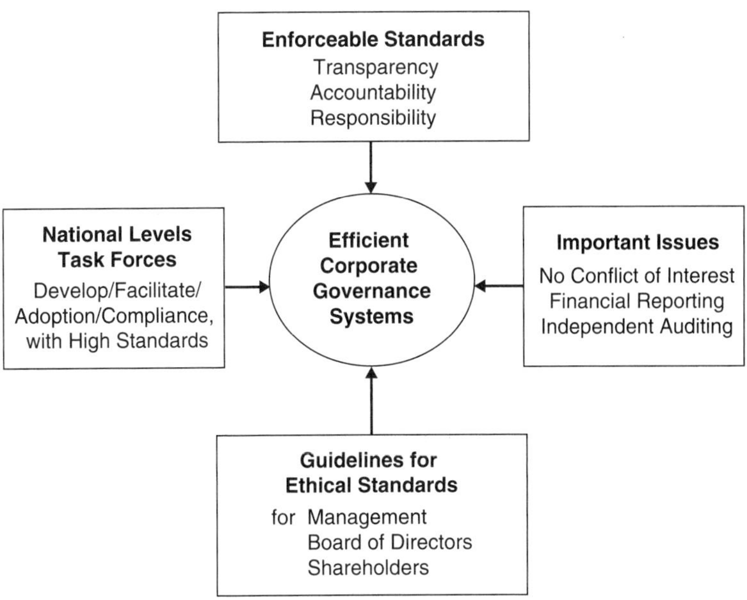

Figure 8.2 The suggested model for a successful corporate governance system in the Gulf countries.

If the corporate governance is good, it should allow shareholders to have access to the information of companies that is necessary for them to form an opinion, then transparency will help stakeholder to observe the actions of managers. Moreover, better disclosure would allow governments to avoid corporate scandals. Then, any unrestricted capital flows and thus global integration of capital markets can contribute to the spread of best practices in corporate governance, accounting rules, and global traditions, as well as limit the ability of governments to pursue bad policies (Taher 2003).

In 2006, Hawkamah the Institute for Corporate Governance, a subsidiary of Dubai International financial Center, and the Institute of International Finance (IIF) have launched the first-ever corporate governance survey of the Gulf Cooperation Council (GCC) countries (Charalambous 2006). They issued a memo of understanding to propagate corporate-sector reforms and improve corporate governance in the Gulf region. It outlines the following three main objectives (ibid.):

1. Improve the corporate governance practices of private- and public-sector entities.
2. Help develop corporate governance frameworks in accordance with best practice for the public and the private sectors in order to promote open and transparent markets and a fair, rule-based, and enforceable corporate governance regime.
3. Cooperate on institution building, a critical component of sound financial markets, in keeping with good corporate governance practices.

This memo of understanding will be a major contributor to the improvement of corporate governance practices in the region. By promoting a higher standard of financial reporting, accounting, and regulation, the corporate sector in the GCC can ensure sustained regional economic growth and the attraction of foreign direct investment and trade (Charalambous 2006). However, in October 2006, the results of a survey conducted by the IIF showed that corporate governance systems in the six Gulf countries are poor and the region generally complies with only half the internationally accepted best-practice codes. The IIF indicated that Gulf countries' average for the compliance with international best practices is 50 percent, lower than in other emerging markets, like India's 75 percent and 65 percent in China (Sharif 2006).

In the UAE, the market regulator Securities and Commodities Authority is drafting a legal code for all listed companies while Abu Dhabi Securities Market has already issued one; the Dubai Financial Market is also drafting a code and the UAE Ministry of Economy will introduce a corporate governance code in its new company law (ibid.). This weak adherence to corporate governance rules may be because the stock markets across the Gulf region are young. In Bahrain, the companies' law is being revising and a new corporate governance code will be introduced. In Saudi Arabia, a draft corporate governance code was issued in August 2006 and will be enforced shortly for listed companies (ibid.).

Summary and Conclusions

Since the beginning of the twenty-first century, failures of corporate governance have been at the root of several well-known cases of management defrauding the shareholders in the United States, United Kingdom, and other most advanced industrialized countries. This behavior was an example of a combination of bad corporate governance and unethical conduct. Where corporate governance works well, it reenforces ethical standards; where it fails, it permits unethical practices. Good governance leads to corporate social responsibility, because a well-governed corporation is expected to adhere to the values and norms of the community. But these values of the community are not with a great deal of precision as they affect corporate behavior, whether in the private or public sector.

The ongoing process of updating the 12 principles of corporate governance issued by the OECD is one step forward for facilitating global adherence to best practices in the Gulf countries. It will also help them in building a culture that respects and rewards transparency (both financial and nonfinancial), disclosure, and accountability, and building sound financial markets and investor confidence. To facilitate the adoption of, compliance with, and effective enforcement of high standards of corporate governance in the Gulf countries, the following guidelines should be implemented:

1. National-level task forces are needed to develop corporate governance codes specific to each country, which should be based on internationally acceptable corporate standards for transparency, accountability, and responsibility and at the same time embrace local realities.
2. All the following groups should be included in establishing and enforcing corporate governance codes: governments, families with large commercial operations, representatives of the small business community, and banks and financial institutions. To be more specific, a stronger commitment to better corporate governance from political authorities is a must.

3. For establishing a successful corporate governance system in the Gulf countries, all the components of the framework of the corporate governance and financial reporting standards for the Gulf countries shown in figure 8.3, including transparency of financial reporting, accountability of management and board of directors, and responsibility of management and independent audit committee should be considered.
4. Codes and standards of corporate conduct must be devised in an inclusive manner by incorporating the ethical standards of the community.
5. Governance legal corporate codes need to be backed up by effective means to ensure compliance. The incentives should be clear, simple, enforced, and transparently directed toward the fundamental objectives of the business entities.
6. National financial institutional laws, regulations, and corporate practices based on international norms and standards should be imparted to professionals and the general public.

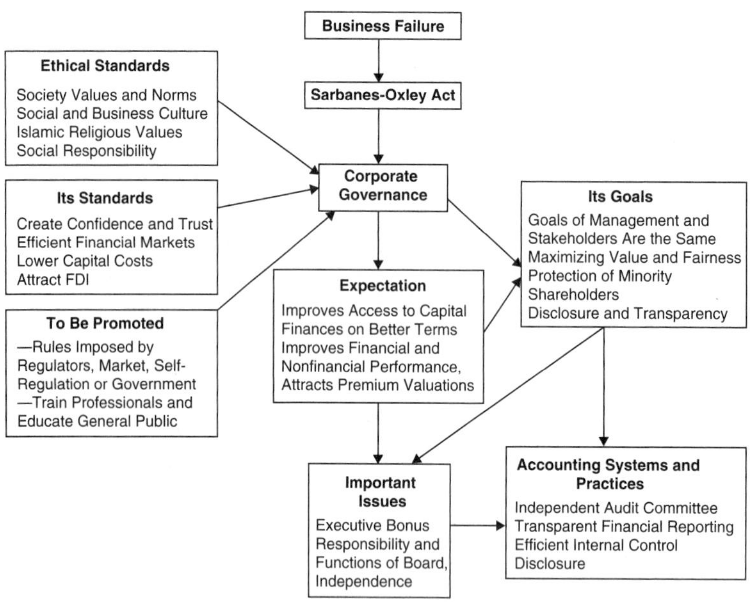

Figure 8.3 The framework of corporate governance and financial reporting standards for Gulf countries.

References

Anonymous 2006. "Corporate Governance." http://www.infobeagle.com/business/corporat-governance.htm, August.

———. 2006a. "Hawkamah Signs MOU with Emirates Securities and Commodities Authority." *Al Bawaba*, London, July 4: 1.

Azzam, Henry T. 2004. "Strengthening Corporate Governance in the Arab Region." *Arab News*, www.arabnews.com, April 12.

Bessire, Dominique. 2005. "Transparency: A Two-Way Mirror?" *International Journal of Social Economics* 32 (5): 424–439.

Charalambous, Lorys. 2006. "Gulf Region's First Corporate Governance Survey Launched." *forLawAndTax-News.com*, Cyprus, July 13.

Cruz, Elfren S. 2006. "Framework." *Business World*, Manila, July 8: 1.

Kaul, Vikas. 2005. "Gulf of Governance." *ITP Business*, April 4.

Knight, Malcolm. D. 2005. "Lessons from International Corporate Governance Standards: The Ethical Perspective in Corporate Governance," http://www.bis.org, presentation at the 2nd Islamic Financial Services Board Summit, Doha, Qatar, May 24.

La Porta, R., F. Lopez-de-Silanes, and A. Shleifer. 1998. "Law and Finance." *Journal of Political Economy* 106 (6): 1113–1155.

Lublin, Joann S. and William M. Bulkeley. 2006. "IBM Ends Director Stock Options, Spotlighting Popular Perk's Decline." *Wall Street Journal* (Eastern Edition), New York, December 21.

McKensey 2000. "Investor Opinion Survey." Included in Clare Roberts, Pauline Weetman, and Paul Gordon. 2005. "International Financial Reporting." *Prentice-Hall Financial Times*, England, 108–115.

Organization for Economic Co-Operation and Development. 2004. "OECD Principles of Corporate Governance, www.oecd.org.

Roberts, Clare, Pauline Weetman, and Paul Gordon. 2005. "International Financial Reporting." *Prentice-Hall Financial Times*, England, 108–115.

Saidi, Nasser. 2004. "Corporate Governance in MENA Countries; Improving Transparency and Disclosure." The Second Middle East and North Africa Regional Corporate Governance Forum, Beirut, June 3–5.

Sharif, Arif. 2006. "Gulf Suffers from Poor Corporate Governance." October 3, www.gulfnews.com.

Taher, Nahed M. 2003. "Corporate Governance & the Saudi Capital Market Law." Special Report to Arab News, November 3, www.arabnews.com.

Timewell, Stephen. 2006. "Middle East & Africa: Corporate Governance-Joint Study Benchmarks Gulf States' Standards—A Ground-Breaking Survey on Corporate Governance Recommends Action to Pull the GCC in Line with Global Best Practice." *The Banker*, London, November 1: 1.

9

Tax Rules and Regulations of the Gulf Countries

Wagdy M. Abdallah

Introduction

In many industrial countries, including the United States and the United Kingdom, sales taxes, individual income taxes, corporate income taxes, and other types of direct and indirect taxes are considered as a part of the daily life. Potential investors, including American and British MNCs, need (1) to decide what types of investments and finance need to be done; (2) to choose the best country, state, or city for investments that will bring back the highest return on invested capital after tax with the lowest political and business risk; (3) to determine the most favorable country for particular investment to achieve corporate long-term objectives; and (4) to look at regional opportunities for cost savings and improvements in efficiency in their tax issues. Comparative tax rates and regulations of the United States and foreign countries are important input factors to help MNCs in making successful investing strategic decisions.

Foreign MNCs have shown every confidence in the Gulf countries market and many are willing to commit to expending serious sums of money on making strategic investments in the Gulf region. Profits can be lost though, by a lack of forethought concerning important and key issues. Some matters involve local equity ownership and tax issues that are not present in other countries. The foreign MNCs should take into account some of the country's tax matters before making investing decisions. Proper planning can alleviate the tax consequences of the home country regulations. At a minimum, the investor's initial purchasing or acquiring considerations and cash projections should take into account these tax implications.

In the best interest of the MNCs, it is necessary to look at each country separately where an investment is contemplated. Tax planning opportunities should be reviewed in the region as a whole, in conjunction with tax planning in each individual country (Bartlett 1997). To achieve long-run objectives, every MNC has to set its tax strategy on the basis of several factors for overseas investments. One of the most important factors is to understand local tax rules and regulations; therefore, tax planning and strategies are just as important in the Gulf countries as in other countries.

Another important factor that requires particular attention when planning an investment in the Gulf countries is technology transfer including know-how, software development and sales, management fees, licensing and royalties. In some countries, license fees and royalties are taxed at the maximum rates with no deductions allowed. Software sales into the Gulf region are often licensed and the whole sale could be subject to tax. It is sometimes possible to have an agreement for technical assistance performed totally outside a particular country. If the agreement is worded carefully and does not call for any local presence, it is not taxable and it may be claimed as a tax-deductible expense in the country from which payments are made. Provisions are often disallowed as an expense (Bartlett 1997).

The Gulf region is considered as one of the most strategic and attractive areas in the world for global business. American and non-American MNCs can be very successful in investing their capital and managing their businesses in the Gulf countries; however, an appropriate tax planning should be done in advance, including the following five major steps:

1. Get access to all up-to-date tax information of the Gulf region and of the selected country.
2. Start your strategic tax planning as soon as your project is initiated.
3. Involve your local partner(s) in your tax planning.
4. Minimize your tax liability by
    a. Choosing the most appropriate investment tools, such as joint ventures or wholly owned subsidiary.
    b. Structuring contracts in the most convenient and appropriate manners.
    c. Taking advantage of all tax holidays and other incentives available.
    d. Coordinating the tax burden in the Gulf countries with that in your home country to take advantage of any tax treaty provisions and other tax credit opportunities.

5. Design your pricing policy, including transfer-pricing strategies, after considering all finance, tax, and custom issues.

The following sections of this chapter are divided into two sections; first, the general characteristics of the tax rules and regulations of the Gulf countries are analyzed. Then, the tax rules and regulations of every one of the six Gulf countries are discussed. Seven selected tax topics are covered with respect to each country; they are taxable income; tax rates; personal income tax, capital gains; dividends, interests, and royalties; transfer pricing, and tax incentives and tax holidays.

General Characteristics of the Tax Rules and Regulations of the Gulf Countries

In this chapter, several issues are emphasized such as (1) tax rules and regulations of the Gulf countries are not coded to the same extent as in the well-developed countries; (2) most of Gulf countries have been trying to reform their tax systems in order to reduce their maximum corporate tax rates to the levels of the industrial countries; and (3) customs and duties in the Gulf countries are unified at 5 percent on goods imported to GCC countries with the exception of the United Arab Emirates (UAE) that imposes a 4 percent rate.

In the United States, to encourage employees to accept overseas assignments, many companies agreed to assume their tax burden and included those costs as part of their compensation packages in addition to cost of living and housing allowances. To help these businesses, Congress increased the foreign earned income exclusion to $75,000, in addition to allowing individuals to exclude excess housing expenses, and shortened the foreign physical presence requirement to 330 days in any 12 consecutive months. In 1997, Congress voted to increase the foreign earned income exclusion from $72,000 for 1998, $74,000 for 1999, $76,000 for 2000, $78,000 for 2001, and $80,000 for 2002. This $80,000 amount was scheduled to be indexed for inflation after 2007. In May 2006, Congress passed the Tax Increase Prevention and Reconciliation Act (TIPRA), which accelerated indexing of the exclusion and resulted in a maximum foreign earned income exclusion for 2006 of $82,400, and the inflation-adjusted amount is $85,700 for 2007 (Dennis-Escoffier 2007).

Most countries offer tax incentives that can be of significant benefit to MNCs investing in the Gulf countries. The main incentive is the tax holiday. Tax holidays, combined with other incentives, such as subsidized loans to finance local expenditure, customs duty exemptions, and a lack of exchange controls in most countries, help to make the Gulf region an attractive place to invest, despite the high tax rates that are still imposed in certain countries (Bartlett 1997).

Table 9.10 summarizes the rates of corporate income tax, personal income tax, customs duties, tax holidays, withholding taxes, and other information about the six Gulf countries. In the following sections, tax rules and tax regulations of every Gulf country are covered including taxable income, corporate tax rates, personal income tax, customs duties, capital gains, transfer pricing, dividends, interests, royalties, tax incentives, and tax holidays.

The Tax System and Regulations in the Six Gulf Countries

Bahrain

General

- No taxes on corporate income, capital gains, interest, dividends, royalties, or fees of foreign companies carrying on a trade or business in Bahrain.
- Exception for certain taxes imposed on oil, gas, and petroleum companies.
- Companies or individuals renting property should pay a municipal tax.
- A 12 percent sales tax on gasoline and service charges of 5 percent and 15 percent levied by the government on persons using hotels.
- No value-added tax, property tax, or production tax.
- Two free-trade zones with a duty-free import of equipment and machines.
- Duty-free access to the GCC members for products manufactured in Bahrain.
- Tax treaties to avoid double taxation with several countries.

Bahrain is the smallest of the Gulf countries' oil producers by volume. It consists of a group of small islands connected to Saudi Arabia from the east by a long bridge. Oil is a major part of Bahrain's economy and its revenues amount to about three-fourths of total Bahraini's government revenues (EIA 2007a). Bahrain imposes no taxes on corporate income with the exception of oil, gas, and petroleum companies.

Taxable Income

Bahrain levies no taxes on corporate income of foreign companies carrying on trade or business in the country. There is one exception; there are certain taxes imposed on oil companies. Therefore, the only corporate tax in Bahrain is levied on oil, gas, and petroleum companies. The tax rate is 46 percent, which is applicable on any oil company conducting business in Bahrain of any kind, including oil exploration, production, and refining regardless of where the company was incorporated, and there are no withholding taxes in the country. For individuals, there is no income tax either for the state or the federal government. There is no value-added tax, property tax, or production tax in the country (Ernst & Young 2007). There are no restrictions on repatriation of profits or capital to the home country.

Deductions are allowed for (1) taxes and customs duties paid by the taxpayer; (2) the costs of raw materials and for all production needs; and (3) management fees. Capital assets, including machinery and equipments, may be depreciated over the expected useful life of assets.

Tax Rates

In Bahrain, there is no corporate or income tax and no restriction on capital or profit repatriations to the home country with the exception of certain taxes imposed on oil companies. Residents and citizens of Bahrain are the least taxed in the world. Oil, gas, and petroleum production companies are taxed at 46 percent. Therefore, for all corporations and businesses other than oil and gas, it is a tax heaven country; and there is no other country in the world that can match Bahrain in this respect.

However, if companies or individuals rent property, they should pay a municipal tax. The municipal tax rate varies according to the nature of the property, whether it is an unfurnished residential, furnished residential or commercial property. There is also a sales tax on gasoline at 12 percent, and the government levy of 5 percent and a 15 percent service charge on persons using hotel facilities and it is generally added to the total bill amount (Ernest & Young 2007).

In Bahrain, there is no existing provision in the tax law to prevent double taxation; however, the foreign tax paid on income subject to tax in a foreign country will be allowed as deductible from the tax levied on taxable income in Bahrain (ibid.). Recently, Bahrain has entered into agreements on double taxation with several countries including Morocco, Egypt, Jordan, Algeria, France, Malaysia, Iran, and China. More discussions and negotiations are still in process, at the time of writing this book, and they will be finalized in the near future with other countries including Tunisia, Syria, Lebanon, Sudan, United Kingdom, and India (Ernst & Young 2007).

Personal Income Tax

In Bahrain, there is no personal income tax on employee earnings.

Transfer Pricing

The tax regulations do not include regulations on transfer pricing. In practice, international market (arm's-length) prices are considered the appropriate standard for transactions between related parties.

Customs Duties

According to the GCC guidelines, the Council established a common external tariff of 5 percent for most imported goods. In December 2002, the member states of the GCC approved the regulations for the implementation of the GCC Customs Union under which the GCC member states agreed to unify the regional customs tariffs at 5 percent of CIF invoice value on all taxable foreign imports. However, implementation of the laws is not uniform in all the member states and some differences still exist. The GCC countries apply the GCC Common Customs Tariff at 5 percent of CIF invoice value for imports of goods from outside the GCC region. Some products, such as tobacco and manufactured tobacco substitutes, are subject to higher rates. Goods and products moving between GCC states are not subject to customs duties (GCC 2003).

The main objective, beyond having a uniform customs, is the concept of a single entry point upon which all customs duties on foreign imported goods are collected, and therefore, goods moving between the GCC States are not subject to customs duties. Commodities and goods produced in any of the GCC member states are treated as "national products," which are not subject to any customs tariffs when transported within the member states (ibid.).

Certain goods or products are exempted from customs; these include (1) basic foodstuffs; (2) imports for diplomatic and consular missions; (3) imports for military and internal security forces; (4) imports for civilian airlines and helicopters; (5) personal effects and used household items; (6) accompanied passenger luggage and gifts; (7) goods required for charitable societies; and (8) ships and other vessels for the transport of passenger and floating platforms (ibid.). The exemptions cover the following: plant and equipment; spare parts; raw materials.

Capital Gains

In Bahrain, there no taxes on any capital gains of investments by individuals or companies.

Dividends, Interests, and Royalties

There are no taxes in Bahrain on interest, dividends, royalties, or fees. Therefore, Bahrain is considered an attractive country in which American companies may establish a Gulf regional office.

Tax Incentives and Tax Holidays

The government of Bahrain encourages foreign investors and companies with high skills and expertise and advanced technologies in several industrial and service fields to boost and diversify the economy, promote tourism, privatize infrastructure projects, and help and encourage small- and medium-sized businesses and industries.

There are two free-trade zones in Bahrain. The first one is Mina Salman, a major port of Bahrain, which provides a free transit zone to facilitate the duty free import of equipment and machinery. The second free zone is located in the North Sitra Industrial Estate. The facilities in the two free zones are used for the temporary import of goods for reexport. All manufacturing businesses in the free zones are exempt from customs duties on the import of raw materials and capital equipment. In an attempt of the government to assist industry, ground rents in the industrial free zones are at very low rates (Ernst & Young 2007).

In general, there are more new incentives being offered to companies to set up industries in Bahrain. Incentives may deal with tax, duty, ownership, government support, labor force amenities, and a developed infrastructure in industry and service. Bahrain does not impose any special performance requirements on foreign companies to qualify for the incentives. They must meet the same requirements and comply with the same regulations as Bahraini-owned companies. There are only three issues that companies should adhere to in order to qualify for the incentives; they are (1) companies must hire a specified percentage of Bahraini employees; (2) must contribute to local value-addition by at least 40 percent; and (3) must export at least 25 percent of their production out of Bahrain (ibid.).

To summarize the tax incentives of the government of Bahrain, the following five major issues make it an attractive place of investment for foreign companies.

1. Absence of individual, corporate, and withholding taxation;
2. No restriction on repatriation of capital, income or profits, royalties, and dividends;

3. A developed infrastructure with well-advanced transportation and communication systems;
4. Permission granted for a 100 percent foreign ownership of a company in certain cases; and
5. Foreigners may own high-rise commercial and residential properties in specific geographic areas.

Kuwait

General

- Foreign companies are liable for tax.
- Companies wholly owned by Kuwaitis and companies incorporated in GCC countries, wholly owned by GCC citizens, are not subject to income tax.
- Kuwaiti income tax is imposed at rates up to 55 percent on taxable profits.
- Private Kuwaiti companies pay 1 percent (*Zakat*) of their annual net income to the state to help improve public service and living conditions of the poor.
- Kuwait has treaties in force for avoidance of double taxation with several countries.
- No personal income tax is levied in Kuwait. A proposal for personal income tax between 5 and 30 percent has been introduced but has not been approved yet.
- No value added tax exists in Kuwait.

Kuwait, with the third largest oil reserves in the world, has a small but relatively open economy dominated by the oil industry and government sector. Oil production generates 90 percent of the government revenue. There are two other major sources of income: payment of war damages by Iraq and revenue from overseas financial investment. The country depends highly on foreign trade (95 percent) and its top three export partners are Japan, the United States, and the Netherlands, and its top three import partners are the United States, Germany, and Japan (FITA 2007a).

In Kuwait, foreign companies are currently subject to a maximum income tax rate of 55 percent, although the government is currently drafting a new tax law that would reduce the tax rate. Kuwaiti-listed companies are not subject to income tax, but are required to make an annual contribution of 2.5 percent of their net profits to the Kuwait Foundation for the Advancement of Sciences (KFAS). They must also contribute 2.5 percent of their net profits toward a National Labor Force Fund.

The initial purpose of the law was to impose an income tax on oil companies operating in Kuwait when no other significant foreign business existed in Kuwait. Since then the law has become, in text and practice, a general tool for the taxation of all foreign companies working not only in but also for Kuwait.

Taxable Income

In Kuwait, foreign companies are subject to tax if they carry on a trade or business in Kuwait, including the islands of Kubr, Qaru, and Umm Al Maradim and in the offshore area of the neutral zone between Kuwait and Saudi Arabia. No income tax is currently imposed on companies incorporated either in Kuwait or in other GCC countries and wholly owned by nationals of Kuwait or other GCC countries. Corporate income tax in Kuwait is levied on foreign companies carrying out trade or business under the under Amiri Decree No. 3 of 1955.

Foreign companies carrying on a trade or business in the Specified Territory are subject to tax under Law No. 23 of 1961 in accordance with the following rules:

- The entire taxable profit derived in the Specified Territory under Kuwaiti control and administration is subject to tax; and
- Fifty percent of the taxable profit derived in the portion of the offshore partitioned zone under the control and administration of Saudi Arabia is subject to tax.

Law No. 23 of 1961 is applicable to the entities carrying on business or trade in the areas known as the "Specified Territory" in the divided neutral zone. The Specified Territory consists of the partitioned neutral zone between Kuwait and Saudi Arabia and the islands of Kubr, Qaru, and Umm Al Maradim and their territorial waters. However, the tax laws of both Kuwait and Saudi Arabia do not specifically provide for rules for filing of tax declarations and assessment of tax on income earned by contractors in the divided neutral zone. The DIT has, however, issued a circular recently ruling that Law 23 of 1961 will be applied only on the revenue earned from the offshore neutral zone between Saudi Arabia and the specified islands. Losses generated from activities in one zone cannot be offset against profits generated from activities in other zones.

The Amiri Decree No. 3 of 1955 and Law No. 23 of 1961 differ primarily with respect to tax rates. Foreign companies can operate in Kuwait (or in the Specified Territory under Kuwaiti administration) either through an agent or as the minority shareholder in a locally registered company. In principle, the method of calculating tax is the same for companies operating through an agent and for minority shareholders. For minority shareholders, tax is levied on the foreign company's share of the profits (whether or not distributed by the Kuwaiti company) plus any amount receivable for interest, royalties, technical services, and management fees.

In the computation of the tax liabilities, it should be based on the profits disclosed in audited financial statements, adjusted for tax depreciation and any items considered nontax deductible by the DIT. Inventories are normally valued at the lower of cost or net realizable value, on a first-in, first-out (FIFO), or average basis. Provisions, as opposed to accruals, are not accepted for tax purposes in Kuwait. With respect to the work-in-process, costs incurred but not billed by an entity at the end of the fiscal year may be carried forward to the subsequent year (or revenue may be estimated provided the revenue is not less than the costs incurred). In general, where less than 20 percent of the contract has been executed in a period, income and expenses relating to the contract may be carried forward.

For depreciations of assets, the allowable rates, applied using the straight-line method, include 4 percent a year for buildings, 10 percent for most plants, 25 percent to 33 1/3 percent for motor vehicles, 20 percent for computers, and 15 percent for office furniture and equipment.

If the company has any losses, it may be carried forward and deducted from subsequent profits without limit, provided there is no cessation of activities. Losses cannot be carried back.

Tax Rates

The corporate tax rates are shown in table 9.1. Kuwaiti income tax is not progressive; consequently, total profit is taxed at the appropriate rate as can be seen from table 9.1.

Kuwaiti income tax is not progressive; consequently, total profit is taxed at the appropriate rate from table 9.1. If taxable profit is only marginally higher than the previous limit, tax is calculated by adding the actual excess to the amount payable on the previous limit. For example, on KD 38,000 of taxable income derived in Kuwait, the tax is KD 37,500 at 10 percent = KD 3,750, plus KD 500, giving total tax of KD 4,250. Within the framework of a joint venture, the initial foreign contracting party will be subjected to the corporate tax in proportion to its contribution in capital. Table 9.2 shows more details of the corporate tax rates under Amiri Decree No. 3 of 1955.

However, the Kuwait Cabinet recently approved to reduce the corporate tax rate from a maximum of 55 percent to a flat rate of 15 percent. This draft has now been referred to the legal and finance committee and will then be presented to The Kuwait National Assembly for review, discussion, and approval.

Table 9.1 Income tax rates of Kuwait

Types of Tax	*Rate (%)*
Corporate income tax	55
Capital gains tax	55
Branch tax	55
Withholding tax	
Dividends	0
Interest	0
Royalties from patents	0
Net operating losses (years)	
Carry back	0
Carry forward	Unlimited

Table 9.2 Corporate income tax rates of Kuwait

Taxable Profits		*Rate (%)*
Exceeding (KD)	*Not Exceeding (KD)*	
0	5,250	0
5,250	18,750	5
18,750	37,500	10
37,500	56,250	15
56,250	75,000	20
75,000	112,500	25
112,500	150,000	30
150,000	225,000	35
225,000	300,000	40
300,000	375,000	45
375,000	—	55

Zakat

In December 2006, Kuwait parliament overwhelmingly voted to pass a controversial law for imposition of *Zakat* in Kuwait, Islamic form of taxation. The law requires private companies to pay 1 percent of their net income annual to the state in order to help improve public services and help the poor. The most important features of the law are as follows:

- Kuwaiti Shareholding Companies (KSC) both public and closed will be liable to pay the *zakat* annually at the rate of 1 percent of their annual net profit.

- Every KSC will be required to submit a *zakat* declaration annually.
- Failure to submit the declaration or falsifying the information submitted will be a criminal offence and carries a prison sentence up to three years and a financial penalty of up to KD 5,000.
- Companies owned by the Government of Kuwait and established under the special laws and the companies subject to income tax under Decree No. 3 of 1955 will not be subject to the *zakat*.

The law does not specify from which financial year the KSC will be liable to pay the *zakat*. It is possible that the executive regulations to be issued by the MOF may provide for payment of the *zakat* from the financial years commencing January 1, 2007.

Based on the experience of the other tax laws in Kuwait it is possible that the executive regulations to be issued by the MOF may include the following:

- Basis of computation of profit liable to *zakat*, format of the *zakat* declaration and audit thereof by the licensed accountants in Kuwait;
- Dates of submission of the *zakat* declaration and payment of *zakat*;
- Books of account to be maintained by the KSC for *zakat* purposes;
- Inspection of the books of account of KSC and issue of the *zakat* assessments by the officials responsible of the Ministry of Finance;
- Filing of objections/appeals against the *zakat* assessments by KSC; and
- Issue of *zakat* clearance certificates by the MOF.

According to the *Zakat* law, the Minister of Finance (MOF) will be responsible for introducing the executive regulations for the implementation of the law within one year of the date of publication of the law in the official gazette, that is, effective from December 3, 2006. However, the tax law does not specify from which financial year the KSC will be liable to pay the *Zakat*. However, it is our understanding that the executive regulations to be issued by the MOF may provide for payment of the *Zakat* from the financial years commencing January 1, 2007.

Personal Income Tax

With respect to personal income tax in Kuwait, generally individuals (residents, nonresidents) are not taxed in Kuwait either on salaries or income from commercial activities, but a project of levy was presented to the National Assembly and has not been approved yet, at the time of writing this book. The tax schedule varies between 5 and 30 percent and is distributed into six brackets, as can be seen from table 9.3.

Table 9.3 Personal income tax rates of Kuwait

Individual Salaries or Income		*Rate (%)*
Exceeding (KD)	*Not Exceeding (KD)*	
0	2,000	5
2,001	10,000	10
10,001	50,000	15
50,001	250,000	20
250,001	1,000,000	25
1,000,001	—	30

The proposed tax law gives deductions or other allowances for individuals. The fixed deductions are as follows:

1. Fixed deduction of 6,000 KD for single people.
2. Fixed deduction of 7,000 KD for married people without dependent children.
3. Fixed deduction of 8,400 KD for couples married with a dependent child.
4. Fixed deduction of 600 KD for every dependent child.

Transfer Pricing

The Kuwaiti tax law does not cover transfer-pricing issue in details. The Kuwaiti tax authorities deem the following profit margins for imported materials and equipments:

- Manufactured and/or imported from head office 10–15 percent of related revenue;
- Manufactured and/or imported from related parties 6.5–10 percent of related revenue; and
- Manufactured and/or imported from third parties 3.5–6.5 percent of related revenue.

With respect to the transfer-pricing policy, the imputed profit described earlier is normally subtracted from the cost of materials and equipment claimed in the tax declaration. If the revenue from the materials and equipment supplied is identifiable, the Department of Income Tax (DIT) normally reduces the cost of such items to show a profit on such materials and equipment in accordance with the percentages described earlier.

In this case, if the revenue from the materials and equipment supplied is identifiable, the DIT normally reduces the cost of such items to show a profit on such materials and equipment in accordance with the percentages described earlier. In cases where the related revenue from the materials and equipment supplied is not identifiable or not stated in the contract, the following formula may be applied to determine the related revenue:

Material and equipment revenue for the year =
Contract revenue for the year × Material and equipment costs for the year......................Total direct costs for the year

With respect to the allocation of head office expenses or management fees, the tax authorities allow the following deductions from income as a contribution toward expenses incurred by the head office of a foreign company or management fees paid by the Kuwaiti subsidiary to the head office in a foreign country:

- Contractors, consultants, and others operating through an agent: 3.5 percent of revenue from the principal activities, reduced by amounts paid or payable to subcontractors and reimbursed expenses;
- Foreign companies participating with Kuwait companies in the execution of a contract: 2 percent of the foreign company's share of the contract revenue reduced by amounts paid to subcontractors and reimbursed expenses;
- Minority shareholders in a share company: 2 percent of the shareholder's share of the company's revenue from the principal activities, net of payments to subcontractors and reimbursed expenses;
- Insurance companies: 3.5 percent of net premiums; and
- Any direct expenses relating to operations in Kuwait that can be fully supported by documentation are allowed by the tax authorities in addition to the percentages stated earlier.

Customs Duties

Customs duties in Kuwait are applied at a standard rate of 5 percent. Most of the imported products can be exempted from customs duties such as food products, staple commodities.

In accordance with GCC guidelines, the Council established a common external tariff of 5 percent for most imported goods. The Government of Kuwait and other GCC states reserve the right to assess certain exceptions until such time as a uniform list of goods exempt from tariff is adopted by all GCC member states. Kuwait officially approved the Single Customs Tariff on April 1, 2003, thereby setting a 5 percent import duty (CIF) on most goods. Exempt from the Single Customs Tariff are certain basic food and medicinal/medical items, which are duty free and tobacco products, which are assessed duty at 100 percent.

Capital Gains

Capital gains on the sale of assets and on the sale of shares by foreign shareholders are treated as normal business profits and are subject to tax at the rates stated earlier. Capital losses incurred on the disposal of capital assets are allowed as deductions from income.

Dividends, Interests, and Royalties

Dividends are not taxed as tax is assessed on the share of profits attributable to the foreign shareholder according to the audited financial statements of a company, adjusted for tax purposes. There is no withholding tax on dividends.

In general, where a foreign company has a minority shareholder interest in a locally registered company, tax is levied on the foreign company's income (whether distributed or not) plus any amounts receivable for interest, royalties, technical services, or management fees. In other words, dividends are not taxed. Tax is assessed on the share of profits attributable to the foreign shareholder according to the audited financial statements of a company, adjusted for tax purposes.

Interest is only usually accepted if it is paid directly by the branch to local banks related to business operations in Kuwait and is reasonable in relation to the activities of the business in Kuwait. According to a previously issued circular interest paid to banks or financial institutions outside Kuwait will be disallowed unless it can be proved that the funds were specifically borrowed to finance the working capital needs of Kuwait operations. We consider that, in practice, it would be difficult to claim interest costs incurred outside Kuwait. Interest paid to the head office or agent is disallowed. Interest paid to local banks that are directly attributable to the acquisition, construction, or productions of an asset are capitalized as part of the cost of the asset.

Tax Incentives and Tax Holidays

In Kuwait, there are several incentives for investors. The first incentive is the "Leasing and Investment Companies. Law No. 12 of 1998," which allows the formation of investment and leasing companies that have their principal place of business in Kuwait, with Kuwaiti or foreign shareholders. The law grants a five-year tax holiday to non-Kuwaiti founders and shareholders of such companies, beginning on the date of establishment of the companies. It is currently difficult to obtain approval of the authorities to form companies under the law.

The second incentive is the "Law No. 8 of 2001" relating to Direct Foreign Capital Investment Law (DFCIL), which allows up to 100 percent foreign ownership of Kuwaiti businesses. The DFCIL has the following interesting features for foreign investors:

1. Possibility of investment by non-Kuwaitis in excess of 50 percent and up to 100 percent in Kuwaiti shareholding companies.
2. Full or partial exemption from customs duties and other government dues for approved projects.
3. Up to ten-year tax holiday on the non-Kuwaiti shareholders' share of profit in the project.
4. Guarantee for repatriation of profit and capital invested in the project.
5. Benefit from Avoidance of Double Taxation Treaties and investment promotion and protection agreements; and
6. Exemption of all or part of the restrictive requirements imposed on exports or imports.

The third incentive is the Free Trade Zones (KFTZ) established by the Kuwaiti government in the vicinity of the Shuwaikh port in Kuwait. The KFTZ offers many benefits and exemptions; they are as follows:

1. Up to 100 percent foreign ownership is permitted and encouraged.
2. Exemption from taxation on all corporate and personal forms of income.
3. Exemption from taxation on all imports to and exports from the KFTZ.
4. Capital and profits are freely transferable outside the KFTZ and are not subject to any exchange price control.

With respect to avoiding double taxation, Kuwait has entered into double tax treaties with several countries, Of these, tax treaties are in force with Austria, Belarus, Belgium, Bulgaria, Canada, China, Croatia, Cyprus, Czech, Egypt, Ethiopia, France, Germany, Greece, Hungary, Indonesia, Italy, Jordan, Korea, Lebanon, Malaysia, Malta, Mauritius, Mongolia, Morocco, Netherlands, Pakistan, Poland, Romania, Russia, Serbia, Singapore, South Africa, Sri Lanka, Switzerland, Sudan, Syria, Thailand, Tunisia, Turkey, Ukraine, United Kingdom, Yugoslavia, and Venezuela. Treaties with several other countries are at various stages of negotiations or ratification.

Kuwait has also entered into treaties with several countries relating solely to international air and/or sea transport. Kuwait is a signatory of the Arab Tax Treaty and the GCC Joint Agreement, both of which provide for the avoidance of double taxation in most areas. The other signatories of the Arab Tax Treaty are Egypt, Iraq, Jordan, Sudan, Syria, and Yemen.

The DIT is very restricted in allowing the Treaty benefits. The DIT is currently concerned that companies from the countries not having tax treaties with Kuwait may be taking an unfair advantage by using their subsidiaries in the countries having tax treaties with Kuwait to sign the contracts in Kuwait. The DIT, therefore, requires to be convinced that the company has substance and is in itself the principal contractor.

Oman

General

- Both foreign and locally owned are taxable.
- The tax system has undergone important changes reflecting the government policy of opening up the economy to foreign investment.
- Companies wholly owned by nationals of the GCC member states will enjoy a lower tax rate of 12 percent irrespective of the nature of their activities.
- Branches of companies registered in GCC states, irrespective of the extent of foreign participation, will be taxed at a rate between 5 and 12 percent.
- Foreign investment projects are exempt from tax on profits for a period of five years.
- No personal income tax, estate tax, or gift tax exists.
- Losses may be carried forward for up to five years; no carry-back option is permitted.

In 1962, Oman's petroleum deposits were discovered, decades after Saudi Arabia, Kuwait, and other Gulf countries. Moreover, Oman's oil fields are generally smaller, more widely scattered, less productive, and involve higher production costs than in other Persian Gulf countries. Oman's oil revenues account for about 75 percent of the country's export earnings and 40 percent of its Gross Domestic Product (GDP). The government continues to be very progressive under demanding circumstances. The development of natural gas sector reserves in Oman has become a central part of the government and is very important to the economy of the country. Its production is likely to expand considerably during the next several years. However, despite the recent rise in production, additional natural gas reserves have not been located as quickly as the government had hoped.

The Omani tax system is considered to be both reasonable and pragmatic in its dealings with taxpayers. The tax system has undergone important changes reflecting the government policy of opening up the economy to foreign investment, and more changes are forthcoming. By and large, taxation is moderate because many of the government's revenues are oil revenues. Therefore, Oman levies no personal income tax, estate tax, or gift tax. All entities, both foreign and locally owned, are taxable in Oman.

Taxable Income

The most important tax in Oman is the tax on business income, which is based upon the Corporate Income Tax Law of 1981 and subsequent Royal and Ministerial Decrees. In September 2003, Oman extended national tax treatment to all companies registered in Oman regardless of the percentage of direct foreign ownership. Royal Decree 54/2003 was issued, which made a series of amendments to the Omani Income Tax Law.

Taxable entities are entities that have a permanent establishment in the country, so that any entity that has personnel present in Oman is taxed. In general, companies, including partnerships and joint ventures, carrying on business in Oman are subject to tax on Omani-source income. Under certain circumstances, income arising outside Oman is deemed to be Omani-source income. The tax rates vary in accordance with the amount of taxable income and the percentage of Omani ownership. Tax holidays granted under the investment incentives laws also provide an official pardon. Some foreign companies are exempted from income taxes in Oman such as shipping and aviation companies, if Omani shipping and aviation companies enjoy similar treatment in the respective foreign countries. If any income is exempt from tax, the related expenses are not tax deductible.

Taxable income includes business profit, interest, royalties, and capital gains, and is computed on the net income arising in Oman after deducting all ordinary expenses, such as expenditure incurred in producing the gross revenue, bad debts, auditors' fees, depreciation, head office expenses, sponsorship fees, and certain donations.

Tax is levied on income that has been realized or has arisen in Oman. Financial statements must be presented on the accrual basis of accounting. Actual expenditure incurred may be deducted. However, special rules exist for allowances such as depreciation, bad debts, donations, head office overhead charges allocated to branches, and sponsorship fees. Any exchange loss relating to head office or related-party balances is normally disallowed.

With respect to inventories, the tax law does not require a specific method of accounting to be used. In general, they should be valued at the lower of cost or net realizable value with cost determined using the weighted-average or first-in, first-out (FIFO) method. However, tax regulations do not allow any provisions to be used to bring down the value to net realizable value. Any provisions relating to accruals, end-of-service benefits, technical provisions based on net premiums for insurance companies, and loan loss provisions for banks are exemptions from this rule.

Losses may be carried forward for five years. No carrying back of losses is permitted. If the business entity incurs net losses during the mandatory tax holiday period of five years, the losses are available for carrying forward against future profits for an indefinite period of time.

Tax Rates

Companies, including partnerships and joint ventures, carrying on business in Oman are subject to tax on Omani-source income. Under certain circumstances, income arising outside Oman is deemed to be Omani-source income. Citizens of other Arab GCC countries are treated as Omanis for tax purposes if engaged in certain specified activities. Companies wholly owned by citizens of other GCC countries and companies owned jointly by citizens of GCC countries are also treated as wholly Omani-owned, subject to certain conditions. The income tax rates in Oman for corporations are shown in table 9.4.

Table 9.5 shows the tax rates for branches of foreign companies in Oman.

The tax rates for branches of foreign companies are not progressive, as can be seen from the table 9.5. Consequently, total taxable income is taxed at the appropriate rate from the table 9.5. For example, tax on RO 80,000

Table 9.4 Income tax rates of Oman

Types of Company	*Rate (%)*
Companies registered in Oman irrespective of the extent of foreign participation and permanent establishments of companies incorporated in the other member countries of the GCC First OR 30,000	0
Excess over OR 30,000	12
Branches of foreign companies (other than companies incorporated in the member states of the GCC)	5–30*

Note: * No tax is payable by a branch of a foreign company if the branch's taxable income is less than OR 5,000.

Table 9.5 Income tax rates on branches of foreign companies in Oman

Taxable Profits		*Rate (%)*
Exceeding (OR)	*Not Exceeding (OR)*	
0	5,000	0
5,000	18,000	5
18,000	35,000	10
35,000	55,000	15
55,000	75,000	20
75,000	100,000	25
100,000	—	30

is RO 20,000 (25 percent of 80,000). However, marginal relief applies if taxable income slightly exceeds the maximum amount in the previous bracket. In such circumstances, tax is calculated by adding the excess to the amount payable on the maximum amount in the previous tax bracket.

If foreign companies do not have a permanent establishment in Oman, they are taxed at a flat rate of 10 percent on gross income from certain types of receipts such as royalties, equipment hire, management fees, and any fees for transfer of technical know-how and research. Companies or permanent establishments in Oman that make such payments must deduct tax at source and remit it to the secretary general of taxation. For oil exploration and production companies, their taxes are computed under special rules covered by the mutual agreements with the Omani government. Joint Investment Accounts (Mutual Funds) established under the Omani regulations or those established outside Oman to deal with Omani Financial Instruments listed on the Muscat Securities Market are exempt from taxation.

Personal Income Tax

In Oman, personal income other than that from business is not taxable. Citizens of other GCC members are treated as Omanis for tax purposes. Companies wholly owned by citizens of other GCC countries and companies owned jointly by citizens of GCC members are also treated as wholly Omani-owned, subject to certain conditions.

All single proprietorship business entities are taxed on Omani-source income. The first RO 30,000 of a sole proprietor's net taxable income is exempt from tax. Amounts in excess of RO 30,000 are subject to tax at a rate of 12 percent. Only an Omani national or, under certain circumstances, a national of a GCC member country may operate a business as a sole proprietor in Oman.

Transfer Pricing

For tax purposes, the amounts charged by a branch's head office or its affiliates are to be allowed only to the extent of cost. The tax administration may require a taxpayer to justify charges between related parties that differ from prices determined at arm's-length basis. If a company carries out a transaction with a related party that was planned to reduce the company's taxable income, the income arising from the transaction is considered to be the income that would have arisen had the parties been dealing at arm's-length price.

All actual expenses incurred by a head office and directly identifiable to Omani operations are allowed, provided such expenses are reasonable and not allocated based on turnover, number of employees, or similar bases indicating the indirect nature of such expenses.

Expenses other than directly identifiable costs are considered as overheads and are restricted to the lower value of the following three amounts:

- Actual expenses charged to the branch;
- Average expenses allowed in the previous three tax years;
- Three percent of the total income of the branch;
- For branches of foreign banks and insurance companies, the allowance may be increased up to 5 percent (the total income of insurance companies for this purpose is total premiums net of reinsurance) and for branches of companies in highly technical fields it may be increased up to 10 percent.

If the tax department determined that the technical staff time fees charged to the Oman branch as significant and unreasonable, the head office auditors are required to confirm such direct costs and these have been identified based on time records.

Customs Duties

Custom duties apply to all importers. Mostly, these are fixed at 5 percent of the Cost, Insurance, and Freight (CIF) value charged for most goods There are exemptions for certain essential goods (e.g., gold, silver bullion, seeds, live plants, refined petroleum products, books, and different foodstuffs). For all alcoholic beverages, tobacco, and pork products, a 100 percent duty is applied as custom duties.

The Omani customs regulations are among the most liberal compared to the other countries of the Gulf. As a matter of fact, the Sultanate neither prohibits the import of alcoholic beverages nor that of pork meat. Some products competing with national production such as cement, plastic and polyethylene products, vegetable and hydrogenated oils, car battery, asbestos products, paints, detergents, and electric lamps are subject to overcharged rates between 5 and 100 percent.

Products exempted from customs duties are live animals, all meats except for pork meat, unsweetened milk, melted butter, seeds, sugar, fertilizers, insecticides, agricultural material, rice, wheat, wheat flour, maize, barley, fresh fruit and vegetables, edible oils, tea, live plants and goods imported by the government. There is also another tax called protective tariffs whose rates are between 10 and 50 percent and the rate on the fruits and vegetables is assessed on seasonal basis.

Capital Gains

No special rules apply to capital gains. Capital gains are taxed as part of regular income at the rates set out earlier. Profit on sale of investments and securities listed on the Muscat Securities Market (MSM) are exempt from tax. Gains on disposal of securities listed in the MSM will be tax exempt.

Dividends, Interests, and Royalties

Dividends received by companies from other Omani companies are not taxed. Under Omani domestic law, withholding tax is not imposed on dividends or interest. Under the France, Mauritius, and U.K. treaties, no withholding tax is imposed on royalties paid to companies resident in those countries subject to the satisfaction of certain conditions. The 10 percent withholding tax on royalties under Omani domestic law applies to royalties paid to companies resident in the other treaty countries.

Tax Incentives and Tax Holidays

There are several tax incentives and tax holidays granted to foreign investors. For example, foreign investment projects are exempt from tax on profits for a period of five years, effective from the date of establishment. There is an additional five-year exemption from tax on income that may be granted by the government if there is reasonable justification for the exemption. In addition, foreign investment projects may be exempt from customs duties on imports of machinery and equipment required for their establishment. If the raw materials required for the productions of products are not available in Oman, they are exempt from customs duties. The aforementioned exemptions are also applicable to new extensions in projects.

Tax holidays are available to colleges, universities, and other private higher education institutions, as well as to companies engaged in industrial activities, mining, exporting, tourism, agricultural farm production, farm processing, animal husbandry processing and manufacturing of animal products, fishing, fish processing, and certain services such as public utility services. The performance of management contracts and construction contracts in tourism and public utility projects and project companies covered by the Sector Law do not qualify for tax holidays.

The Omani government encourages foreign expertise and technology in several fields to develop and diversify the economy and to help the country benefit from its natural resources. To encourage foreign and local investment, a modern and sophisticated infrastructure has been developed to provide a suitable business environment. In these cases, interest-free loans and other incentives are granted to certain projects and businesses. Tax-free contracts are available in exceptional situations. A tax holiday, or exemption, is granted for certain projects up to a maximum of 10 years.

Joint Investment Accounts (Mutual Funds) are tax exempt. Companies engaged in the educational and medical sectors are tax exempt. Fish farming and aquaculture are eligible for tax exemption. Foreign airline companies will be exempt from tax, subject to reciprocal treatment. Losses on disposal of securities listed in the MSM will not be tax deductible.

Commercial banks and investment and brokerage joint stock companies that are registered in Oman may establish funds, which are registered with and regulated by the MSM. Non-Omanis may own up to 49 percent of these funds. Such funds are exempt from tax.

With respect to tax treaties to avoid double taxation, Oman has entered into several tax treaties with Algeria, Canada, China, France, India, Italy, Lebanon, Mauritius, Pakistan, Singapore, South Africa, South Korea, Thailand, Tunisia, Turkey, the United Kingdom, and Yemen. Oman has signed double tax treaties with Egypt, Iran, the Russian Federation, Seychelles, Sudan, and Syria but these treaties are not yet in force. The double tax treaties signed with Brunei, Germany, and Kazakhstan have not yet been ratified. Several countries, including the United States, allow a measure of unilateral relief against their own taxes for income tax paid in Oman.

Qatar

General

- A wholly owned branch of a foreign company is taxable in full.
- For joint ventures between foreign and local partners, the allocated portion to the foreign investor (based on the percentage of ownership) is the only one taxable.
- Foreign companies are allowed to own 100 percent equity in key sectors.
- There is no personal income tax on employees' earnings.
- Tax exemption of corporate income tax is allowed for approved projects for a period of up to 10 years.
- Losses may be carried forward for up to 3 years, but the carry-back option is not allowed.

While Qatar is a member of the Organization of the Oil Exporting Countries (OPEC) and is a significant oil producer, it holds the world's largest natural gas reserves and is the single largest supplier of liquefied natural gas (LNG) (EIA 2007d). In 2006, Qatar reportedly surpassed Indonesia to become the largest exporter of LNG in the world. Revenues from the oil and natural gas sectors together amount to 60 percent of the country's GDP (ibid.).

For tax purposes, neither expatriates nor Qatari nationals are subject to individual taxation, although foreign investors, other than GCC-owned companies, are required to pay corporate income tax up to a maximum of 35 percent. However, several agreements for tax-free zones are in the process of being set up, which will allow business firms to benefit from a tax holiday (for both direct and indirect taxes) for 20 years. Moreover, banks in Qatar Financial Center (QFC) are exempted from tax up to April 2008, after which time an independent tax regime (a flat rate of 10 percent) will be applicable (EIU 2006).

Taxable Income

Corporate income taxes are imposed on foreign firms operating in Qatar at rates ranging from 5 to 35 percent of net profits, including profits from majority-owned Qatari joint ventures exceeding 100,000 Qatari riyals (approximately US$30,000). All Qatari-owned firms and joint ventures are exempt from corporate income taxes.

Foreign companies, including partnerships and joint ventures, carrying on business activities in Qatar are subject to corporate income tax. Tax is imposed on a foreign entity operating in Qatar regardless of whether it operates through a branch or in a joint venture with a locally registered company. For a company with Qatari and foreign shareholders, tax is assessed on the total profits of the company. The resulting tax liability is allocated between the foreign and local partners. The foreign investor must pay their share of the tax liability to the tax authorities, but the Qatari shareholders are exempt from tax. Citizens of other GCC countries are exempt from tax in the same way as Qatari citizens. Consequently, foreign companies wholly owned by locals and other GCC nationals are exempt from tax.

Normal business expenses are allowable and must be determined under the accrual method of accounting. Agency fees paid to a Qatari agent are deductible if they are supported by a valid agreement and if they do not exceed 5 percent of the reported contract revenue for the year. An agent's commission is allowed without limit if supported by a valid agreement. Inventories may be valued using any internationally accepted method applied in the relevant case. Depreciation is calculated using the straight-line method. Intangible assets are depreciated on a straight-line basis over the estimated duration of the company benefiting from the asset. If a taxpayer's accounting rates are lower than those permitted, no additional claim is allowed. Accelerated rates are not allowed.

General provisions, such as bad debts and stock obsolescence, are not allowed. Specific bad debts that are written off are deductible to the extent that they satisfy strict conditions specified by the tax rules. Deductions by banks for loan loss provisions are the subject of periodic instructions from the Central Bank of Qatar. Losses may be carried forward for up to three years. Carrying back of losses is not allowed.

Tax Rates

Corporate income is subject to tax at progressive rates in Qatar. Table 9.6 presents the tax rates in Qatar.

Qatar does not impose estate, gift, or social security taxes.

Table 9.6 Corporate income tax rates of Qatar

Taxable Incomes		*Rate (%)*
Exceeding (QR)	*Not Exceeding (QR)*	
0	100,000	0
100,000	500,000	10
500,000	1,000,000	15
1,000,000	1,500,000	20
1,500,000	2,500,000	25
2,500,000	5,000,000	30
5,000,000	—	35

Personal Income Tax
In Qatar, there is no personal income tax on employee earnings.

Transfer Pricing
The tax regulations do not include regulations on transfer pricing. In practice, international market (arm's-length) prices are considered the appropriate standard for transactions between related parties. The tax administration may require a taxpayer to justify charges between related parties that differ from prices determined at an arm's-length basis.

Allocated expenses of head office to its Qatar branch are allowed as deductions, if they do not exceed 3 percent of turnover less subcontract costs. For banks, the limit is 1 percent. If a project derives income from both Qatari and foreign sources, the limit is 3 percent of the total revenues of the project, less subcontract costs, revenues from the supply of material and equipment overseas, revenues derived from services performed overseas, and other income not related to activities in Qatar.

Customs Duties
Qatar imposes a 5 percent tariff on a wide range of products. Basic food products such as wheat, flour, rice, feed grains, and powdered milk are exempted from tariffs. The tariff on alcoholic beverages and tobacco products is 100 percent and on 12-millimeter steel bars it is 20 percent. Projects funded by the Qatar Industrial Development Bank (QIDB) can be granted a customs duty waiver for the import of machinery, raw materials, and other industrial inputs.

Capital Gains
In Qatar, capital gains are aggregated with other income and are subject to tax at the regular corporate income tax rates.

Dividends, Interests, and Royalties
Dividends are not taxed in Qatar. Tax is assessed on the share of profits allocable to foreign investors according to the financial statements of a company, as adjusted for tax purposes.

Tax Incentives and Tax Holidays
In Qatar, a tax holiday may be granted for up to 10 years for new foreign investments in key sectors. Other foreign companies may be granted tax exemptions on a case-by-case basis. However, the law regulations allow for exemptions from the general rule where it is in the public interest to allow a foreign company to conduct business without a local partner or where the state grants the task of extraction, exploitation, or management of natural resources to a foreign contractor.

The Foreign Capital Investment Law includes a range of investment incentives for projects that involve inward investment by foreign investors. The Law sets out the general principle that foreign participation in business activities in Qatar is allowed in all sectors of the national economy with the exception of banking, insurance, commercial agency, and real estate trading sectors. In general, the percentage of foreign ownership in business activities in Qatar should not exceed 49 percent of the capital. A resolution from the minister of finance, economy, and commerce is required in order to increase the foreign investment share above the general limit of 49 percent. The percentage of foreign ownership may be increased to 100 percent in designated business sectors such as agriculture, education, healthcare, manufacturing, mining, power, and tourism.

Exemption of corporate income tax is allowed for approved projects for a period of up to 10 years. Each application may be evaluated for tax exemptions by considering the following factors:

- Whether the project provides social or economic benefits to Qatar;
- Whether the project falls within the planned development and economic objectives of the government and has the approval of the appropriate government department;
- Whether the project contributes to the national economy;
- Whether the project uses modern technology; and
- Whether the project creates employment opportunities for Qatari citizens.

Several agreements for tax treaties have been signed with France, India, Pakistan, Syria, and Senegal. Other agreements have initiated double tax treaties with Algeria, Belgium, Cyprus, Egypt, Italy, the Russian Federation, Turkey, and the United Kingdom. However, these treaties have not yet been ratified. An interesting fact is that under the treaty with France, Qatari taxpayers may obtain relief from certain taxes paid in France. However, no reduced withholding tax rates are provided with this treaty. In contrast, the treaties with India and Pakistan provide for a withholding rate of 10 percent for dividends, interest, royalties, and technical services fees.

Saudi Arabia

General

- Corporate income tax is assessed on profits of foreign partnerships, foreign corporate entities, and on profits attributable to foreign shareholders at rates up to 20 percent.

- Taxable income includes all income and profits derived from operations inside Saudi Arabia or from operations inside and outside Saudi Arabia at the same time.
- Non-GCC companies are taxable on taxable income.
- Nationals of GCC countries are treated as Saudis and are subject to a religious tax (*Zakat*) of 2.5 percent.
- There is no income tax on salaries and wages of employees in Saudi Arabia. There are social security taxes.
- In practice, no company not directly engaged in the production of crude oil or gas and petrochemicals is known to have been required to pay income tax under the corporate income tax regulations.
- Taxes are imposed on oil-producing companies at rates agreed directly with their host government.
- Losses may be carried forward without any time limits.
- No VAT, indirect tax, or sales tax exists in Saudi Arabia.

Saudi Arabia has the world's largest proven oil reserves. It is the largest producer of crude oil in the Middle East and is likely to remain so in the foreseeable future. Oil accounts for more than 90 percent of the country's exports and nearly 75 percent of the government revenues. Driven by strong government spending, rising foreign investment, increasing oil production, and high oil prices, the country's economic growth will remain robust in the coming years. The IMF forecasts a growth of 6.5 percent in 2007. The kingdom will also generate large oil-export driven current-account and fiscal surpluses (EIA 2007b).

As a result of the improving climate for foreign investment in Saudi Arabia and sustained high oil prices, foreign direct investment has boomed since 2000. After years of rhetoric without substantial change, Saudi Arabia made its first real allowances to foreign investors with the Foreign Investment Act of 2000.

In Saudi Arabia, only foreign-owned corporations and the foreign-owned portion of joint ventures are subject to the corporate income tax, which ranges up to 30 percent of net profits. Local corporate partners are subject to a 2.5 percent tax on assets (*zakat*). In April 2000, a resolution was issued by the Council of Ministers to eliminate the 10-year tax holiday previously enjoyed by companies and to provide instead the loss carry-forward provisions without any time limits.

Taxable Income

Income tax is assessed on profits arising or deemed to arise in Saudi Arabia that are earned by foreign partnerships, joint ventures, limited partnership, and foreign corporate entities, and on the share of a foreign shareholder in the profits of a Saudi corporate entity. However, for income tax purposes, foreigners do not include citizens (nationals) of countries that are the members of the GCC. In the case of a company incorporated in a GCC state, the share of profits attributable to interests owned by GCC nationals in that company is subject to *zakat*. The share of profits attributable to interests owned by non-GCC nationals in that company is subject to income tax.

In general, under Saudi tax regulations, income tax is assessed on profits of the following six cases:

1. A resident capital company (such as a Joint Stocks Company, Limited Liability Company, etc.) on the non-Saudi shareholders share;
2. A resident non-Saudi natural person who does business in Saudi Arabia;
3. A nonresident who does business in Saudi Arabia through a permanent establishment;
4. A nonresident who derives income subject to tax from a source in Saudi Arabia;
5. An entity engaged in the field of natural gas investment; and
6. An entity engaged in the production of oil and hydrocarbonic materials.

From the Department of Zakat Income Tax (DZIT) perspective, the most acceptable basis for assessing tax liabilities is profit as per the accounting books and records, including the audited financial statements, as adjusted for the Saudi tax purposes. In certain cases, such as foreign airlines and foreign freight and land and marine transport companies operating in Saudi Arabia, tax may be assessed under the "presumptive basis." Under the presumptive basis, no financial statements are presented, and the tax liability is assessed on deemed profit calculated at rates specified in the tax regulations.

The DZIT listed in their regulations some of the common items that are not allowed as deductible expenses; they are as follows:

- Expenses not connected with the earning of income subject to tax;
- Payments or benefits to a shareholder, a partner, or their relatives for property and services if they do not represent an arm's-length payment;
- Entertainment expenses;
- Expenses of a natural person for personal consumption;

- Income tax paid in Saudi Arabia or another country;
- Financial penalties and fines paid or payable to any party in Saudi Arabia except those paid for breach of contractual terms and obligations; and
- Payments of bribes and similar payments, which are considered criminal offences under the laws of Saudi Arabia, even if paid abroad.

With respect to inventories, they should be valued at the lower value of cost and market value. Cost should be determined on the weighted average cost method, or any other acceptable method with prior approval from the DZIT. Items such as provisions for doubtful debts, termination benefits, and other similar items are not deductible. Specific write-offs and actual employment termination benefit payments that comply with Saudi Arabian labor laws are deductible. Depreciation is calculated for each group of fixed assets by applying the prescribed depreciation rate to the remaining value of each group at end of the fiscal year. Assets developed in respect of build-operate-transfer (BOT) or build-own-operate-transfer (BOOT) contracts are allowed to be depreciated over the period of contract or the remaining period of contract.

Technical expenses have a special treatment under the Saudi tax rules. In general, technical costs that are related to engineering, chemical, geological, or industrial work and research, even if incurred wholly abroad by the main office or other offices, are deductible provided they can be substantiated by certain documents. When payments are made for technical and consultancy services rendered by the head office and affiliated non-resident entities, they are subject to 15 percent withholding tax. However, if the payments are made for technical and consultancy services rendered by nonaffiliated third parties, they are subject to withholding tax at a rate of 5 percent, regardless of the place of performance of the services.

Losses may be carried forward indefinitely. However, the maximum loss that can be offset against a year's profit is 25 percent of the tax-adjusted profits for that year. Saudi tax regulations do not provide for the carrying back of losses. If a change of 50 percent or more occurs in the underlying ownership or control of a capital company, no deduction is allowed for the non-Saudi share of the losses incurred before the change in the tax years following the change.

Tax Rates

The DZIT assess corporate income tax on the share of profit attributable to interests owned by foreign persons and assess *zakat* on the share attributable to the interests owned by Saudis and GCC nationals. Saudis and GCC nationals and their interests are subject to *zakat* but not income tax.

The tax rates on the non-Saudi and non-GCC corporations since the new tax law came into effect on July 30, 2004, are described in table 9.7.

Saudis and GCC nationals are not subject to income tax. Foreign employees are not taxed on their wages and salaries. Self-employed foreigners who are resident in Saudi Arabia are not taxed on income from non-Saudi sources but only on Saudi-source income. Wherever applicable, the tax rate is progressive from 5 to 30 percent and is divided into six brackets.

As can be seen from the table 9.7, the maximum corporate tax rate is 20 percent. It applies to taxable income over SR 36,000 (US$9,600). However, table 9.8 shows the detailed rates of corporate income tax that are applicable to non-Saudis (excluding citizens of GCC states).

Natural Gas Investment Tax (NGIT) applies to natural or legal persons (including GCC nationals and entities) engaged in natural gas, natural gas liquids, and gas condensates investment activities in Saudi Arabia. NGIT does not apply to a company engaged in the production of oil and other hydrocarbons. The NGIT rates range from 30 to 85 percent and are

Table 9.7 Income tax rates of Saudi Arabia

Types of Tax	*Tax Rate (%)*
Corporate income tax	20
Capital gains tax	20
Branch tax	20
Withholding tax	
Dividends	5
Interest	5
Royalties from patents	15
Net operating losses (Years)	0
Carry back	Unlimited time
Carry forward	

Table 9.8 Corporate income tax rates of Saudi Arabia

Taxable Income		*Tax Rate (%)*
Exceeding SR	*Not Exceeding SR*	
0	6,000	0–5
6,001	16,000	5
16,001	36,000	10
36,001	—	20

determined on the basis of the internal rate of return on cumulative annual cash flows. The NGIT rate includes income tax of 30 percent.

Companies engaged in the production of oil, gas, and other hydrocarbons are taxed at a rate ranging from 30 to 85 percent. Also, corporate tax rates up to 20 percent are imposed on profits made by the branches of foreign companies in Saudi Arabia.

Zakat is a religious wealth tax assessed on Saudi and GCC nationals and companies entirely owned by Saudi or GCC nationals. If companies or partnerships are owned by Saudis or GCCs nationals or both, as well as by other foreigners, *zakat* is assessed in proportion to equity interest of Saudis and GCCs nationals in the company. *Zakat* rates are 2.5 percent of capital employed, not invested in fixed assets, long-term investments, and deferred expenses, as adjusted by net results of operations for the year.

Personal Income Tax

There are no income taxes on salaries and wages of employees in Saudi Arabia. The tax regulations states that income tax at the standard rate of 20 percent is assessed on profit earned in Saudi Arabia by self-employed foreign professionals and consultants from their activities conducted in Saudi Arabia.

Customs Duties

Customs duties in Saudi Arabia, like the other GCC members, are applied at a standard rate of 5 percent. In accordance with GCC guidelines, the Council established a common external tariff of 5 percent for most imported goods. Alcoholic drinks and pork products are not allowed in Saudi Arabia based on the Islamic belief.

Transfer Pricing

When a Saudi company deals with the head office or any affiliated company of foreign shareholders, it is expected to trade on an arm's-length basis. The company is required to submit to the DZIT a certificate from the seller's auditors confirming that the materials and goods supplied to the Saudi Arabian company were sold at the international market price prevailing at the date of shipment. This requirement is also extended to foreign branches importing materials and goods from the head office for the fulfillment of their Saudi contracts.

However, there are certain provisions with respect to measures against tax avoidance that empower the DZIT to challenge transactions between related parties. Under these circumstances, the DZIT has the right to (1) disregard a transaction that has no tax effect, or reclassify a transaction whose form does not reflect its substance; and (2) allocate income or deductions between related persons or persons under common control as necessary to reflect the income that would have resulted from a transaction between independent persons.

The allocation of costs by a head office to a branch is not allowed for tax purposes However, certain costs incurred abroad directly relating to the Saudi Arabian operations are deductible subject to adequate documentation support and verification.

Moreover, any reimbursements to the head office and affiliated nonresident entities for services provided to the Saudi resident entity are subject to 15 percent withholding tax. However, a credit will be given against the tax liability of the Saudi branch for withholding tax settled on payments made to the head office, which are not tax-deductible expenses in the Saudi branch tax declaration.

Capital Gains

Overall, long-term capital gains from the sales of business assets and business interest are considered as ordinary income and are taxed at the regular corporate tax rates. Tax on capital gains will be assessed at 20 percent if there is a change/sale in the shareholding in the company. The tax on capital gains will be determined as the difference between the higher value of (1) contractual sale value; (2) market value of share; or (3) book value of share, and the cost base of the shares. Capital gains on sales by non-Saudi shareholders of shares in a Saudi joint stock company traded on the Saudi stock exchange are exempt from tax if the shares had been acquired after the effective date of the new tax regulations, which is July 30, 2004. However, gains on the disposal of property other than assets used in the business activity are exempt from tax.

Dividends, Interests, and Royalties

On July 30, 2004, the DZIT issued a new tax law to tax dividends for the first time in the history of Saudi Arabia. In general, dividends paid by Joint Stock Companies and limited liability partnerships to a nonresident party are subject to 5 percent withholding tax. Also, remittance of after-tax profits of branches of foreign companies (including GCC registered companies) is subject to 5 percent withholding tax. The DZIT has recently clarified that any undistributed profit of the company that is attributable to the outgoing shareholder on the date of sale/change in the shareholding will be subject to 5 percent withholding tax.

Interest paid to foreign affiliates or nonresidents' third parties is usually subject to a final withholding tax rate of 5 percent. Interest paid to foreign banks that have no presence in Saudi Arabia is not subject to the deemed profit tax. Royalties, management fees, or any other services are deemed to be 100 percent profit. Consequently, withholding taxes are applied at different rates. Royalties paid to the head office is taxed at 15 percent, management fees at 20 percent, and any payments for other services at 15 percent.

Tax Incentives and Tax Holidays

A number of incentives are available to foreign investors in Saudi Arabia. A tax holiday is granted for a period of 5 or 10 years, depending on the industrial, agricultural, or other projects in which investment has been made by the foreign investor, only if Saudi participation in the capital is at least 25 percent. For industrial and agricultural projects, the tax holiday period is 10 years; otherwise, it is 5 years. Additional tax holidays are granted to foreign shareholders in industrial projects and banks if additional capital is invested and if certain other conditions are met. During the tax holiday period, the foreign shareholder is subject to tax if it carries out any activities not specifically covered by its license, which is issued by the Ministry of Industry and Electricity on the recommendation of the Foreign Capital Investment Committee (this license is known as the Foreign Capital Investment License [FCIL] or the Industrial License).

The Saudi government, for the sake of encouraging new technology in industrialization, grants the following incentives to approved industrial projects that include technology transfer:

- Financing assistance: Low-cost financing through the Saudi Industrial Development Fund (SIDF) and the Public Investment Fund (PIF);
- Industrial facilities: Nominal rent on industrial sites and low fees for water and electricity;
- Duty exemption: Exemption from customs duties on imported production equipment and raw materials;
- Protective tariffs: Tariff protection once the local product achieves an approved standard;
- Tax credit: As a part of a major government drive to boost development in certain areas, it indicated that a tax credit will be granted to foreign investors based on their investment, employment, and training to Saudi nationals.

Until recently, the only effective tax treaty was with France, which covers corporate tax, personal tax, inheritance tax, capital tax, and *zakat*. The treaty was renewed for an additional five years from December 31, 2003. More new tax treaties have been signed between Saudi Arabia and several other countries including Austria, China, India, Pakistan, Malaysia, and

Turkey. At this time, the Government of Saudi Arabia is negotiating double tax treaties with Germany, Italy, the Netherlands, Russia, and the United Kingdom. Moreover, Saudi Arabia has entered into limited tax treaties with the United Kingdom, United States, and certain other countries for the reciprocal exemption from tax on income derived from the international operations of aircraft and ships (FITA 2007).

The United Arab Emirates

General

- Oil companies pay up to 55 percent tax on UAE sources' taxable income and pay royalties on their proceeds.
- Foreign banks pay 20 percent tax on their profits.
- There are no withholding or capital taxes.
- Income tax is assessed only on the profits of oil and gas and related petrochemical companies and on branches of foreign banks.
- The federal government of the UAE has not promulgated any tax laws.
- Each Emirate has its own tax legislation, however, in practice, personal income is not subject to taxation in the UAE.
- Several of the Emirates have free zones, which offer tax and business incentives including tax holidays for a guaranteed period.
- There is no VAT in the UAE at present and the federal government is considering introducing VAT at 5–7 percent.

The UAE is a high-income, stable federation with the second largest Arab economy in the Middle East. The non-oil sectors grew by 18.6 percent in 2006 and have tripled during the last three years. However, the country remains dependent on oil revenue, and the government has announced large oil-production capacity increases within the next seven years. Abu Dhabi is the major hydrocarbon and industrial power while Dubai is the trading, financial, and tourist center of the Emirates. Abu Dhabi and Dubai account for 80 percent of the UAE's income. Hydrocarbon revenues account for around one-third of the UAE's GDP, though the non-oil finance and service sectors in Dubai are making the city an attractive base for MNCs in the Gulf region (EIA 2007c).

From the tax perspective, each Emirate has its own tax legislation; however, in practice, personal income is not subject to taxation in the UAE. American citizens are, however, liable to taxation on their worldwide income. Most Emirates charge a municipal tax on the annual rental for residential properties. Entertainment (including hotels and restaurants) is also taxed. Customs duty rates on imports are low.

A number of tax-free trade areas exist aimed at stimulating commercial activities. Standard Chartered Bank has predicted that a 3–5 percent sales tax could be introduced within the next 18 months in the UAE as customs tariffs are dropped as part of planned free-trade agreements with its leading trading partners (Kerr 2007). Moreover, the UAE was ranked fifteenth in the world out of 144 countries in UNCTAD's inward FDI performance index. The UAE has low tariffs, low currency risk, extremely low financial risk, no restrictions on repatriation of profits or capital, and numerous double-taxation agreements (Siddiqi 2007).

However, in Dubai, with its enormous oil revenues the government has no need to raise income through direct taxation. Accordingly Dubai is now a "no tax" emirate characterized by an almost complete absence of taxation. There are no withholding or capital taxes. It had been suggested in August 2005 that the UAE was thinking about the introduction of a national sales tax, and reports suggested that the IMF had been asked by the UAE authorities to help develop a value-added tax system in an attempt to widen the country's tax base (Law and Tax 2007).

The IMF also reportedly urged the UAE to introduce a property tax and widen the corporate tax net across all sectors, warning that state budget surpluses, which have been dependent on high oil prices in recent times, are unsustainable without longer-term sources of tax revenues. However, the overall impression was that the emirate will at least remain free from income taxes for non-oil firms and individuals for the foreseeable future.

With the exception of banks and oil companies no corporate income tax is payable by businesses in Dubai (ibid.). In most of the Emirates, property tax is payable by residential and commercial tenants by reference to the annual rent of residential property, generally at a rate of 5 percent and for commercial property at a rate of 5–10 percent payable to the local municipality.

For hotels in the UAE, municipal taxes are imposed on their services. Service charge percentages vary among the Emirates. A service charge of 5–10 percent is charged on food purchased in restaurants. Hotels charge a 10–15 percent service charge per night on room rates. These charges are usually included in the customer's bill, which the municipality will collect from restaurants and hotels. Individuals living and working in Dubai, for example, pay a 10 percent service charge on food purchased in most restaurants. Hotels also charge an additional 15 percent service charge on the services they provide.

Taxable Income

In general, the federal government of the UAE has not promulgated any tax laws. Each emirate issues its own tax regulations and rules. However, with the exception of foreign banks and oil, gas, and petrochemical companies, no corporate income tax is payable by businesses in the UAE. The taxable income of banks is as per the audited financial statements whereas that of oil companies is as per the concession agreement. Oil companies also pay royalties on production (FITA 2007).

Most of the seven Emirates have issued their corporate tax decrees, but, in practice, taxes are only imposed on oil- and gas-producing companies at rates set forth in their government concession agreements, and on branches of foreign banks at rates set out in specific tax decrees or fixed in agreements with the Rulers of the Emirates in which the branches operate (Ernst & Young 2007).

The income tax decrees that have been enacted in each of the seven Emirates provide for tax to be imposed on the taxable income of all corporate businesses wherever incorporated, and their branches that carry on trade or business, at any time during the taxable year through a permanent establishment in the relevant Emirates. Companies are taxed if they carry on trade or business directly in the Emirate or indirectly through the agency of another company.

Tax Rates

In the UAE, there is no tax imposed either on individual incomes or on the profits of companies except oil, gas, and foreign banks. The only tax applicable to all the companies is the right taken by the municipality in every Emirate during the initiation or the renewal of a commercial license. This rate amounts to 10 percent of the annual amount of the offices and stores rent as well as 5 percent of the annual amount paid by the company to accommodate its employees (FITA 2007). Business properties pay a municipal tax set at 10 percent (2006) of annual rental value.

The corporate taxable income will be discussed for the three most important emirates: Abu-Dhabi, Dubai, and Sharjah; the other four emirates are almost the same. With respect to Abu-Dhabi, the Income Tax Decree imposes income taxes on all corporate entities carrying out trade or business in Abu Dhabi. However, in practice, corporate income tax is mainly imposed on two major businesses: Oil production and foreign banks. Oil- and gas-producing companies pay income taxes at rates specified in the relevant concession agreement with the Emirates' officials. Moreover oil companies also pay royalties on production. For foreign banks, corporate income taxes are imposed at rates specified in the relevant concession agreement with the government.

According to the Abu Dhabi Income Tax Decree, every chargeable person who conducts trade or business, including the rendering of any services in Abu Dhabi shall be subject to a sliding scale up to a maximum of 55 percent as shown in table 9.9.

A "chargeable person" means a business entity wherever incorporated, or each and every branch thereof, carrying on trade or business of any type during an income tax year through a permanent establishment physically located in the Emirate whether directly or through the agency of another business entity. However, some business may be entitled under an agreement with the ruler to an exemption from liability to income tax; in this case, they are not required to pay income taxes. According to the Abu Dhabi tax regulations, "Carrying on trade or business" means:

1. Selling goods or rights in such good in the the United Arab Emirate;
2. Operating any manufacturing, industrial, or commercial enterprise in the Emirate;
3. Renting any property located in the Emirate; or
4. Rendering services in the Emirate.

Taxable income is computed after the deduction of all costs and expenses incurred by a business entity earning such income. For tax purposes, deductible costs and expenses include acquisition cost of goods sold, the expenses of operating the business, allowances for depreciation, obsolescence, and exhaustion of both tangible and intangible assets and losses sustained by the business entity in connection with the business.

Dubai's tax-free environment makes the emirate an attractive place to live and work. Living in such a tax haven makes it easy to forget that the matter of taxes cannot be completely ignored for many foreign nationals. Quite often the tax laws of the investor's home country must be considered before taking the investment plunge into the Dubai property market (Jeker 2004).

Table 9.9 Corporate income tax rates of Abu Dhabi-UAE

Taxable Incomes		*Rate (%)*
Exceeding (DHS)	*Not Exceeding (DHS)*	
0	1,000,000	0
1,000,000	2,000,000	10
2,000,000	3,000,000	20
3,000,000	4,000,000	40
5,000,000	—	55

Both Dubai and Sharjah Emirates have similar income tax decrees; all companies carrying on trade or business in Dubai or Sharjah are required to pay tax on their earnings. The rates of tax are on a sliding scale up to a maximum of 55 percent. In practice, however, only

- Oil- and gas-producing companies pay tax at rates specified in the relevant concession agreement. Oil companies also pay royalties on production;
- Branches of foreign banks pay tax at a flat rate of 20 percent on annual profits. The taxable income of banks is calculated by reference to their audited financial statements.

For more details of the tax regulations in Dubai, Sharjah, and the other emirates, the tax regulations of Abu-Dhabi can be used as a reference because they are very much the same as the ones of the other emirates and there is no reason to repeat them again here.

Personal Income Tax

In general, there is no individual income tax or consumption tax in the UAE. Foreign banks pay 20 percent tax on their profits, and foreign oil companies with equity in concessions pay taxes and royalties on their proceeds (FITA 2007).

Transfer Pricing

There are no any specific tax regulations on transfer pricing other than the corporate tax regulations discussed earlier.

Customs Duties

Import duties have been largely standardized at 4 percent, but there are many exemptions, including food, building materials, medical products, and any item destined for the three free zones: Jebel Ali Free Zone, Dubai Internet City, and the Dubai International Financial Centre. Food products must carry dates of manufacture and expiry and meat for the local market must have a certificate to prove compliance with Islamic law. Dubai (as part of the UAE) and under an agreement with the GCC is required to levy 10 percent duty on all luxury goods (Law and Tax 2007).

By law, 70 goods have been exempted from tariffs, including medicines, agricultural machinery, pesticides, fertilizers, periodicals, wood, unstrung pearls, unworked silver and gold, iron and steel for use in construction, and raw or partially worked materials for use by local manufacturers. Goods produced within the GCC are also exempt from duties as are goods destined for the Jebel Ali Free Zone. Cigarettes are the exception to the general rule with the federal government approving a 100 percent tax. A 50 percent tax is levied on alcohol in Dubai (ibid.). In Sharjah alcoholic beverages are not allowed.

Capital Gains

There is no capital gains tax in the UAE. For tax-paying entities, capital gains are taxed as part of business profits.

Dividends, Interests, and Royalties

There is no tax on dividends distributed in the UAE. Interest is treated as a business expense and is deductible for tax purposes if the company's profits are taxable under the specific regulations of the emirate. Oil companies pay royalties on the production in addition to its corporate income tax liabilities. The rate of royalties is determined by the concession agreement with the ruler of the emirate.

Tax Incentives and Tax Holidays

Foreign MNCs have shown every confidence in the UAE market and many are willing to commit to expending serious sums of money on purchasing properties in Dubai. Profits can be lost though, by a lack of forethought concerning certain issues. Some matters involve local real estate property issues that are not present in other countries. The foreign MNC should take into account the country's tax matters before purchasing. Proper planning can alleviate the tax consequences of the home country regulations. At a minimum, the investor's initial purchasing considerations and cash projections should take into account these tax implications (Jeker 2004).

The potential investor should be aware that the UAE law is still a bit unsettled with regard to foreign ownership of real property. While the federal law does not prohibit the ownership of UAE property by a foreign national, to date, registration procedures have not yet been formulated (ibid.).

For tax incentive purposes, several of the Emirates in the UAE have free zones, which offer tax and business incentives aimed at making the UAE a global business and commercial center. The incentives usually include tax holidays for a guaranteed period (most free zones offer a tax holiday of 50 years), 100 percent foreign ownership, no customs duty within the free zone, and "one stop shop" administrative services (Ernst & Young 2007).

To avoid double taxation, the UAE has signed tax treaties with a growing list of countries, including Algeria, Armenia, Austria, Belarus, Belgium, Canada, China, the Czech Republic, Egypt, Finland, France, Germany, India, Indonesia, Italy, Korea, Lebanon, Luxembourg, Malaysia,

Mongolia, Morocco, Mozambique, Netherlands, New Zealand, Pakistan, Philippine, Poland, Romania, Singapore, Sri Lanka, Sudan, Switzerland, Syria, Tajikistan, Thailand, Tunisia, Turkey, Turkmenistan, Ukraine, the United States, and Yemen. Treaties have been concluded with Bosnia, Malta, Mauritius, Seychelles, and Spain but not formally ratified (ibid.).

The purpose of the treaties is to promote investment and trade between the parties to the treaty by eliminating double taxations. The treaty agreements benefit the residents in the UAE whose income arising in the UAE is subject to tax in a foreign country of the treaty countries. The benefits of the treaties may cover dividends, business income, and certain other types of income including personal income.

Summary and Conclusions

This chapter examines the tax rules and regulations of the six Gulf countries. The purpose of this chapter is fourfold: (1) to understand the taxation rules and regulations of the Gulf countries, (2) to guide MNCs and all other businessmen how to implement strategic tax planning for the purpose of investing and managing their businesses successfully within the Gulf countries' tax regulations and end up with the highest rate of return on their invested capital with the lowest possible business and political risks; (3) to help and guide potential investors to determine the most favorable country for particular investment; and (4) to look at regional opportunities for cost savings and chances for improvements in making tax affairs more effective for both host countries and investors.

First, this chapter discussed taxation in general and emphasized the essential need for a successful and effective tax planning for MNCs in the preliminary stage of feasibility study and, before they start investing in the Gulf countries, to take advantage of low tax rates, tax differences, holidays, tax treaties, and other incentives. Second, the characteristics of the tax rules and regulations of the six Gulf countries in general were analyzed. Regional tax coordination and trends and most of the potential advantages of well-designed regional tax planning were discussed.

Third, the tax regulations and rules of each country of the six Gulf countries were discussed separately. As can be seen from table 9.10, both Bahrain and the UAE have no corporate income taxes with the exception of the oil and gas companies with a maximum tax rate of 46 and 55 percent, respectively. Moreover, the UAE imposes tax on foreign banks at 20 percent. Ranking the Gulf countries in terms of the lowest corporate tax rates to the highest, Saudi Arabia is ranked first with the lowest tax rate of 20 percent; both Oman and Qatar come in second with a tax rate of 30 percent; Bahrain is ranked

Table 9.10 Gulf countries taxation at a glance

Countries	*Corp. Tax Rates*	*Personal Income Tax*	*Customs Duties (%)*	*Tax Treaties*	*Losses Carry Back*	*Losses Carry Forward*	*Tax Holiday*	*Other Taxes (d)*	*With-holding Taxes*
Bahrain	No except for Oil and Gas (46%)	No	5	(a)	No	No	No	12% Sales tax on gasoline	No
Kuwait	Up to 55%	No until now	5	(a)	No	Unlimited	10 yrs	No	No
Oman	Up to 30%	No	5	(a)	No	5 yrs	5 yrs	Yes	Yes
Qatar	Up to 30%	No	5	(a)	No	3 yrs	10 yrs	No	No
Saudi Arabia	Up to 20%	No	5	(a)	No	Unlimited	5–10 yrs	No	No
United Arab Emirates	Up to 55% on Oil and 20% on foreign banks	No	4	(a)	No	No	No	No	No

Source: (Ernst and Young 2007; EIA 2007; and FITA 2007).

Note: The table of footnotes should only be used as a guide.
(a) Double tax treaties have been signed with various countries.
(b) Withholding taxes are calculated at corporate tax rates on a deemed profit basis between 15 and 100% on the payments to non-residents.
(c) New customs duty regulations will be introduced soon.
(d) Other taxes include stamp duties, municipal taxes, and so on.

fourth with 46 percent; and both Kuwait and the UAE are ranked last with the highest tax rate of 55 percent. All the six countries have a low rate of customs duties of 5 percent, with the exception of the UAE that has a rate of 4 percent. There is no personal income tax in all the six countries as of today.

Finally, this chapter urges MNCs and any potential investor to pay attention to the design of an appropriate strategic tax planning. To be successful, the plan should fit into the Gulf region's political, cultural, and tax environment.

References

Bartlett, Sam. 1997. "Middle East Low Tax Myth Dispelled." *International Tax Review* London, Euromoney Publications PLC, March: 19–22.

Dennis-Escoffier, Shirley. 2007. "Tax Planning Opportunities for U.S. Taxpayers Working Abroad." *Practical Tax Strategies* (78) 1 (January): 12–13.

Economic Intelligence Unit (EIU). 2006. "Qatar: Country Fact Sheet." New York, November 6.

Energy Information Administration. 2007a. http://www.eia.doe.gov/emeu/international/bahrain.html. April 2007.

———. 2007b. http://www.eia.doe.gov/emeu/cabs/Saudi_Arabia.html. February 2007.

———. 2007c. http://www.eia.doe.gov/emeu/cabs/UAE/Background.html. July 2007.

Ernst & Young. 2007. "Corporate Taxation in the Middle East." January 1. http://www.ey.com/me.

Federation of International Trade Association (FITA). 2007. "Kuwait." January. http://www.fita.org/countries/kuwait.html.

———. 2007a. http://www.fita.org/countries/kuwait.html, January 2007.

———. 2007b. http://fita.org/countries/saudi.html, January 2007.

———. 2007c. http://www.fita.org/countries/UAE.html, January 2007.

———. 2007d. http://www.eia.doe.gov/emeu/cabs/Qatar/pdf.pdf.

GCC (The Cooperation Council of the Arab States of the Gulf) 2003. "Common Customs Law of the GCC States," http://library.gcc-sg.org/English.

Gordon, Michael. 1999. "No Representation without Taxation." *Middle East*, London, March: 19–20.

Jeker, Virginia La Torre. 2004. "The UAE Property Buying Frenzy," September issue of *UAE MONEY works* at http://www.getyourmoneyworking.com.

Kerr, Simeon. 2007. "Fiscal Clouds Loom over Gulf Expats." *Financial times*, London, U.K., June 29: 11.

Law and Tax. 2007. http://www.lawandtax-news.com/html/dubai/jdblatdctx.html#customs-August.

Siddiqi, Moin. 2007. "The Success Story Surges Onwards and Upward." *Middle East*, Issue 379, London, June: 36–42.

10

The Development of Securities Regulations in the Gulf Countries

Sivakumar Velayutham and Thoraya Al-Hajj

Introduction

While capital markets have been established in GCC (Gulf Cooperation Council) countries since 1977 (Kuwait Stock Exchange was established in December 1977) the enactment of codified securities regulation and establishment of independent securities regulators is rather a new phenomenon. In Oman, the Capital Market Law establishing the Capital Market Authority was enacted in 1998. This was followed by the establishment of the Emirates Securities and Commodities Authority in the United Arab Emirates (UAE) in 2000. The Securities and Exchange Commission in Saudi Arabia was inaugurated in 2003 and the Qatar Financial Markets Authority (QFMA) in 2005 through Law No. 33 of year 2005. This is an indication of tremendous interest in securities regulation in the last seven years although stock markets have been in existence in GCC countries for more than 20 years. Recent studies also suggest that the GCC stock markets are strongly co-integrated (Hammoudeh, Al-Eisa, and Al-Nsour 2003).

The GCC is a security-economic grouping of six countries (Saudi Arabia, Oman, UAE, Bahrain, Qatar, and Kuwait) between the Red Sea and the Arabian Gulf, which was formed in 1981. The six countries share a common language (Arabic) and religion (Islam) and political systems (monarchies). Furthermore unlike most economies in the world where the government is reliant on taxation for its revenue, the main source of government revenue in all the GCC countries, with the exception of Bahrain, is from the export of oil and gas, as they possess nearly half of the world's proven oil reserves. Many of the companies listed on the stock exchanges are also substantially state owned or have substantial state investment. The role of the stock market in this context is slightly different from that in many other countries and the recent development in securities regulation is of particular interest.

The purpose of this chapter is to evaluate the recent interest in the development of securities regulation and evaluate the regulatory approach adopted in the GCC countries. This essay examines the capacity of "public interest" and "group interest" theories to explain the origins of development of securities regulation in the GCC countries. The first hypothesis follows from the view that regulation can be attributed to market failure and, therefore, regulation means to prevent market failure and in the process maximize social welfare. The second hypothesis suggests that individuals form coalitions or constituencies, to protect and promote their interests by lobbying the government. This essay also evaluates the quality of the regulation. It is shown that the political-economic contingency model best explains the development of securities regulation in GCC countries.

The next section provides a brief overview of the theories of regulation and the purpose of securities regulation. The third section provides a background of the development of securities markets in GCC countries. The fourth section examines the capacity of "public interest" and "group interest" theories to explain the origins of development of securities regulation in GCC countries. The fifth section provides an overview of the specific economic features of GCC countries and highlights the inability of the state to supply funds for investment as the driver for the recent interest in securities regulation in GCC countries. The sixth section consists of an evaluation of the securities regulation using IOSCO principles as a benchmark and the performance of the stock markets since, with some concluding remarks in the final section.

Rationale for Securities Regulation

The International Organization of Securities Commissions (IOSCO) identifies three core objectives of securities regulation, which are (1) protecting investors; (2) ensuring that markets are fair, efficient, and transparent; (3) reducing the extent of systemic risk. Fair, efficient, and transparent markets are recognized as critical to efficient flow of capital within an economy. A major impediment to financial markets working properly is information asymmetry (Scott 1995). When this occurs investors would recognize that the market is not a "level playing field" and would either withdraw from capital markets or lower the amount they are willing to pay for any security. This would seriously undermine the useful role financial markets can play in the development of the economy (ibid.). Securities regulation is, therefore, the means through which governments attempt to reduce information asymmetry in the markets and ensure that capital markets are functioning properly.

Regulation generally suggests some form of "intentional restriction of a subject's choice of activity, by an entity, not directly party to, or involved in that activity" (Mitnick 1980), implying that a third party is involved. Mitnick (1980) further points out that at the base of most regulatory instruments there is some formal rationalization that the regulation is to proceed in the "public interest." The standard "public interest" theory of regulation is based on two assumptions (Shleifer 2005). First, unhindered markets often fail because of the problem of monopolies or externalities. Second, governments are benign and capable of correcting these market failures through regulation. This view has a historical antecedent: regulation in the past (and even today) had almost always followed some form of crisis or public dissent. For example the Securities and Exchange Commission in the United States was formed after the stock market crash in 1929 (Carosso 1970; Galbraith 1955) and the Food and Drug Act was passed following the drug accident in 1937.

To achieve its aim, regulation in the public interest should aim at providing the public with all relevant information necessary for decision making and/or strive to protect the public from monopolies or industries that generate substantial external costs or benefit (Uche 2000). This does not always happen in practice (Posner 1974). Public-interest theories have, therefore, been subjected to a number of criticisms, associated mainly with the Chicago School of Law and Economics. These criticisms proceed in three intellectual steps (Shleifer 2005). First, markets and private orderings can take care of most market failures without any government intervention at all let alone regulation. Second, in the few cases when markets might not work perfectly, private litigation can address whatever conflicts market participants might have. Third, even if markets and courts cannot solve all problems perfectly, government regulators are incompetent, corrupt, and captured. So regulation would make things even worse.

Following from this, weaknesses of the explanatory power of the public-interest theory, Stigler (1971) asserted that "as a rule, regulation is acquired by the industry and is designed and operated primarily for its benefits." This proposition has come to be known as the "group interest" or capture theory of regulation. From this perspective, regulation, far from supporting the general public interest by achieving efficiency gains, is enacted and implemented in the interest of specialist producer groups. Proponents of this theory argue that people in their political behavior cannot be assumed to be motivated by fundamentally different forces other than in their private choice-making behavior. Self-interest is usually put above all other interests (Stigler 1971). It is pointed out that persuading a customer to utilize one's services will no doubt produce a payoff, but the same can also be achieved by getting the government to impose some form of tariff on your competitors or to grant subsidies. Ricketts and Shaw (1984) conclude that the choice between market and political action is essentially an economic one and will depend upon the relative costs involved and the chance of success in each case. The major problem with this theory is that it is notoriously difficult to prove (McCraw 1975; Skowronek 1982).

Recent evidence suggests that neither the public-interest hypothesis nor the group-interest hypothesis can by itself account for the complex social processes at work to establish regulation (McCraw 1975; Burk 1985; Uche 2000). Uche (2000) shows how regulation serves different purposes for different interest groups on different occasions. It is pointed out that regulation imposed on the grounds of public interest may sometimes end up serving the interest of the regulated group (for example, the Prohibition of Advertising Act 1971 regulating the tobacco industry). Burk (1985) in his study of the origins of the federal securities regulation in the United States (Securities Act of 1933 and Securities Exchange Act of 1934) ties the origins of this regulation both to moral concerns to protect the public interest and to instrumental concerns to safeguard the tenure of elected government officials. This highlights the importance of case studies and comparative studies to better understand the forces that drive regulation.

Development of Securities Markets and Regulation in GCC countries

The first official Stock Exchange in a Gulf country was established in Kuwait in 1977. The establishment of the stock exchange followed a long period (since the 1950s) of domestic equity trading (Al Rimawi 2001). The establishment of the official stock exchange was motivated by spiraling levels of speculation in the stocks of local companies ending with the first market collapse in early 1977 when share values dropped by nearly 20 percent (Al-Yahya 1993). Al Rimawi (2001) attributes the lack of official interest in regulating the domestic Kuwaiti securities market to Kuwait's official active interest in investing substantial funds abroad. In December 1977 the government opened and regulated an official stock exchange and intervened to maintain share prices (Seznec 1987).

Strict regulations, however, contributed to equity trading on an *ad hoc* nonofficial local Kuwaiti market known as Souk Al Manakh, which ended in a crash in 1982 with aggregate bad debts amounting to US$7.7bn (Seznec 1987). Al Rimawi (2001) observes that the collapse of the Souk Al-Manakh (and the colossal financial bailout that the Kuwaiti government undertook in its aftermath) sent shock waves beyond Kuwaiti domestic markets and made other Gulf countries more skeptical about equity markets. The extensive financial bailout undertaken by the government resulted in state-owned companies holding between 48 and 50 percent of traded shares (Azzam 1997). The Kuwaiti government issued new Decrees in 1983 establishing the Kuwaiti Exchange as an autonomous juristic person and enhancing the powers of the exchange with the minister of commerce and industry chairing the Kuwait Stock Exchange Committee.

This did not, however, hinder the formation of the Saudi Arabian Stock Market in 1985 although informal trading has been in existence since the 1950s. The formation of the Saudi Arabian Stock Market was followed by the Muscat Securities Market in Oman in 1988 and the Bahrain Stock Market 1989. Qatar and the UAE, however, did not establish their official stock markets until 1997 and 2000, respectively. In Saudi Arabia and Bahrain the respective monetary agencies Saudi Arabian Monetary Authority (SAMA) and Bahrain Monetary Agency (BMA) were charged with the day-to-day regulation of the Market. In Oman, the Muscat Securities Market (MSM) was set up as an independent self-regulating organization.

The first GCC country to issue a formal securities law and establish an independent securities regulator was Oman in 1998. Royal Decree 80/98 dated November 9, 1998, provided for the establishment of two separate entities: a regulator, to be named the Capital Market Authority (CMA), which will be a governmental authority responsible for organizing and overseeing the issue and trading of securities in the Sultanate, and an exchange, to be named the Muscat Securities Market (MSM) where all listed securities shall be traded. The exchange will also be a governmental entity, financially and administratively independent from the authority but subject to its supervision. The board of directors of the Capital Market Authority is chaired by the minister of commerce and industry.

The UAE Federal No. 4 of 2000 established the Emirates Securities and Commodities Authority (ESCA) in February 2000. The UAE is probably one of few countries to establish an independent securities regulator prior to formation of stock exchanges. This could probably be attributed to the UAE being made up of seven semiautonomous emirates (states). The desire by both Abu Dhabi and Dubai to have independent stock exchanges probably contributed to a feeling in the federal government that an independent securities regulator would contribute to the development of a more organized securities market in the UAE without resulting in undue competition between the two stock exchanges. Following the establishment of the ESCA in February 2000 the Dubai Financial Market commenced operation in March 2000 and Abu Dhabi Securities Market was established in November 2000.

The Saudi Arabian government followed Oman and the UAE in establishing an independent regulator—the Saudi Arabian Securities and Exchange Commission (SASEC)—by passing the Capital Markets Law in June 2003. The Commission is to be governed by five commissioners, who will be appointed by Royal Decree. The commissioners were only appointed in April 2004 and are to be chaired by deputy chairman of the Saudi Arabian Monetary Authority.

In February 2004, the Capital Market Supervision Directorate of the Bahrain Monetary Agency (renamed the Central Bank of Bahrain) issued a Consultation Paper on the Securities and Exchange Regulations, which are expected to be adopted soon. The consultation paper provides for a comprehensive securities regulation although it does not envision the establishment of an independent regulator. The Bahrain Monetary Agency is to continue regulation of the securities market. The youngest securities regulator in the GCC is the Qatar Financial Markets Authority (QFMA) created in 2005 through Law No. 33 of year 2005. It is to operate as an independent regulatory authority managing the regulatory regime of financial markets in Qatar. The securities market in Kuwait is regulated by the Kuwait Stock Exchange Committee, which is chaired by the minister of commerce and industry, and includes representatives from the Ministry of Finance and the Central Bank. The Committee issues orders relating to share dealings, work of jobbers, and related areas.

It is also important to note that Qatar and Dubai have also created offshore financial centers called the Dubai International Financial Center (DIFC) and the Qatar Financial Center (QFC), respectively. The DIFC also includes the Dubai International Financial Exchange (DIFX), which is a stock exchange. These centers are regulated by their own independent regulatory authorities: the Dubai Financial Services Authority (DFSA) and the QFC Regulatory Authority, respectively. These authorities are not included in the study that focuses on national regulatory authorities regulating local stock exchanges.

The preceding review highlights a recent interest in securities regulation and independent securities regulators although stock markets have been in existence since the 1970s. The next section provides an overview of the specific economic features of the GCC countries and evaluates the recent interest in securities regulation in the GCC countries.

Public Interest or Group Interest

Public interest has been the most frequent argument used to explain the development of securities regulation in the United States following market failures disclosed by the stock markets crash in 1929 (Carosso 1970; Galbraith 1955; Philips and Zecher 1981). Three kinds of market failures have been identified to explain the development of the Securities Act of 1933 in the United States. The first was the perception that there was an excess of speculation during the 1920s, that is, a "speculative orgy" (Cowing 1965). Congressional leaders observed that bankers and the Federal Reserve had fed excess speculation by diverting credit from productive purposes to sustain the stock market boom.

Fraudulent sale of securities was a second kind of market failure disclosed during Senate investigations into stock exchange practices during 1933 and 1934 (Carosso 1970; Mintz 1981). Bankruptcies and defaults made clear that many new securities sold were worthless. Investment banks were blamed for not carefully verifying the values underlying securities they underwrote, creating opportunities for unscrupulous issuers to misrepresent (or siphon) their corporate assets.

Finally, manipulation of stock prices was identified as the third kind of failure. Senate investigations revealed the formation of double markets in some securities, for example, when J.P.Morgan & Co "sold" securities below market price to a "preferred list" of customers (Burk 1985).

More evidence, however, indicates that the market never failed. First, recent economic history documents that even large departures from the ideal of "perfect markets" do not cause markets to fail to produce prices closely approximating prices to be expected from perfect competition (Hawke 1980). Furthermore quantitative research also indicated that speculative trading during the 1920s did not lead to excessive overvaluing of securities (Sirkin 1975). A review of the evidence on fraudulent or misleadingly prepared financial statements prior to the enactment of the 1934 Act has also revealed very little evidence of abuses in reporting (Benston 1973).

Similar to the situation in the United States in 1929 there was no major market failure in the GCC stock markets. From table 10.1 it can be observed that there was a decline of stock market indices in all the GCC countries in 1998 but not really a crash with the exception of Oman, which saw the index halved. Table 10.1 also shows that there was no excessive speculation in the

Table 10.1 Arab Monetary Fund Index for GCC stock markets

	2006	*2005*	*2004*	*2003*	*2002*	*2001*	*2000*	*1999*	*1998*	*1997*	*1996*	*1995*	*1994*
Abu Dhabi Stock Exchange	211	353	228	136	107	100	—	—	—	—	—	—	—
Bahrain Stock Exchange	187	183	160	135	111	97	109	122	123	137	96	91	100
Saudi Stock Market	403	878	410	202	133	130	128	120	91	136	113	100	
Kuwait Stock Market	402	435	287	259	158	134	102	96	97	157	147	118	100
Dubai Financial Market	379	828	350	156	121	100	—	—	—	—	—	—	—
Muscat Securities Market	198	186	139	115	84	64	89	112	115	265	127	104	100
Doha Securities Market	368	554	307	206	135	100	—	—	—	—	—	—	—

Source: Arab Monetary Fund.

GCC stock markets, again with the possible exception of Oman. The effect of the decline in the GCC stock markets on the general economy was also small because market capitalization as a percentage of GDP is smaller than in OECD and East Asian countries. There is also considerable evidence to suggest that the decline in share price could be attributed to decline in the price of oil (figure 10.1). Hammoudeh, Al-Eisa, and Al-Nsour (2003) found that the GCC stock markets are strongly co-integrated or have many long-run relations and are co-moved over time by three common forces namely the price of oil, U.S. interest rates, and political news. Furthermore, there were no major bankruptcies that have caught public attention. This could be partly attributed to the fact that many of the companies listed on the GCC stock markets have been banks, and listed companies in trouble have been rescued early.

As highlighted earlier, an alternative explanation for regulation has been the operation of group interest or frequently referred to as capture theory. This theory focuses on the interests of the group/s to be regulated. In the case of the Securities Act 1933, the influence financiers exercised in framing the legislation was primarily negative (Burk 1985). Similarly in the GCC countries the only interest group with sufficient influence would be family businesses with close affiliation to the state. The family businesses have generally benefited from their close affiliation to the state through cheap finance from the state to expand their business interests and have little to benefit from securities regulation enacted in the various GCC states.

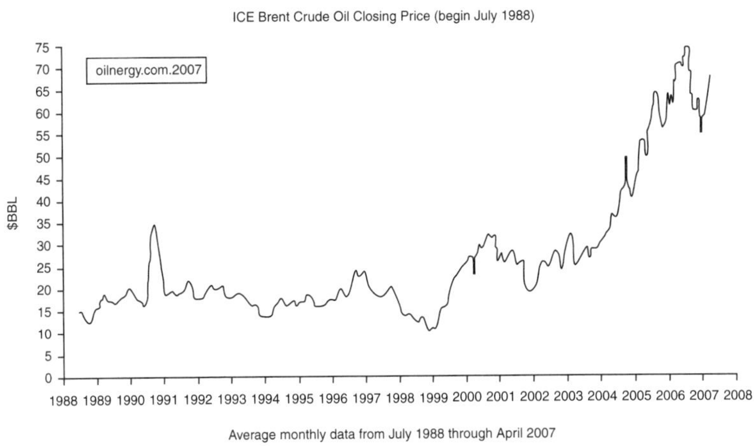

Figure 10.1 ICE Brent crude oil closing prices.

Source: (http://www.oilnergy.com/1obrent.htm#since88, 2007).

Professional bodies have generally been weak with little influence in the decision-making process (Velayutham and Al Segini 2002).

This review highlights that neither the public-interest theory nor the group-interest theory can provide a complete explanation for the recent interest in securities regulation and independent securities regulators in the GCC countries.

The Role of Political-Economic Contingency, Oil Revenue and Government Investment

Unlike explanations for the adoption of regulation in parliamentary democracies that rely heavily on government and parliamentary reports, explanations in the GCC countries have to be based on economic developments alone since there is a scarcity of government reports. There is also frequently a lack of public debate. This section is, therefore, mainly based on economic developments in the GCC countries prior to the adoption of securities regulation.

Political-Economic contingencies play an important part in shaping the expansion of government roles. Based on his analysis of the federal government's growth and transformation during the populist and progressive eras, Skowronek (1982) argues forcefully that "state building remains at all times a political contingency, a historical structural question." It is pointed out that officials try to alter the institutions of government in response to perceived crisis or class conflict, and they do so in order to maintain their power and legitimacy. But whether they will successfully refashion institutions and relations between state and society is always a matter of uncertainty (Skowronek 1982). It is emphasized that the correlation between intentions and outcomes is unpredictable because attempts to reform are mediated by preexisting institutional and political arrangements that cannot easily be foretold (Skowronek 1982). Burk (1985) concludes that the success of officials at expanding the government's role depends on political contingencies that are not determined entirely by the perception of crisis or by the structural interests to which officials would respond.

As highlighted in the introduction, the GCC is a security-economic grouping of six countries (Saudi Arabia, Oman, the UAE, Bahrain, Qatar, and Kuwait) between the Red Sea and the Arabian Gulf formed in February 1981, a few months after the war between Iraq and Iran had started. The six countries share a common language (Arabic) and religion (Islam) and have similar political systems (monarchies). The UAE is a federation of seven emirates, each with its own ruler. The Federal Supreme

Council (FSC) consisting of the rulers of the seven emirates is the highest constitutional authority in the UAE. The FSC appoints the president and vice president and sanctions federal legislation. Saudi Arabia and Qatar are absolute monarchies with appointed advisory councils (Majlis Al-Shura) while Oman has an appointed and elected advisory council. Kuwait and Bahrain are monarchies, with elected parliaments and head of government appointed by the monarch.

The GCC countries, while rich in oil reserves, are not highly populated in comparison to its neighbors and, therefore, the grouping was a means to collective security. While security was the main stimulus of the new organization, its declared objective was to effect the social and economic integration of the member states (Zahlan 1998). With respect to social and economic integration, the GCC has made major strides. The Unified Economic Agreement signed in 1983 committed the countries to freedom of movement, work, and residence, free movement of capital, a free-trade zone, customs union, and harmonization of investment rules and regulations. The agreement also contains clauses relating to the establishment of a monetary union of GCC members and the launch of a single currency.

All the GCC countries except for Bahrain have major reserves of oil and gas, which accounts for a major portion of their respective Gross Domestic Products (GDP), for example, 62 percent in Qatar, 42 percent in Saudi Arabia's GDP, and 23 percent in Bahrain's GDP (http://library.gcc-sg.org/gccstatvol15/EcoStat/eco76.htm, 2004). Oil and gas exports also account for the major portion of government revenues ranging from 80 percent in Saudi Arabia to 67 percent in UAE. Due to the high oil revenues, the GCC governments are not reliant on taxation for its funding of government expenditure and investment. Growth in most GCC economies is driven by public-sector investment rather than by private-sector investments. Figure 10.2 shows the ratio of private investment to public investment to be less than 2 while the same ratio in OECD countries is close to 6 and in the fast-growing east Asian economies it is close to 5 (Sala-I-Martin and Artadi 2003). Most studies of financial-sector development in GCC and other Middle East and North African countries highlight the dominance of the financial system by banks (frequently public banks) and the poor development of capital markets (Chalk et al. 1996; Nashashibi, Elhage and Fedelino 2001; Creane et al. 2004). Hakura (2004) in her study of growth in the Middle East and North Africa observes that in GCC countries, where oil revenues are significant, large governments have been a key factor stifling private-sector growth and impeding diversification.

The state rather than private investors became the major source of funds for many state-owned and even private companies. For example, in Kuwait the state-owned Kuwait Investment Authority has major equity

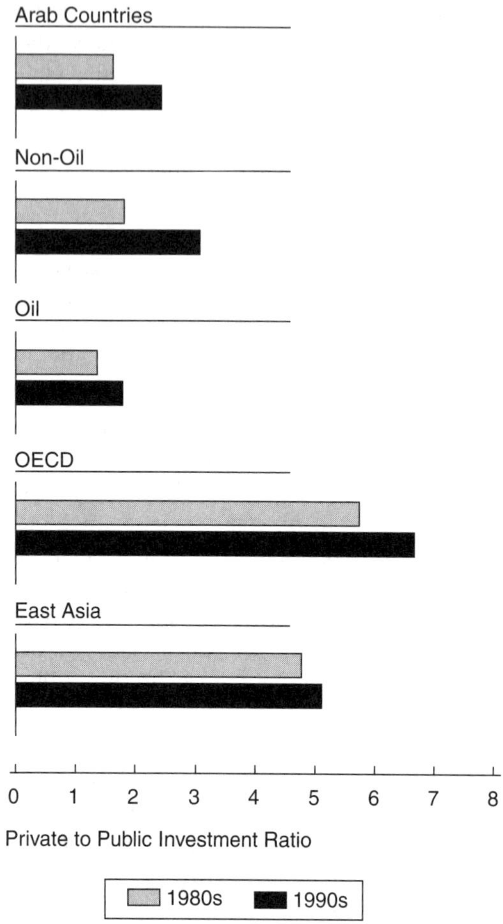

Figure 10.2 Private to public investment ratio over time.

Source: X Sala-I-Martin and E.V. Artadi (2003).

stakes in many local companies either directly or through subsidiaries such as the Kuwait Investment Company (incorporated in 1961) (Wilson 1983). The driver for the establishment of securities markets in the GCC countries was, therefore, not to mobilize funding for investments but rather to provide citizens with investment opportunities in government-owned companies, formalize the trading of shares in joint stock companies, and prevent future market collapses like that which occurred in Kuwait in 1977. This is reflected in the early companies listed on the GCC stock markets. These were companies with a high level of government ownership such as the National Bank of Kuwait and Kuwait National Airways, and banks. The high oil revenue not only enabled the state to be a major source of funds for investments but also enabled the state to undertake major financial bailouts in the case of a market collapse through active intervention in the market, as in the case of Kuwait in 1977 and 1982.

High government expenditure also attracted a lot of foreign companies interested in meeting consumer demand for household and luxury goods. The governments in the six GCC countries generally restricted foreign investment in local business to 49 percent, to promote local participation in the businesses. Since many of the foreign companies were focused on marketing their goods and services in the GCC countries they sought out influential local family businesses to be the local partners. A number of family businesses, therefore, came to dominate the GCC business scene.

In the late 1990s, however, oil prices hit new lows not seen since the 1970s, as shown in figure 10.1. IPE Brent Crude Oil closing prices dropped as low as US$12 per barrel in 1999. GDP growth rates also plunged in 1998 as illustrated in table 10.2. GDP growth rates for all GCC countries were negative for 1998, not seen since the first Iraq war in 1990–91. The economic situation required the GCC countries to rethink their economic policies. The drop in oil prices reduced government revenues considerably in many GCC countries and forced the budgets in many GCC countries into big deficits as illustrated in table 10.3. In an IMF report on the Middle East, Iqbal (2001) observes that before the 1997–98 downturn in oil price

> the major oil-exporting countries responded to episodes of falling oil prices with a combination of financing and adjustment. Substantial external reserves and the low level of public debt allowed room to finance external current account and fiscal deficits. Adjustments were largely undertaken through cuts in capital outlays, which also adversely affected private sector growth and did not correct the underlying structural weaknesses of the economy. The adjustment strategy during these earlier episodes of declining oil prices thus did not seek a lasting solution....

Iqbal (2001) observes that the oil price downturn of 1997–98 spurred a policy response "that sought to fundamentally reform underlying structural distortions—not only to deal with the short term adverse effects of fluctuating oil price receipts, but also to establish a firm foundation for reducing dependence on oil and facilitating sustained growth of the non-oil sector." A central plank of this reform strategy was to narrow the role of the government sector since the state could not afford to finance investment in the economy. The role of the government was narrowed through public-sector restructuring and privatization,

Table 10.2 Annual growth rates of gross domestic product of the GCC countries

Country	*2005*	*2004*	*2003*	*2002*	*2001*	*2000*	*1999*	*1998*	*1997*	*1996*	*1995*	*1994*
United Arab Emirates	15.4	11.1	171	8.8	–1.4	27.8	13.8	–5.3	6.7	12.1	11.9	7.1
Bahrain	19.7	15.2	14.8	6.5	–0.5	20.4	7.1	–2.6	4.1	4.3	5.1	7.0
Saudi Arabia	24.7	16.6	13.7	3	–2.9	17.1	10.3	–11.5	4.6	10.7	18.5	1.4
Oman	24	13.7	7.2	1.8	0.4	26.5	11.5	–11.1	3.7	10.7	6.8	3.4
Qatar	20.7	20	20.3	11.1	–0.1	43.3	20.8	–9.2	24.7	11.3	10.4	3.0
Kuwait	35	22.5	31.3	3.2	–7.9	22.9	16.1	–14.5	–3.5	16.1	9.2	3.3

Source: Arab Monetary Fund.

Table 10.3 Overall government revenue, expenditure, and surplus/deficit of the GCC countries between 1994 and 2004

Country		*2004*	*2003*	*2002*	*2001*	*2000*	*1999*	*1998*	*1997*	*1996*	*1995*	*1994*
UAE	Revenue	25,349	20,513	15,580	18,688	20,255	12,182	11,630	15,301	17,556.5	14,271.3	12,557.6
	Expenditure	24,905	24,180	23,585	25,993	22,891	20,222	19,461	17,533	19,479.7	16,925.6	14,925.6
	Surp/def	444	−3,666	−8,005	−7,305	−2,636	−8,040	−7,830	−2,233	−1,923.2	−2,654.6	−2,368
Bahrain	Revenue	2,954	2,579	2,263	2,678	2,885	1,838	1,474	1,809	1,637	1,400.5	1,266.8
	Expenditure	2,761	2,638	2,433	2,760	2,709	2,193	1,784	2,142	1,833.2	1,837.2	1,521.8
	Surp/def	193	−59	−170	−82	175	−355	−310	−333	−146.3	−336.7	−155.1
Saudi Arabia	Revenue	104,611	78,667	56,875	60,842	68,909	39,373	37,812	54,873	47,823.8	39,060	34,441.9
	Expenditure	76,053	66,667	62,350	68,037	62,836	49,089	50,750	59,085	52,897.2	46,385	45,681.2
	Surp/def	28,558	12,000	−5,475	−7,195	6,073	−9,716	−12,938	−4,211	−5,073.4	−7,325	−11,239.3
Oman	Revenue	10,423	8,596	7,827	6,605	5,956	4,671	4,802	5,896	5,155.4	4,765.6	4,570.6
	Expenditure	9,230	8,294	7,645	7,439	6,908	5,901	5,778	6,001	5,659.6	6,062.4	5,859.3
	Surp/def	1193	303	183	−833	−953	−1,230	−979	−104	−504.1	−1,296.9	−1,288.7
Qatar	Revenue	8,140	6,882	7,288	5,517	5,043	4,196	4,176	4,050	3,065.7	3,315.4	2,804.9
	Expenditure	5,166	5,221	5,532	5,393	4,862	4,841	4,698	4,972	3,912.4	3,672.5	3,591.2
	Surp/def	2,974	1,660	1,756	124	181	−645	−522	−922	−846.7	−357.1	−786.3
Kuwait	Revenue	23,367	20,597	17,394	16,170	17,169	9,197	11,837	14,479	11,597.8	10,387.6	9,324.9
	Expenditure	18,602	16,320	15,471	10,382	13,136	13,281	13,051	12,819	13,779.9	14,047.6	14,250
	Surp/def	4,765	4,277	1,923	5,788	4,033	−4,084	−1,214	1,660	−2,182.1	−3,660	−4,925.1

Source: Arab Monetary Fund.

correcting prices of officially supplied inputs to reduce implicit subsidies, strengthening the financial sector's ability to mobilize and allocate savings more efficiently (Iqbal 2001). The countries also introduced regulatory reform to encourage the foreign direct investment that will deepen and diversify the economic base.

The 1998 oil price crash was also preceded by the East-Asian economic crisis of 1997, which saw the currencies of Thailand, South Korea, Malaysia, and the Philippines dive by 35–50 percent against the American dollar. Furthermore the stock markets in all five countries lost 60 percent of their market capitalization in American-dollar terms. Whilst the collapse of the East-Asian and South-East Asian economies was attributed to huge overseas debt, wasteful use of resources, speculative property investment, and the over-expansion of industrial capacity, the finger was also pointed at the lack of accountability in state and corporate governance. An IMF staff report (1998) identified "a lack of enforcement of prudential rules and inadequate supervision of financial systems, problems resulting from the limited availability of data and a lack of transparency, as well as problems of governance" (19) to be principal causes of the financial crisis.

A recent World Bank Report (2003) reported that better governance was critical to development in MENA countries and that improved governance could contribute to a 1 percent increase in economic growth. The report emphasized the importance of accountability and inclusiveness to governance. The report observed that when compared with countries that have similar incomes and characteristics—the main competitors in the global marketplace—the MENA region ranks at the bottom on the index of overall governance quality, as can be seen from figure 10.3.

The preceding review highlights the internal economic pressures from a downturn in oil prices, external economic events such as the East-Asian economic crisis, and the pressure of economic reports from international bodies such as the IMF and World Bank—all playing a role in the enactment of securities regulation. The enactment of securities regulation in GCC countries was also part of a wider economic reform process. There was a realization that the state could not only finance investment in the economy but also would be hard-pressed to bail out investors and companies in case of a market collapse. Following conventional wisdom that for the stock market to be an effective mobilizer of private capital for investment, there must be regulation to protect investors and ensure that markets are fair, efficient, and transparent (IOSCO 1998), the GCC countries started enacting securities regulations and the establishment of independent regulators.

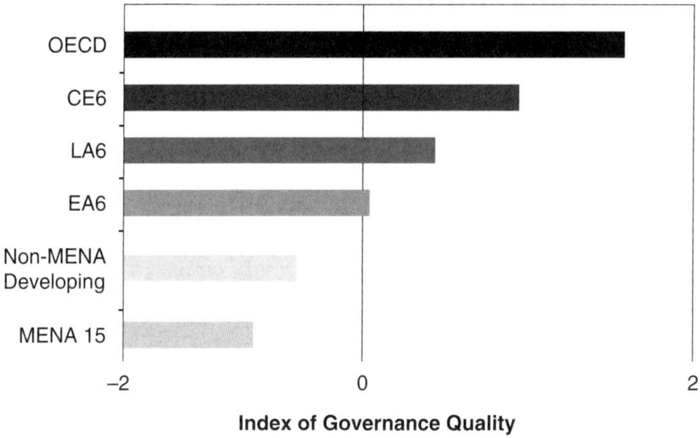

Figure 10.3 Compared with other regions, MENA shows a clear governance gap.

Source: World Bank (2002).

Notes: (CE6) include Bulgaria, the Czech Republic, Hungary, Poland, Romania, and the Slovak Republic. Latin American countries (LA6) include Argentina, Brazil, Chile, Mexico, Republica Bolivariana de Venezuela, and Uruguay. East Asian countries (EA6) include Indonesia, Malaysia, the Philippines, Singaphore, Thailand, and Vietnam. (MENA 15) includes Algeria, the Arab Republic of Egypt, Bahrain, the Islamic Republic of Iran, Jordan Kuwait, Lebanon, Morocco, Oman, Qatar, the Republic of Yemen, Saudi Arabia, the Syrian Arab Republic, Tunisia, and the United Arab Emirates.

An Evaluation

The earlier review highlights the political and economic contingencies that contributed to the enactment of codified securities regulation and establishment of independent securities regulators in GCC countries. However, it is not clear whether the securities regulation enacted are cosmetic and the independent securities regulators have had an impact on the development of the securities market. The International Organization of Securities Commissions was formed in 1983 and has become the leading international grouping of securities market regulators. Its current membership comprises regulatory bodies from more than 90 countries. In September 1998 IOSCO produced its statement of Objectives and Principles of Securities Regulation as a benchmark standard of regulatory best practices against which regulators around the world can reliably measure their own regulations.

IOSCO identifies the following three core objectives of securities regulation:

- The protection of investors;
- Ensuring that markets are fair, efficient, and transparent;
- The reduction of systemic risk.

The statement identifies the desirable attributes of a regulator as follows (IOSCO 1998):

1. The responsibilities of the regulator should be clear and objectively stated.
2. The regulator should be operationally independent and accountable in the exercise of its functions and powers.
3. The regulator should have adequate powers, proper resources, and the capacity to perform its functions and exercise its powers.
4. The regulator should adopt clear and consistent regulatory processes.
5. The staff of the regulator should observe the highest professional standards, including appropriate standards of confidentiality.

Overall the securities laws in the GCC countries are very general, with few specific provisions providing the regulator with wide powers to develop rules. The responsibilities of the regulators in each country are clearly and objectively stated. The laws in all the five countries have the general objectives of investor protection, securities market development, and regulation. The regulators in all of the five countries enjoy juristic personality, and financial and administrative independence. While the regulator in Bahrain is not a separate body, the Capital Market Supervision (CMS) Directorate has it own independent resources (Chapter 2, Article 42). A board consisting of five to nine members with a term of three to five years administers the regulators in the five countries. In the UAE, Qatar, and Oman the Board is chaired by the minister for commerce and dominated by representatives from the Ministry of Finance and Central Bank. In Saudi Arabia the Board is chaired by the deputy governor of the Central Bank. From this it can be observed that while the regulators in Oman, Saudi Arabia, and the UAE are established as independent statutory bodies—separate from the executive government—they are closely attached to the executive government by nature of their membership. Furthermore, the regulators in the four countries are accountable to the council of ministers or prime minister.

The regulation establishing the regulators in the UAE, Oman, and Saudi Arabia provide the regulators with wide-ranging powers, perhaps too much power with few checks because the regulation is very brief and general and the relationship between the executive government and the regulator is very close through membership. Among GCC states the Capital Markets Law in Oman most clearly spells out the authority of the regulator to carry out investigation and disciplinary action as well as provisions for the establishment of a grievance committee to hear complaints made by parties concerned against resolutions made by the regulator. The Capital Markets Authority in Oman and the Securities and Commodities Authority in the UAE have good websites in which organizational structure and responsibilities of the various departments are clearly stated. In addition the Capital Markets Authority in Oman articulates its views, interpretations of the law, and approach to enforcement formally through circulars and decisions. The reasons for the decisions are, however, frequently not stated.

The securities regulation in the UAE and Saudi Arabia require Board members to disclose their interests in securities and changes in ownership of securities. The regulations in Oman are silent on the issue. Other than this there is little mention of confidentiality. In terms of transparency the regulator in Oman appears to be the most transparent with the publication of a monthly bulletin highlighting all decisions taken by the authority with respect to investigations, disciplinary action, and also decisions of the grievance committee headed by a judge. The ESCA in the UAE also publishes a monthly bulletin, mainly highlighting trading activity and new issues.

With respect to the performance of stock markets, the stock markets in all the GCC countries have witnessed a boom since 2001 particularly between 2003 and 2005 (IMF 2006). As can be seen from table 10.1 there was little change in the AMF Index of GCC stock markets between 1994 and 2002. Between 1994 and 2002 the index of the best-performing stock market—the Kuwait Stock Market—only increased 58 points with a major dip in 1998. Whereas between 2002 and 2005 the AMF index for the Saudi Stock market more than quadrupled from 132.9 to 878.4 and the market capitalization went from $74 billion to $646 billion. In 2006, however, there was a major correction in all the GCC stock markets except in the case of the Muscat Securities Market (MSM) and the Bahrain Stock Market (BSM). There is, however, a continued interest by government-linked and private companies to list on the stock markets and the number of listings has continued to grow. The stock market boom also attracted many new investors between 2002 and 2005.

The IMF (2006) report observed that the stock market boom partly reflect improved fundamentals and substantial privatization programs. The report also highlighted the role of high oil prices on high levels of liquidity and strong credit growth. The IMF (2006) report also recognized that the broad range of legal, regulatory, and supervisory changes in the region had improved the markets' transparency, increasing foreign and domestic investors' confidence alike.

Summary and Conclusions

The forces contributing to economic regulation have been of considerable interest to historians, economists, and political scientists (McCraw 1975). Two conflicting theories have dominated attempts to explain the origins and practice of economic regulation: the public-interest and group-interest or capture theories. Recent evaluations of the two theories have pointed to problems with both. McCraw (1975) in his review concludes that neither theories nor the two in combination adequately characterize the American experience with regulation over the last century. Burk (1985) suggests that political contingency has a major role to play in the origins of the Securities Act of 1933.

In this study we do not only look at the forces contributing to the development of securities regulation in a single country but a few countries within an economic grouping—the Gulf Cooperation Council (GCC). The study first evaluated the ability of the public-interest theory and group-interest theory to explain the recent interest in securities regulation. We found that both theories could not sufficiently explain the recent interest in securities regulation.

It is argued that political contingency provides the best explanation for the recent interest in securities regulation within the GCC countries. It is pointed out that the downturn in oil prices in 1997–98 placed major stress on the government budget, reducing the states' traditional role of funding investment in the economy, thereby contributing to negative growth rates of the GDP. The study also highlights the role of economic events, principally the East-Asian economic crisis and the pressure from international bodies on the need for reform. The state was forced to promote private-sector investment in the economy, following conventional wisdom that effective securities regulation was essential for the stock market to be an effective mobilizer of private capital.

An evaluation of the securities regulation highlights that the independence of the regulators is questionable. The performance of the securities markets since the enactment of the regulations has, however, been impressive although it is difficult to determine whether it is due to fundamentals or whether it is the formation of a bubble.

References

Al-Rimawi, L.M. 2001. "Jordanian, Kuwaiti and Omani Securities Regulation: Can They Be the Subject Matter of a Viable Comparative Study with EU Securities Regulation." *Journal of Financial Regulation and Compliance* 9 (3): 253–273.

Al-Yahya, M. 1993. *Kuwait: Fall and Rebirth*. London: Kegan Paul.
Azzam, H. 1997. *The Emerging Arab Capital Markets: Investment Opportunities in Relatively Unplayed Markets*. London: Keegan Paul.
Benston, G. 1973. "Required Disclosure and the Stockmarket." *American Economic Review* 63 (1): 132–155.
Burk, J. 1985. "The Origins of Federal Securities Regulation: A Case Study in the Social Control of Finance." *Social Forces* 63 (4): 1010–1029.
Carosso, V.P. 1970. *Investment Banking in America*. Boston: Harvard University Press.
Chalk, N., A. Jbili, V. Treichel, and J. Wilson. 1996. "Financial Structure and Reforms." In *Building on Progress: Reform and Growth in the Middle East and North Africa*. Washington: International Monetary Fund.
Cowing, C. 1965. *Populists, Plungers and Progressives*. Princeton: Princeton University Press.
Creane, S., R. Goyal, A.M. Mobarak, and R. Sab. 2004. "Financial Sector Development in the Middle East and North Africa." *IMF Working Paper WP/04/201*. Washington: International Monetary Fund.
Galbraith, J.K. 1955. *The Great Crash: 1929*. Boston: Houghton Mifflin.
Hakura, D.S. 2004. "Growth in the Middle East and North Africa." *IMF Working Paper WP/04/56*. International Monetary Fund: Washington.
Hammoudeh, S., E. Al-Eisa, and R. Al-Nsour. 2003. "Links and Volatility Transmission among the GCC Stock Markets and the Nymex Oil Futures." *Topics in Middle Eastern and North African Economies, Electronic Journal* 5 (1).
Hawke, G.R. 1980. *Economics for Historians*. Cambridge: Cambridge University Press.
International Monetary Fund Staff Report. 1998. "The Asian Crisis: Cause and Cures." *Finance and Development 35 (2)*: 18–21.
International Monetary Fund. 2006. "Regional Economic Outlook: Middle East and Central Asia." Washington: International Monetary Fund.
International Organizations of Securities Commissions (IOSCO). 1998. Statement of Objectives and Principles of Securities Regulation. www.iosco.org/library/pubdocs/pdf/IOSCOPD154.pdf.
Iqbal, Z. 2001. "Economic Challenges in the Middle East and North Africa—An Overview." In Z. Iqbal, ed., *Macroeconomic Issues and Policies in the Middle East and North Africa*. New York: International Monetary Fund.
McCraw, T.K. 1975. "Regulation in America: A Review Article." *Business History Review* 49 (2): 159–83.
Mintz, I. 1981. *Deterioration in the Quality of Foreign Bonds Issued in the United States, 1920–1930*. National Bureau of Economic Research.
Mitnick, B.M. 1980. *The Political Economy of Regulation*. New York: Columbia University Press.
Nashashibi, K., M. Elhage, and A. Fedelino. 2001. "Financial Liberalization in Arab Countries." In Z. Iqbal, ed., *Macroeconomic Issues and Policies in the Middle East and North Africa*. Washington: International Monetary Fund.
Phillips, S.M and J.R. Zecher. 1981. *The SEC: An Economic Perspective*. Boston: MIT Press.

Posner, R.A. 1974. "Theories of Economic Regulation." *The Bell Journal of Economics and Management Science* 5 (2): 330–359.

Ricketts, M. and K. Shaw. 1984. "The Theory of Regulation." In A. Peacock, M. Ricketts, and J. Robinson, eds., *The Regulation Game: How British and West German Companies Bargain with Government*. Oxford: Basil Blackwell Publishers.

Sala-I-Martin, X. and E.V. Artadi. 2003. "Economic Growth and Investment in the Arab World." In P.K. Cornelius, ed., *The Arab World Competitiveness Report 2002–2003*. Oxford: Oxford University Press, 22–33.

Scott, W.R. 1995. *Financial Accounting Theory*. New Jersey: Prentice Hall.

Seznec, J. 1987. *The Financial Markets of the Arabian Gulf*. London: Croom Helm.

Shleifer, A. 2005. "Understanding Regulation." *European Financial Management* 11 (4): 439–451.

Sirkin, G. 1975. "The Stock Market Crash of 1929 Revisited." *Business History Review* 49 (2): 223–231.

Skowronek, S. 1982. *Building a New American State*. Cambridge: Cambridge University Press.

Stigler, G. 1971. "The Theory of Economic Regulation." *Bell Journal of Economics and Management* 2 (1): 3–21.

Uche, C.U. 2000. "The Theory of Regulation: A Review Article." *Journal of Financial Regulation and Compliance*. 9 (1): 67–80.

Velayutham, S. and S. Al-Segini. 2002. "The Contribution of Professional Bodies to the Development of a Knowledge Economy in the United Arab Emirates: The Case of the Accountants and Auditors Association." Proceeding of the 5th Annual CBE Conference, March 24–25, in Al-Ain, United Arab Emirates, 948–973.

Wilson, R. 1983. *Banking and Finance in the Arab Middle East*. London: Macmillan Publishers.

World Bank. 2003. *Enhancing Governance in MENA*. Washington: World Bank.

Zahlan, R.S. 1998. *The Making of the Modern Gulf States*. Reading: Ithaca Press.

Part IV

Looking Ahead

11

The Future Outlook of the Business Trends in the Gulf Countries and Its Impact on the Developments in Accounting, Finance, and Tax

Wagdy M. Abdallah

The purpose of this chapter is twofold: (1) to present a summary of the key issues of accounting, auditing, tax, and finance in the six Arab Gulf countries, excluding Iraq and Iran, by providing MNCs' corporate and financial executives with guidelines to help them in planning, managing, and controlling their Gulf region's international business activities; and (2) to state general conclusions from the research on the future outlook of the global business trends in the Gulf countries and its impact on accounting, finance, and tax in the Gulf countries.

In chapter 1, it was noticed that the primary purpose of the book was to provide the latest information on accounting, finance, and tax of the six Arab Gulf countries with emphasis on cultural and economic issues and their effect on accounting standards and practices, auditing, financial institutions, harmonization of accounting standards, stock markets, and accounting profession and education. The economic and political characteristics of the Gulf countries and their impact on accounting and management were covered in chapter 2. The Islamic business ethics and its impact on management and accounting of national and multinational companies in the Gulf countries were discussed in chapter 3. Accounting systems and practices of the Gulf countries with coverage of the International Financial Reporting Standards (IFRSs) and their relevance to the Gulf countries were discussed in chapters 4 and 5. The developments of auditing standards and practices of the Gulf countries were reviewed in chapter 6.

Accounting professions and accounting education in the Gulf countries were discussed in chapter 7. Corporate governance systems in the Gulf countries, tax rules and regulations of the Gulf countries, stock markets and financial institutions of the Gulf countries were covered in chapters 8 through 10. In this last chapter, we take a global view of accounting, auditing, and tax of the Gulf countries to summarize major findings from the research on the following topics:

- The effect of Islamic business ethics on accounting and management in the Gulf countries;
- Accounting and financial reporting of the Gulf countries and IFRSs and their relevance to the environment of the Gulf countries;
- The developments of the auditing standards and practices of the Gulf countries;
- Accounting education of the Gulf countries and its impact on the development of the accounting professions;
- Corporate governance systems and financial reporting transparency of the companies of the Gulf countries;
- Tax planning and strategies of the MNCs for investing in the Gulf countries;
- The developments and efficiencies of the stock markets of the Gulf countries within the new global business environment; and
- Global business and the expected development of accounting, auditing, and finance in the Gulf countries in the twenty-first century.

Some general conclusions from the research will be provided in the last topic listed—global business and accounting in the Gulf countries in the twenty-first century.

Major Finding from the Research

The Effect of Islamic Business Ethics on Accounting and Management in the Gulf countries

In chapter 3, religion, especially Islam, is one of the most significant cultural values that has considerable effect on a country's accounting practices, tax rules, and financial institutions, and, therefore, should not be ignored. This chapter seeks to briefly survey the business ethics enjoined by Islam on its followers. Given nearly 1.5 billion followers of Islam, Muslims, around the world and their history—which dates back to the birth of Islam—the chapter has space only to discuss very aspects of Islam's history and behavior of Muslims.

In recent years Islamic banking has been making news. In order to introduce readers to Islamic business ethics and how they impact Muslims' behavior, the chapter started with an update on Islamic banking. The chapter then discussed other aspects of Islamic business ethics and its impact on accounting, tax, and finance. Major cultural and religious issues affecting accounting can be summarized as follows:

- Islam is one of the most significant determinants of cultural values and practices throughout the nations that border the Persian Gulf. It is having a growing impact on the trade and business practices, judging from the major growth in the availability of not only Islamic banking but various financial and investment products. Life for any individual, worker, manager, or an officer, is often influenced by many variables, and for a majority of people in any Islamic country, including the Gulf countries, the influence of culture (especially Islam) is apparent in many of their personal and public activities, actions, decisions, and behavior. Therefore, a businessman or an MNC doing business in the Gulf countries will undoubtedly encounter this influence during interpersonal interactions with Muslim individuals both within and outside the workplace, and a sensitivity to and understanding of these influences and preferences may contribute to improved personal and successful business relations.
- Unfortunately, Islam is largely misunderstood not only by non-Muslims but also by many Muslims themselves. Since September 11, 2001 such misunderstandings seem to have exponentially increased. But a great deal, if not all, of the negative views being spewed by the preachers, politicians, and media pundits is based on lies and stereotypes going back 1,200 years, rather than on facts. This can easily be shown by looking at words Islam and Allah. For the Islamphobes, both are evil and Satanic terms.
- With respect to finance, a telling development in Islamic banking is the emergence of the term Islamic Financial Services Industry to describe what used to be called Islamic banking. The change is symptomatic of the changes taking place in the industry and activities that are being carried out not only by the Islamic banks indigenous to Islamic countries but also by the subsidiaries of major Western

banks, such as Citi Bank and HSBC who have joined what was for all intent and purpose a niche market.

- Along with the international banks, accounting and consulting firms have arrived, among them Ernst & Young and KPMG. Such Western players in the financial service game are employing Islamic scholars to give themselves an aura of credibility and Islamic Law (Shari'ah) compliance, a phrase very much in vogue in the Islamic Financial Services sector. In 1996 Dow Jones launched its index of Shari'ah-compliant stocks and since then others have emerged around the world. This has allowed mutual funds to become a feature of Islamic financial industry and available to Muslim investors. The Islamic indexes now number more than 40.
- The current spurt in Islamic finance started after 9/11 when wealthy Muslims brought their money back home to the Gulf region fearing the seizure of their assets by American politicians seeking to please their voters and the supporters of Israel. This movement of capital seems to have reversed what took place in the aftermath of the First Gulf War, which led to the transfer of a large proportion of the capital in the Middle Eastern Banks to Swiss banks.
- Even though one cannot as yet fully answer the question about the long-term viability of Islamic financial services, one can say that there are developments taking place and many of them are positive. What is beyond doubt is the strong emphasis given to their religious beliefs by Muslims and their willingness to act in compliance to those beliefs. The emergence of Western banks as major players in the industry is a testimonial to the significant level of money involved. It is also a comment on the relative distrust of their indigenous banks by investors in Muslim countries, which is to a large extent due to the absence of effective regulatory oversight and accountable governance in these countries.
- The Islamic prohibition against cheating others is grounded in the same spirit as is the Islamic injunction against transactions involving usury. Both would encroach upon the basic right that Islam, in effect, grants to all human beings, namely, the right to be free from economic exploitation.

Islam, in encouraging ethical economic activities to keep it from being exploitive as well as becoming a target in itself, has prohibited Muslims from *Riba* (usury or interest) because it is considered as unlawful or unacceptable gains from the Islamic point of view. The prohibition against it must not be construed as applying only to transactions involving usury or even interest. The prohibition against *Riba* is intended to promote ethical economic activities that do not exploit other human beings in order to create wealth for an individual.

- Taxes (*zakah*) was the primary source of revenue for the Islamic State during the time of Prophet Muhammad [pbuh] and the four caliphs (companions) who succeeded him, Abu Bakr, Umer, Uthman, and Ali, collectively known as the Pious Caliphs. Initially, in the Islamic State governed by the Prophet [pbuh] there were no "taxes" to provide revenue for the community's needs. The Qur'an exhorted and the Prophet [pbuh] encouraged Muslims to perform charitable acts and to spend for the sake of Allah.
- Taxes are hardly the cherished symbol of the allegiance citizens owe to their states. Throughout the world, professional tax experts seek to aid citizens in avoiding or at least minimizing taxes. Tax avoidance through legal and illegal means is and has been a global reality. Such desires to avoid taxes pose problems for nations of all stripes, developed as well as developing. The act of paying *zakat* is taken seriously by a vast number of Muslims throughout the world. Even though it is fair to say that among Muslims there are those who seek to avoid paying taxes—both religious taxes such as *zakat* and others imposed by contemporary governments—still it would appear that making financial contributions to one's community a form of worship and a requirement of belief cannot but help lessen the problem of tax avoidance.
- If the national cultural values of Islamic society shape and reinforce both accounting systems and practices, it will be a rational decision to harmonize the accounting standards of these countries as one subgroup of the international community. Therefore, it is the time for the IASB to consider not harmonizing international accounting standards but rather establishing Islamic International Accounting Standards (IIASs). IIASs will be helpful for Muslims around the world (1.5 billion) including South Asian, Africa, Arab countries, and the remaining 545 million Islamic adherents. IIASs should be based on the Holy Qur'an and the Sunna of the Prophet Mohamed (PBUH).

Accounting and Financial Reporting of the Gulf Countries and International Financial Reporting Standards

In chapters 4 and 5, accounting standards and practices of the six Arab Gulf countries, the International Financial Reporting Standards (IFRSs) promulgated by the International Accounting Standards Board (IASB), and their relevance to the business environment of the Gulf countries were examined. Comparisons of financial reporting standards in the Gulf countries with IASs/IFRSs were included. The major issues of financial reporting can be summarized as follows:

- Five accounting issues have been discussed using the accounting standards of the six Gulf countries as compared with the IASs and Gulf Countries Council Accounting and Auditing Organization (GCCAAO).
  1. For accounting treatment of investments, Kuwait, Oman, Qatar, and Saudi Arabia are in compliance with IASs; GCCAAO requires using the fair market value for long-term investments.
  2. Accounting treatment for inventory: all Gulf countries follow IFRSs. IFRSs is using the LIFO as a permissible alternative.
  3. Asset valuation: All six Gulf countries follow the same pattern as the IASs, except Saudi Arabia, which uses the cost method for financial reporting.
  4. Foreign Currency Translations: Kuwait, Oman, and Qatar are consistent with the IASs. The GAAP of both Saudi Arabia and UAE do not cover the foreign currency translation; however, foreign firms and joint ventures are allowed to use IFRSs.
  5. Consolidation: In all selected countries, financial statements are consolidated if the voting controls 50 percent or more of subsidiaries.
- Some Gulf countries consider the IFRSs as a replacement for their domestic standards, while others accept IFRSs financial statements from foreign companies for listing purposes in their stock exchanges. The national standards of some countries are either based on or are similar to IFRSs even though they may not have adopted IFRSs. Only one of the six Gulf countries, Saudi Arabia, does not permit the use of the IFRSs for their listed and unlisted domestic companies.
- It is suggested that the GCC should adopt a new IASs regulation requiring listed Gulf companies, including banks and insurance companies, to prepare their consolidated accounts in accordance with IFRSs from 2008 onward. The goal is to eliminate barriers to cross-border trading in securities by ensuring that the Gulf company accounts throughout the Gulf region are reliable, transparent, and comparable. The GCC should have the force of law without requiring transposition into national legislation by establishing a new mechanism to assess IASs to give them legal endorsement before they can be used. It is recommended that if Gulf countries are

looking forward to having one single regional standard setter and one set of international financial reporting standards, the following four principles are essential in achieving this ultimate goal:

1. All Gulf countries involved in a global financial reporting must have a common mission or objective of financial accounting and reporting.
2. Gulf countries must have a process for implementing and adapting the IFRSs that are accepted and trusted by all constituents and one that assures that the mission of the standard setter is fulfilled.
3. Gulf countries should establish a mechanism to assess IFRSs that achieve high quality.
4. Gulf countries should ensure establishing efficient corporate governance systems, including financial disclosure and transparency for all listed domestic companies in Gulf stock exchange markets.

Auditing Standards and Practices in the Gulf Countries

In chapter 6, the developments of auditing standards and practices were discussed. The major issues of the development of auditing standards and practices can be summarized as follows:

- Bahrain is the leading country in the area of Islamic accounting and auditing standards for financial institutions.
- In Kuwait, Oman, and Qatar, there are no professional organizations in charge of setting accounting and auditing standards.
- Saudi Arabia may be considered the only Gulf country that has established a framework for its accounting and auditing standards. The Saudi Organization for Certified Public Accountants (SOCPA) is the professional body that has the responsibility of developing the accounting profession. Its basic responsibility entails organizing, regulating, and monitoring professional practices.
- In the UAE, the basic power of setting accounting and auditing standards rests with the Ministry of Commerce and Economics. Therefore, to establish a national professional body that is empowered to develop accounting and auditing standards, from the government's point of view, is not justified.
- Auditing standards for banks in the UAE have varied widely and the banking industry has been dominated by the Big Four international accounting firms. These firms audit most of the local commercial banks in the UAE. Most banks have not changed their auditing firm

for several years, and the central bank does not require them to do so (Islam 2003).

- In general, the actual practices and services of the auditing profession in the Gulf countries are not that different from the practices known in the Western societies. However, there is one unique culture-based characteristic of actual auditing practices in the Gulf countries that is less known in the Western society; this refers to auditing services related to the Islamic banking.

Accounting Education and Accounting Professions of the Gulf Countries

In chapter 7, the development and contribution of the accounting profession and accounting education to the economic development of GCC countries were covered. It was highlighted that in the last 15 years the GCC economies have experienced high growth rates as well as high population growth, which has contributed to a huge demand for accounting professionals. Much of the demand has mainly been met by a growing expatriate workforce. The major issues of accounting education and accounting profession can be summarized as follows:

- In the past five years, the higher education sector has gone through a major change, mainly with the opening up of many private universities. While the opportunities for higher education in accounting has grown exponentially, the approach to accounting education has not changed much. The focus of accounting education has continued to be the mastery of knowledge rather than the mastery of skills.
- It is argued that the weak state of the accounting profession could be a reason for the aforementioned point as well as little connection between the practice environment and the academic programs that are based on the traditional American accounting curriculum.
- A major reason for the weak and poorly developed accounting profession in the Gulf countries is the government control over registration of accountants and auditors and the non-requirement of membership of the local body, which provides little incentive for accountants to be members of the local professional body.
- The small size of the professional accounting organizations and hence their limited financial resources does not allow them to carry out the normal activities of a professional body, such as improving accounting education, funding research and knowledge development, developing and enforcing work and ethical standards, and quality control.

Corporate Governance Systems and Financial Reporting Transparency of the Companies in the Gulf Countries

In chapter 8, the most important corporate governance issues and financial reporting transparency of the companies in the Gulf countries were examined. The practice of corporate governance and the key drivers for the changes in corporate governance of the Gulf countries were analyzed. The major issues of corporate governance systems of the Gulf countries can be summarized as follows:

- The ongoing process of updating the 12 principles of corporate governance issued by the OECD is one step forward for facilitating global adherence to best practices in the Gulf countries and will also help them in building a culture that respects and rewards financial reporting transparency, disclosure, accountability, and build sound financial markets and investor confidence.
- To facilitate the adoption of, compliance with, and effective enforcement of high standards of corporate governance in the Gulf countries, the following guidelines should be considered and implemented:
  1. National-level task forces are needed to develop corporate governance codes specific to each country. At the same time, these should be based on internationally acceptable corporate standards;
  2. Governments, families with large commercial operations, representatives of the small business community, and banks and financial institutions should be included in establishing and enforcing corporate governance codes;
  3. For establishing a successful corporate governance system in the Gulf countries, all key factors including transparency of financial reporting, accountability of management and board of directors and responsibility of management, and independent audit committee should be considered.
  4. Codes and standards of corporate conduct must be devised in an inclusive manner by incorporating the ethical standards of the community.
  5. Governance legal corporate codes need to be backed up by effective means to ensure compliance. The incentives should be clear, simple, enforced, and transparently directed toward the fundamental objectives of the business entities.
  6. National financial institutional laws, regulations, and corporate practices based on international norms and standards should be imparted to professionals and the general public.

Tax Planning and Strategies of MNCs for Investing in the Gulf Countries

In chapter 9, the tax rules and regulations of the six Gulf countries were investigated. The purpose of this chapter was fourfold: (1) to understand the tax rules and regulations of the Gulf countries, (2) to guide MNCs and all other businessmen how to implement strategic tax planning for the purpose of investing and managing their businesses in the Gulf countries; (3) to help and guide potential investors to determine the most favorable country for particular investment; and (4) to look at regional opportunities for cost savings and chances for improvements in making tax affairs more effective for both host countries and investors. The major issues of tax rules and regulations of the Gulf countries can be summarized as follows:

- Both Bahrain and the UAE have no corporate income taxes with the exception of the oil and gas companies with a maximum tax rate of 46 and 55 percent, respectively. Moreover, the UAE imposes tax on foreign banks at 20 percent.
- To rank the Gulf countries in terms of the lowest corporate tax rates to the highest, Saudi Arabia is the lowest, with a tax rate of 20 percent; both Oman and Qatar are ranked second, with a tax rate of 30 percent; Bahrain is ranked fourth with 46 percent; and both Kuwait and the UAE are the last, with the highest tax rate of 55 percent. All the six countries have a low rate of customs duties of 5 percent, except the UAE, which has a rate of 4 percent. There is no personal income tax in all the six countries as of today.
- MNCs and any potential investor in the Gulf countries are urged to pay attention to the design of an appropriate strategic tax planning. To be successful, the plan should fit into the Gulf region political, cultural, and tax environment. Tax strategic planning should be done in advance and should include the following five major steps:
  1. Get access to all up-to-date tax and economic information of the Gulf countries and of the selected country;
  2. Start your strategic tax planning as soon as your project is initiated;
  3. Involve your local partner(s) in your tax planning;
  4. Minimize your tax burden by
     a. Choosing the most appropriate investment tools, such as joint ventures or wholly owned subsidiary;
     b. Structuring contracts in the most convenient and appropriate manner;

   c. Taking advantage of all tax holidays and other incentives available;
   d. Coordinating the tax burden in the Gulf region with that in your home country to take advantage of any tax treaty provisions and other tax credit opportunities;
5. Design your pricing policy, including international transfer-pricing strategies, after considering all tax, custom, political, and social issues.

The Developments and Efficiencies of the Stock Markets of the Gulf Countries

In chapter 10, research on the development of the stock markets of the Gulf countries did not only look at the forces contributing to the development of securities regulation in a single country but also investigated a few countries within an economic grouping—the Gulf Cooperation Council (GCC). The chapter first evaluated the ability of the public-interest theory and group-interest theory to explain the recent interest in securities regulation. Both the theories could not sufficiently explain the recent interest in securities regulation. The major issues of developments and efficiencies of the stock markets of the Gulf countries can be summarized as follows:

- Political contingency provides the best explanation for the recent interest in securities regulation within the GCC countries. It is pointed out that the downturn in oil prices in 1997–98 placed major stress on the government budget to reduce the states' traditional role of funding investment in the economy, thereby contributing to negative growth rates of the GDP.
- However, stock markets, in general, are predictive mechanisms driven by several forces, including greed and fear. Therefore, they tended to anticipate future events, and were not solely concerned with the economic situation on a particular day. The dilemma was how could you explain the current Gulf puzzle of stock market crashes at a time of record oil prices? In short, government revenues were surging, which had to be good for local business, and yet at the same time investor confidence was weakening. The truth is that potential investors were looking forward and saying that oil prices may go up to $100-a-barrel, but what happens after that? Would we accept a recession? (Cooper 2007).
- The chapter also highlights the role of economic events principally the East-Asian economic crisis and the pressure from international

organizations on the need for reform. The state was forced to promote private-sector investment in the economy, following conventional wisdom that effective securities regulation was essential for the stock market to be an effective mobilizer of private capital.

- An evaluation of the securities regulation highlights that the independence of the regulators was questionable. The performance of the securities markets since the enactment of the regulations had, however, been impressive although it was difficult to determine whether it was due to fundamentals or whether it was the formation of a bubble.

Global Business and the Expected Development of Accounting, Auditing, and Finance in the Gulf Countries

In the twenty-first century, private businesses, not governments, should lead the Gulf countries to the most significant long-term business success, as long as their central value of benchmarking lies in determining their strengths and weaknesses and identifying the areas where improvements are needed and investments have to be made if the country is to boost its economic and social environment.

First of all, it is so obvious that due to the significant oil price windfall, the Gulf countries' economies have been growing at levels not reached since the 1970s. However, can Gulf countries sustain this strength with heightened expectations and deal with outside pressures for a long time? For them to have a successful global business environment, they are and will be facing many challenges and now it is the time for them to know how to deal with them and find out the appropriate and effective solutions.

The Gulf countries can have a strong, stable, and global business environment, if they are willing to be leaders, not followers, build real global business environments, face their challenges, remove obstacles to growth while at the same time foster the development of sectors with high potential. If national and multinational companies are willing to help them in achieving this ultimate goal, then the following powerful key drivers are essential:

1. The GCC should adopt a new IAS Regulation requiring listed Gulf companies, including banks and insurance companies, to prepare their consolidated accounts in accordance with IFRSs from 2008 onward. In other words, it is urgent to enforce a relevant set of IFRSs to ensure that the information upon which local and foreign investors and other stakeholders base their decisions is transparent,

relevant, comprehensive, reliable, consistent, and internationally comparable. Moreover, the accounting profession organizations in Gulf countries should play an important role in this trend and participate in the implementation of the appropriate IFRSs for the Gulf countries, and cooperate with accounting firms serving the business community in the area in implementing these standards.

2. Based on the unique Islamic culture-based characteristics of actual auditing practices in the Gulf countries, the Islamic banking and its related auditing services should be included in the accounting and auditing curriculum of the United States and Schools of Business of all other developed industrialized countries. These norms should be taught to all accounting and finance major students to enable them to promote successful global businesses. These standards should not be ignored any longer.
3. For the Gulf countries' stock market to be efficient, it is essential for these countries to pursue reforms, particularly in compliance with effective corporate governance standards and codes in order to have transparent financial reporting of all national and multinational companies operating in the Gulf countries. To establish and enforce effective corporate governance codes and standards, participation is a must for all Gulf countries' governments, families-owned businesses, professional accounting organizations, and banks and financial institutions.
4. For MNCs to implement relevant and appropriate strategic tax planning of their business activities in the Gulf countries, they have to balance between two things: (1) Cost savings with chances for improvements in making tax affairs more effective for both host countries and investors and their social responsibilities toward helping to improve and meet the economic and social needs of the Gulf countries.
5. All Gulf countries have a fixed exchange rate system with their rated pegged to the U.S. dollar. In 2010, the combination of using a single currency and the diversification of their economies with less dependence on oil can be the key drivers for the Gulf countries to maintain stronger economies and deeper regional integration, which will lead to reduction in business costs and help the global competitiveness of Gulf countries.
6. The Gulf countries should continue to reform their education systems, including accounting and auditing. The local and international colleges and universities operating in the Gulf countries must aim to develop leaders more effectively. Building business leaders is more important than the scarce resources. The truth

is that successful organizations need talented people a lot more than talented people need organizations (Colvin 2007). In the private and public sectors, business institutions must become more transparent and relevant to the market needs and reduce the employment rates (World Economic Forum 2007).

7. Professional accounting organizations should not be managed and controlled by the government. To improve accounting education, funds for scholarly and practical research, to develop and enforce professional ethical standards, and quality control on practitioners, all professional accounting organizations should be independent and funded by the required membership of all CPAs. In addition, money should be donated from most corporate business entities operating in the Gulf countries in a way similar to the AICPA and FASB of the United States.

In the twenty-first century, the recommendations of this book, if used as practical guidelines and a reference, are expected to have many implications for all national and multinational companies operating in the Gulf countries, potential international investors, the Big-Four-accounting firms, the Gulf countries' local investors, the Gulf region's professional accounting organizations, accounting education, management organizations, stock markets, financial institutions, and, last but not the least, the governments of the Gulf countries, by thriving in a global business environment and encouraging different kinds of honest and transparent foreign investments.

References

Colvin, Geoff. 2007. "Leader Machines." *Fortune*, October 1: 98–106.

Cooper, Peter. 2007. "Why Are Gulf Stock Prices Falling When Oil Prices Are Hitting Record Highs?" May 26 at http://www.ameinfo.com/83651.html.

Islam, Mazhar M. 2003. "Development and Performance of Domestic and Foreign Bank in GCC Countries." *Managerial Finance* 29 (2/3): 42–73.

World Economic Forum. 2007. "Arab Competitiveness Roundtable" in Doha, Qatar, April 9–10; Geneva, Switzerland, at www.weforum.org.

Index